D1479756

Peasants No More

Chandler Publications in
ANTHROPOLOGY AND SOCIOLOGY
Leonard Broom, Editor

FIGURE 1. Map of Italy

Peasants No More

Social Class and
Social Change in an
Underdeveloped Society

JOSEPH LOPREATO
The University of Texas

CHANDLER PUBLISHING COMPANY
124 Spear Street
San Francisco, California 94105

 Science Research Associates, Inc., 259 East Erie Street, Chicago, Illinois 60611
A Subsidiary of IBM   Distributors

Copyright © 1967 by Chandler Publishing Company
Library of Congress Catalog Card No. 67–17741
Printed in the United States of America

Book designed by Joseph M. Roter

HD
676
L65

To Gregory and Marisa, in gratitude
for their patient affection

223274

Contents

❀

TABLES

❀

FIGURES

Preface

Among the many transformations shaping human society today, one stands out both for its intensity and for its generality: Everywhere agricultural people are being seduced from all directions with products, ideas, and values manufactured in the great urban centers of the industrial world. Human society seems to have every intention of transforming itself into one colossal city of teeming bureaucracies and industrial complexes. Peasants want to be peasants no more. At least, they are no longer willing to suffer the privations—economic, social, and political—that have been the secular characteristics of their status. At the first opportunity they leave their fields to seek the economic and social opportunities of the city. Some take their families, never to return to the old village. Others shuttle back and forth between village and city, playing a direct role in the "urbanization" of the agricultural world.

This book analyzes social change in southern Italy as a consequence of emigration. This region of the peasant world has long been a source of migrants to the four corners of the earth. The book reveals a people traditionally characterized by the most abject poverty, the deepest sense of hopelessness, and the most complete servility. But at the present—because of the material and cultural benefits derived through emigration—they are upgrading their position in the stratification system, developing more resolute attitudes toward their traditional superiors, gaining an invigorating sense of economic security, and displaying a marked degree of achievement motivation.

While I have been specifically concerned with southern Italy, the problem I have investigated is to a large extent common to peasant society in general. My basic aim has been not merely to illuminate the specific case but also to make a contribution to the growing literature on social change in developing societies as a whole. As such, I hope that my endeavor will be useful both to those concerned with the practical problems of economic and social development, and to those involved in a variety of more purely theoretical pursuits in such fields as social change, community organization, social stratification, and peasant societies and cultures.

Various organizations and institutions have given financial support to this study. A Fulbright research scholarship for the period 1962–1964 made it possible to bring to completion a program of research begun in 1959. I am deeply indebted to the Fulbright program, and especially to Dr. Cipriana Scelba, the Italian executive director in Rome, whose efforts on my behalf were untiring during the two-year stay in Italy. The University of Connecticut Research Foundation and the University of Texas Research Institute kindly provided me with funds for research and clerical assistance during the final stages of the study. For part of the material included in this volume, appreciation is also extended to the Social Science Research Council and the National Science Foundation, which have provided the funds for a broader study of social class and social change in Italy as a whole, to be discussed in another book.

Grateful acknowledgment is due to Professor Luigi M. Lombardi Satriani for permission to translate and reprint the material on folklore appearing in Chapter IV. Some passages scattered throughout the book appeared in preliminary form in several journal articles. For permission to use those materials I am grateful to the American Sociological Association, the Rural Sociological Society, and the Society for Applied Anthropology.

A number of people have given help at various stages of the study, and I wish to record my grateful appreciation to them. Lionel S. Lewis and Sidney Tarrow have helpfully criticized the book in manuscript form. Professor Pierpaolo Luzzatto Fegiz of the University of Rome, director of the DOXA Statistical Institute in Milan, was always generous with encouragement and constructive suggestions. The contributions of my research assistant, Janet E. Saltzman, are especially worth mentioning, and my gratitude to her can hardly repay her for all her toils at various stages of the research and writing.

Leonard Broom read the manuscript in its "final" form, and his keen eye discovered many linguistic and substantive infelicities. Their correction has resulted in a much improved book, and for that I am deeply grateful to him.

Finally, my greatest debt is to Carolyn, my wife, who contributed, at all stages of the work, her research abilities, her typing skills, and a truly stoic patience.

Part One

The Legacy

I HISTORICAL SKETCH

Southern Italy, as an essentially agricultural but industrializing region within a modern society, may be said to bestride two worlds: industrial society on the one hand, and the peasant underdeveloped world on the other. Since the end of World War II, when old as well as new nations emerged from age-long feudal or colonial somnolence, Italy has thrust herself into an "economic Renaissance" and, because of the government activities in the underdeveloped South, has arrested attention as a school for developing societies. I hope, therefore, that the findings from southern Italy will lend themselves to a wide range of theoretical and practical applications. Through a detailed examination of the southern Italian case, we can attempt a clarification of some of the theoretical and methodological issues surrounding contemporary peasant societies in general.

Until recent decades, the peasant of southern Italy, like peasants elsewhere, had led a traditionally precarious existence within an essentially static economy. Poverty, along with an accompanying isolation from the centers of civilization, resulted in a set of circumstances whereby the peasant had occupied the lowest status in the prestige and power structures of his society, and had received little or none of the social recognition that his toils, tenacity, and contributions would merit. The combination of economic poverty and social castigation, in turn, had produced in the peasant a deep sense of deprivation and despair and, in his own group, a system of interpersonal relations based on tension, conflict, and rampant insecurity. Thus it has often been said of the southern Italian peasant, as of many peasants elsewhere, that he is an inveterate individualist and pessimist, hopelessly alienated from his society. Above all, he is said to be endowed with a low level of achievement motivation, at the basis of which the interest of his small family nucleus is the major driving force.

The central thesis to be established in this book is that whatever the validity of this argument for the past, it is no longer applicable to the southern Italian peasant today. When the opportunities for achievement recently came in his direction, the peasant was quick to avail himself of them. As a result, though remnants of a forbidding past still linger on, the peasant now shows pronounced signs of a willingness and capacity to enjoy with his fellow citizens the conditions and the promise of an achieving society.

Until now, the major source of achievement for the southern Italian peasant has been emigration. By leaving his peasant society and then returning with the earnings from his labor abroad and with new cultural standards, or merely by remitting these from abroad, many a peasant has achieved in his society a degree of economic well-being and independence unimaginable a few decades ago. Through emigration, he has rapidly achieved a degree of social recognition that until recent times seemed to be the monopoly of the signorial class. He has achieved the social and psychological vitality with which to challenge the old social order and to demand the recognition that his achievements deserve. Finally, and more important, through emigration the southern Italian peasant has achieved a warm and invigorating sense of security in relation to the present and the future as well. In short, through emigration, the peasant has broken the formidable bonds of his secular poverty, and actively entered the current of a larger civilization. More important still, by releasing shares of previously very scarce goods through his departure from the village, he has also helped spread the new advantages to a considerable portion of those who have not themselves been directly involved in the phenomenon of emigration.

In the ensuing pages, these and several other aspects of peasant society in the South of Italy will be discussed in some detail. The approach will be one of particular sensitivity to the importance of the time dimension, the roots of social phenomena that time conceals, and the social changes that it comprises. Man is an historical animal, with a profound sense of time and a great capacity to be influenced by it. Very little in his life is meaningful today if it is not first understood as part of a larger whole whose roots lie deeply in the past. Accordingly, to create a better understanding of the genesis and the magnitude of many of the social conditions and problems with which the present-day peasant of southern Italy is confronted, this chapter begins with a brief historical examination of his region.

The Years before the National Unification

The known history of the southern Italian peoples [1] begins, quite significantly, with their region under foreign domination. By the eighth century B.C., Hellenic civilization had established, all along the southern Italian coast, a network of rich and prosperous cities very likely serviced by an equally prosperous peasantry. Beginning with the third century B.C., however, a series of less

---

[1] The South of Italy, *Il Mezzogiorno*, traditionally comprises the regions of Campania, Abruzzi, Molise, Apulia, Lucania (or Basilicata), Calabria, and the islands of Sicily and Sardinia, while the remainder of the country is generally referred to as "northern Italy." This chapter does not give the history of the remarkable variety of people, but merely points out some common features and a few historical and economic highlights that will later allow better understanding of the socioeconomic conditions of the present-day South.

beneficial invasions, lasting well into modern times, ravaged the southern regions to such an extent that the area has still not fully recovered. The first onslaught was ushered in by the Romans, whose destruction of Lucania and Apulia was so complete that historians in the first century A.D. could find no trace of the previous cultures of these regions (Schachter, 1965, 29). So devastating in its effects was the Roman conquest that, according to Schachter, even before the Roman Empire started to decay, southern Italy was properly considered a backward region.[2] The subsequent barbarian invasions of the entire Italian peninsula further eroded the conditions of the region. In the ensuing centuries, first the Arabs, then the Normans, followed by a host of other foreigners, including the Germans, the Spanish, and the French, overran the area in a succession of waves. They caused a continuous state of chaos, widespread demoralization, and a series of violent transfers of property (Vöchting, 1955, 32). The result was the most indescribable poverty. For the masses of people, ownership of land and all other forms of property were almost completely nonexistent. This condition was to persist until the beginning of the nineteenth century, when feudalism, that peculiar culmination of southern evils, was finally abrogated.

In the thirteenth century and the era of Hohenstaufen domination, the Holy Roman Emperor Frederick II, whom Burckhardt once styled "the first modern man to sit upon a throne" (1961, 41), attempted to resuscitate and reorganize the southern economy. In the most thoroughly systematic fashion he proceeded to destroy serfdom and the feudal state, abolishing, too, many of the trade restrictions and hindrances so detrimental to the economy of the region. In the process, however, Frederick's policies served also to transform the people into a multitude destitute of any will and of all means of resistance, directed as they were to the sole consideration of being "profitable in the utmost degree to the treasury" (Burckhardt, 1961, 42). Despite the fact that he was at least moderately successful in reviving the

---

[2] Schachter here cites Giuseppe Maria Galanti, *Relazioni sull'Italia Meridionale* (Milan: Universale Economica, n.d.), pp. 59ff.

southern economy, his authoritarian state, built as it was on an extremely rigid administrative structure and on an extensive network of strict monopolies, militated against occupational diversification, a sense of social conscience, a spirit of self-reliance, and public trust (Vöchting, 1955, 34). To make matters worse, after Frederick's death, his son became embroiled in nineteen years of civil war, during which time those few economic gains achieved earlier were lost. Southern Italy slipped back into the status quo which had preceded Frederick (Schachter, 1965, 30).

Under Charles of Anjou, who assumed authority as King of Naples and Sicily in 1268, bringing to an end the Hohenstaufen rule, further chaos was added to the picture. To the old ills he added a new and more virulent one. Within a short time, his kingdom was so dependent on the financial and commercial capital of the North that, writing in 1902, George Yvers could refer to the situation as "colonial imperialistic" (1902). In order to help him reach southern Italy, the great Florentine banks had provided Charles of Anjou with large sums of money. Consequently, upon ascending the throne, he repaid his creditors with handsome privileges, all very costly to the southern population. The Florentine banks, already creditors to half of Europe, found in the South of Italy a market lending itself to the utmost exploitation. They were given the right to coin money, administer the saltworks and salt monopoly, collect port charges, and levy taxes on the proceeds from state lands in Apulia, and, what is far worse, to manage the exportation of grain, the basic produce of the South, which since the days of Frederick II had been administered by the state.

The Florentines were further entrusted with paying salaries to state employees and soldiers; they supplied the needs of the army and the luxury items for the court itself; and they appropriated as many other privileges and rights as they were pleased to receive. Their lust for excessive profit and the lack of scruples with which they collected taxes, administered offices, and plundered monopolies gave rise in the general population to an intense hatred of the state, the merchant, the public official, and all public institutions. Even a somber scholar like Vöchting (1955, 36–38) was recently led to state that Florentine finance extended its tentacles, like an octopus, over all of southern Italy, sucking the riches from this economic colony and leaving behind nothing but squalid destitution.

With the rise of the Aragonese hegemony in southern Italy in the fifteenth century, the Florentine banks gradually lost their choking grip on the southern economy. Not until the middle of the sixteenth century, when the economic exploitation of the South was taken over by Genoa on the western coast and by Venice on the eastern, did they lose it entirely.

The effects of the Florentine economic domination of the South were not all negative. To some extent, Florence brought southern Italy into contact with the social, artistic, and scientific Renaissance of Tuscany. The southern culture, to that time largely based on the decaying traditions of the Arabo-Byzantine style, was to a degree revived and brought into the orbit of Florentine culture. It is also true, however, that the feudal structure, which the Florentines had served to strengthen in the South, effectively resisted a full blooming of the new spirit. It is likely that the failure of Florentine culture to become more deeply entrenched in the South was to a large extent due to the distaste of southern intellectuals for everything Florentine, an attitude which must have developed during the Florentine reign of economic exploitation.

Aragonese rule proved to be no improvement over the earlier dynasties. Extravagant and degenerate (Burckhardt, 1961, 60–61), its demise in 1503 marked the end of an era. If, as is sometimes said, modern European history begins at the end of the fifteenth century, coinciding with the discovery of America, the modern history of southern Italy begins with the Spanish domination that was part of the general colonial expansion of the Spanish kingdom. With the beginning of Spanish ascendancy in 1503, the economic and social difficulties of southern Italy were exacerbated.

For a while, the Spaniards succeeded in effecting certain beneficial changes such as taming the southern barons, who had at least equaled the conquerors in their selfishness and arrogance toward the masses. But in the long run, the old ills remained, and the Spanish dynasty added to them a few more. A brief listing of some of the more serious wrongs perpetrated by the new regime might include (1) an arbitrariness of the laws so that they never applied to the *gran signore* (powerful lord) and other privileged individuals; in cases of quarrel between employer and worker, for instance, the employer was all too often both the accuser and judge; (2) all manner of rights of preemption, banishment, and coercion which lent themselves to every kind of oppression; and (3) a system of excessive and abusive taxation.

Although the southern economy remained essentially static during the first 120 years of Spanish domination, state revenues increased from 800,000 ducats to 5,000,000. The burden of those taxes fell naturally on the poorest classes, the peasants. In 1575, for instance, the hearth tax alone represented 45 percent of the ordinary state income. The tax was collected with indescribable brutality, as exemplified by the practice of appropriating and selling at public auctions the very roofs from the houses of those unfortunate enough to be in arrears.[3]

At about this time, a new scourge arose to plague the already overburdened peasantry. Largely as a result of the never-ending litigations among the aristocracy for possession of unclearly demarcated state territories, a class of lawyers arose, mostly from the masses, who gradually became one of the most powerful and wealthy groups among the rising bourgeoisie. So powerful was this group that a duke of Brunswick quipped, around the end of the eighteenth century, that to be socially and economically successful it was enough to be a soldier in Berlin, a priest in Rome, or a lawyer in Naples (Fortunato, 1926, I:82). These successful lawyers, together with a small group of rich merchants, soon learned to compete with the nobility for titles. So marked indeed was this competition by the end of the sixteenth century, that in 1597 it was said that "the Court received applications for titles which offered as much as half a million in gold. . . . And the

---

[3] For a discussion of taxes imposed on the population, see Pino-Branca (1938), pp. 472–474.

King sold the title of prince for 20,000 *scudi*, of duke for 15,000, of marquis for 10,000, and of count for 5,000" (Pino-Branca, 1938, 458).

In having their ambition for an aristocratic title satisfied, these petty lords enjoyed not merely social advantages but, what was far worse for the already overtaxed masses, appreciable reductions in taxes as well. As a result, the peasant masses paid increasingly higher bills at the same time that they were defrauded of those very elements in their ranks whose greater energy and political capacity might otherwise have led them to protest against the general corruption and exploitation.[4]

Conditions were worsened by the Spanish monarchs in yet another, more direct, fashion. Due to a most singular characteristic, a never-ending obsession with the danger of conspiratorial activities, they were forever ready to proceed with the utmost severity against enemies and suspects alike. Fully understanding that the populace could not engage in effective political action without the nobles, who in turn could not act without the support of the populace, the monarchs took every opportunity to create conflict between the two classes and, further, to encourage disharmony among the nobles themselves by creating contrasts within their group, exciting their envy and favoring the enemies of one or another. This policy did indeed have the intended effect of weakening nobility and populace alike, impeding their agreement for any concerted action. It also had the effect of augmenting the arrogance and the arbitrariness of the nobles toward the populace, as well as permitting the provincial officers to enrich themselves by selling favors (Pino-Branca, 1938, 467–468). The end result of this policy of divide and rule was a state of generalized disintegration and conflict, with the masses defenseless against the arrogance and avariciousness of the nobles, old and new, as well as against the tendency within their own ranks to transfer aggression onto weaker parties.

---

[4] For a theoretical discussion of this issue, see Pareto (1935), Vol. II, Sections 2178–2179, where Pareto discusses the difficulties involved in overthrowing a governing class that is adept in absorbing the best men of the governed class and in the shrewd use of chicanery, fraud, and corruption.

To the above circumstances must be added yet another endless succession of Spanish viceroys. During the slightly more than 200 years of direct Spanish hegemony, no less than sixty viceroys ruled for an average duration of less than four years apiece. On the one hand, instability prevented the development of any lasting policies beneficial to the state and the population. On the other hand, it resulted in an unhindered contest among the viceroys to amass riches and to procure for themselves, cheaply and at the expense of the population, the favor of the distant Spanish court (Vöchting, 1955, 42). Again the brunt of the added burdens fell on the already overburdened and impoverished masses. The result was their total demoralization together with a boundless hatred of their peasant lot and of all persons in positions of power and authority. What is far worse, however, as we shall have further occasion to see, this situation also gave rise to a particularly critical form of social pathology that made of every man—fellow peasant as well as superior—a dangerous and despicable competitor and enemy.

Nor was the situation helped at all by the slight economic intelligence of the Neapolitan kings. The principle followed was simple and incredible: cut down the tree before it yields. Toward the end of the sixteenth century, for instance, a new tax imposed on the exportation of silk was so heavy that it marked the end of the exportation of this product and, of course, all revenues from it. The production of silk was reduced to one-fifth of the original volume. Again, toward the end of the eighteenth century the duty imposed on raw silk from the region of Apulia had reached such a level that it was more than 50 percent higher than that imposed on imported silk. Such a policy could hardly encourage internal production. In fact, while other states encouraged the exportation of finished products, the Neapolitan state exported its grains, oil, fruits, and fibers largely as raw materials, later reimporting them in a finished form (Dal Pane, 1932, I:50ff.).

Private initiative was, under such circumstances, quickly destroyed. When attempts were made to improve techniques of olive pressing, to plant potentially profitable trees, or to expand the cultivation of cotton, new and heavy taxes choked initiative at its birth, forestalling every attempt at innovation and improvement. To make things worse, rights of taxation and monopolies were often leased to third parties, the right of tax collection coming to be equal to the right of exploitation.[5]

With respect to the peasant's relation to the land, by the eighteenth century, fifty-nine out of every sixty families did not own enough land in which to be buried (Vöchting, 1955, 45). In changing hands, the land almost invariably went from one noble to another or from the aristocracy to the Church. It is estimated that by the end of the eighteenth century the Church, the *Manomorta*, had in some provinces achieved control of as much as 80 percent of all tillable land (Ricchioni, 1946, 238). It is true that in contrast to the excessive cruelty of the secular masters, the Church was a somewhat more benign master. It is no less true, however, that the Manomorta was particularly active in discouraging all but the most traditional and inefficient techniques of cultivation (Vöchting, 1955, 45). The land of southern Italy was never very fertile, but the failure to develop rational techniques of farming made impossible an already difficult situation.

Things in general went a little better on the lands of secular lords as long as the owners themselves were the administrators of the property and lived on their manors. Toward the end of the seventeenth century, however, a marked tendency toward urban living developed among the nobility. Two factors were probably most responsible for this phenomenon. On the one hand, with a recrudescence of malaria, the urban setting, being less dangerous, became also more attractive. On the other, an increasing tendency developed on the part of the state to intervene in questions regarding the rights and duties of the inhabitants of feudal lands, questions that had previously fallen regularly under the jurisdiction of the lord and required his presence on the land.

To these circumstances two others may be added. First, during this period the lord's rights were frequently challenged,

---

[5] Southern commerce was now in the hands of speculators from the North and other European peoples, such as the French, the Dutch, and the English. See Arias, 1919, I:83.

and as a consequence it became increasingly necessary for him to go to Naples in order to attend to legal matters. Eventually, he found it convenient to settle permanently in the city. Second, residence in the city involved also a number of economic and social advantages. The pomp and pleasures of court life attracted the more socially ambitious, while others saw occupational advantages in the proliferation of official positions. For these reasons and others, absenteeism, which previously had been an exception, became widespread among the landed nobility by the end of the eighteenth century (Vöchting, 1955, 46–47). Concomitantly, the impoverished peasants were left without capital and farming guidance, each pursuing his own avocation according to his ancient beliefs and with one goal overshadowing all others: minimize all risks in order to insure survival.

The urbanization of feudal lords had still another deleterious consequence. As the nobles moved to the city, they found it necessary to entrust the administration of their properties to overseers. These individuals could conceivably have performed the functions of the lord with respect to the improvement of the land and farming techniques. Instead, however, they were most often ignorant persons motivated only by a desire to enrich themselves in the shortest possible time at the expense of the noble and the peasant both. Genovesi attributes to the lords' absenteeism and to the accompanying phenomenon of the feudal administrator one of the major causes of the agricultural backwardness of the South, arguing that the peasants had neither the education, the spirit of enterprise, nor the capital to engage in rational cultivation of the land (Genovesi in Villari, 1963, 3–11).

The administrator's main concern was with his own self-enrichment and aggrandizement. All considerations of human regard, justice, or charity were therefore largely irrelevant. So successful were the overseers that not infrequently they became sufficiently rich to buy a title, thus achieving the loftiest of their goals. If the administrator himself failed, the climb was often made by his children. As a financially successful individual, he sometimes sent his children away to school to be trained as doctors or lawyers. With a little perseverance, luck, and some pushing, the lawyers might then become high magistrates, and to such persons titles were quite regularly accorded (Blanch in Croce, 1945, I:42–45). In general, it may be said that, once the peasant station was abandoned—for one reason or another—many a climber's aim was to gain a position in the aristocratic estate. And in relation to the peasant, the individual in "the third estate" was, as Mumford says of the European townsman of the twelfth and thirteenth centuries, "something of a snob, with such snobbery as only the upstart and the *nouveau riche* can achieve" (Mumford, 1938, 27).

A bird's-eye view of the Italian South toward the end of the eighteenth century, that is, in the final years of the feudal period, shows that, barring very few exceptions, the Church and the nobles owned all the land. The peasants worked the land to satisfy their minimal needs, in return for which they had to pay to the limits of their energy in toil, as well as to tolerate all manner of abuse, humiliation, and occasionally physical punishment. For, in addition to the old "royal rights" of the lord, which in the course of the centuries had been expanded to include the absolute ownership of peasant holdings and the communal lands as well as the demesne lands, there were also the "personal rights." These included a great variety of privileges that went all the way from the right to the best fruit of the land to the famous right of the first night. Such rights were further reinforced by the prevailing custom among the southern nobility of keeping large numbers of armed bodyguards (Anderson, 1962, 39).

As far as the peasant was concerned, the lawyers and local overseers were second only to the lord—sacred or secular—in power and influence. In their never-ceasing drive to enrich themselves and join the ranks of the aristocrats, these men often rendered the peasant's lot most precarious. The only other group of any importance in southern Italian society consisted of a small group of professionals and clerks, who were usually either the descendants of noble families gone in decay or newly mobile protégés of feudal lords.

The number of persons engaged in commerce was insignificant. More insignificant still were the craftsmen and enlightened intelligentsia. Elsewhere in Europe, and to some extent in northern Italy, these groups were acquiring the character and functions of a capitalistic bourgeoisie, essentially oriented toward the abolition of feudalism. In southern Italy, they were involved in an antibaronial struggle, too, but usually as individuals for strictly personal motives.

Finally, at the bottom of the hierarchy, stood the mass of peasants languishing in hunger, disease, and exhaustion. Lacking the leadership, the legal support, the education, and the moral strength to organize a protest, they accepted as given and unalterable the existing order of things. But existing in a state of constant oppression, at the least provocation they struck out against one another and applied to each other criteria of treatment analogous to those applied against them by their superiors. *"Prega lu galantomu ca si scaza: non pregari a lu villanu ca s'innaza,"* goes an old Calabrian proverb. ("Beg of a gentleman, and he will give you his shoes; do not beg of a villein, for he will act superior.") The peasants learned to play among themselves the game of the wolf and the lamb; and so it was that they turned to making all manner of prestige gradations within their own estate. Those who possessed even a small *"fazzoletto"* (handkerchief) of land were superior to those who did not; those who tilled certain particularly fertile plots were better than others; those whose strips of land were situated near the village were more important than those whose land was farther away. Those who were on amicable terms with the landlords were superior to those who were not. Finally, those very few who—whether through their own savings or through the proprietor's capital—owned a team of oxen, and possibly a cart to go with it, constituted what amounted to a caste of their own, practicing the strictest endogamy well into recent decades.

With the invasion of the revolutionary French in the last decade of the eighteenth century, a new era began in the history of southern Italy. On February 18, 1799, during the ill-fated Neapolitan revolution, the Legislative Council of the Neapolitan republic discussed, for the first time, the problem of land reform. A small group of Jacobins argued in vain for a vigorous reform which would abolish all feudal rights and distribute all feudal lands to the peasants. A majority of the Republicans, on the other hand, had a more moderate program, which was approved as law on April 25, 1799. This law abolished the jurisdiction and the privileges of the barons, allowing them, however, to keep possession of all their holdings except the communal lands on which the population had originally exercised the rights of usage. A few months later, however, the revolution failed, and with the restitution of the Bourbon monarch that same year, both Jacobins and moderates found themselves together on the executioner's scaffold. The law on land reform—inadequate as it was—did not go into effect.

In 1806, Napoleon installed his liberal brother Joseph on the Neapolitan throne, driving the Bourbons into exile. During his two-year reign, Joseph attempted many administrative reforms, by far the most critical of which consisted of the official abolition of serfdom, made law on August 2, 1806. At that time, too, an agrarian reform was instituted, and some of the feudal lands were finally distributed to the landless (Fortunato in Villari, 1963, 161–170). The reform, however, was from the very beginning ill-fated, resistance against it being so strong that as late as 1843 much smoke and very little fire surrounded this problem. No wonder that the agrarian question has risen time and again in the history of the South, and still remains unsolved. It came up again immediately after the unification of Italy in 1861, again especially in 1884, 1893, 1897, 1902, 1904, 1924, and finally after World War II, to mention but some of the more important dates.

Writing in 1879, Giustino Fortunato, one of the most illustrious minds of "the southern question," had reason to state:

. . . those peasants who since 1806 were fortunate enough to profit from the distribution of state lands have not yet come out of their abject conditions; quite the opposite. The shares assigned to the peasants, which vary from 83 ares to 1½ hectares,[6] according to the fertility of the land, are much too small for the subsistence of a

---

[6] 100 ares = 1 hectare; 1 hectare = 2.47 acres.—J. L.

family; and even considering the larger shares, the peasants entirely lack the capital necessary for the proper care of the land. Production is scant; the soil is soon exhausted; the town and government taxes are high and inescapable. As a result, one of three things happens: (1) the share is taken back by the town for unfulfilled payment; (2) it is sold for an insignificant amount to a local landowner; (3) finally, it is surrendered to the usurer to pay for contracted debts. And let us not speak of the frauds which happened, and still happen, whereby the distribution is favorable to the better off . . . (Fortunato, 1911, I:88).

Such hardships did the new petty proprietor have to endure that, according to Vöchting, he "felt such an irresistible need to breathe freely even for a short period of time, that he often considered the piece of land given him a sort of warrant for cash payment rather than a guarantee of a better and more independent existence, previously so ardently desired" (Vöchting, 1955, 55–56). In sum, he sold the land. Thus, a certain irony is involved in the land reform of southern Italy, as initiated in 1806, for the reform had an effect which was in some respects the very antithesis of the one intended. The process of usurpation of the communal lands, initiated by the feudal lords around the middle of the seventeenth century, was intensified after the land reform of 1806, so that by 1879 only about 300,000 hectares remained in tillable public lands, with an immense residue of resentment and hatred (Fortunato in Villari, 1963, 161–170) and indescribable "moral disorder" (Franchetti, 1950, 171). Likewise, the peasants' small shares—both those received on the basis of the land reform and those few previously held—fell gradually and increasingly into the hands of the large proprietors.

To be sure, laws had been instituted which forbade the sale of distributed shares, but these were easily evaded, the more so since evasion was in the interest of the upper class. Thus, on December 3, 1808, a decree by Joseph's successor, King Joachim Murat, forbade the sale or mortgaging of lands for a period of ten years from the time of the grant. Ferdinand I, the restored Bourbon monarch, reinforced the decree in a law promulgated on December 12, 1816. On December 6, 1852, Ferdinand II extended the period of inalienability from ten to twenty years. Neverthe-less, ways and means were found by the nobles, the bourgeois proprietors, the town, and the Church to transfer ownership of the land from the peasants to themselves.

A few examples will clearly indicate the extent of this trans-fer. According to Fortunato, the land previously distributed in the town of Atella had by 1879 passed almost in its entirety into the possession of the municipality—this within only a twenty-year period. In Barletta, at least 600 of the 800 shares previously distributed to peasants had fallen into the hands of latifundists. The numerous shares distributed in Eboli, the town rendered famous by Carlo Levi's mordant account of life in southern Italy in the Mussolini era (Levi, 1947), had soon become the possession of two or three large landowners of the Salerno plains. Again, of the 7260 shares distributed in the province of Teramo, only 2777 were still held by the original grantees in 1879 (Fortunato in Villari, 1963, 167).

The political situation in the Neapolitan kingdom subsequent to the fall of the Napoleonic rulers only served to exacerbate the situation and render effective reform virtually impossible. The restored Bourbon monarchy—ruled first by Ferdinand I and after 1825 by his son, the "brutal and treacherous" Francis I—was under the actual control of reactionary Austria, whose troops were garrisoned there. Two abortive revolts, one in 1820 and the second five years later, served as witness to the misery and chaos of the area. In fact, the Neapolitan state of 1825 has been charac-terized as having

. . . its prisons full, its civil and ecclesiastical offices in the hands of the most venal administrators, its towns swarming with spies, and its provinces infested with outlaws. . . . (Artz, 1934, 246).

Given the circumstances of the times, no law, reform, or decree in favor of the peasantry could have had its desired effect. The peasant was prostrate, demoralized, and ignorant before his usurers, his deceitful lawyers, his vain and avaricious barons, and before a Church whose secular and religious roles he could hardly reconcile. The peasant saw justice as merely the power to make wishes prevail. To the peasant, there was only one right, that of the stronger. What means of self-protection were available to the weakened peasantry?

In my opinion, Vöchting puts his finger on the truth when he argues that it is in this state of mind, and in the manner of acting which derives from it, that the meaning Sicilians give to the concept of *mafia* is to be found. For many Sicilians still today, the mafia does not signify criminality; rather, it expresses an attitude anchored in the belief that one must trust only his own personal strength in order to protect his person and his possessions (Vöchting, 1955, 52). The peasants did not start the mafia. It would seem, indeed, that this odd phenomenon was originally a development among the middle-class customs officers and land-owners. Once it was started, however, the peasants soon learned to respect the legitimacy of its spirit.

This same attitude fostered to a very large extent that strange type of civil war which, under the name of *brigantaggio,* raged in southern Italy throughout the nineteenth century. In the eyes of the common peasant, the brigand justly became a romantic figure. He represented a just and honorable protest against existing injustices, a living confirmation of the human dignity that was so often trampled upon through the person of the peasant. The lack of any forum for the expression of public opinion, the difficulties that were involved in going to a court of justice, the excessive cost of a trial, the weakness of the government in curbing arbitrary actions, and many other such factors had the effect of leaving the victim no other alternative to violence but to lower his head and accept humiliation (Vöchting, 1955, 53), until the brigand assumed his role.

Fundamentally, the phenomenon of brigandage was a vivid form of social protest against the failure of the gentry and the state to restore to the peasant a modicum of economic security and his long-lost rights of human dignity. It is interesting to note that its most virulent peaks were reached immediately after the years 1806 and 1860, periods in which promises of transformation were made but in which the aspirations of peasants were repeatedly frustrated. Brigandage was strongest where poverty and human misery were greatest. It was most excessive, for instance, in the Capitanata zone of Apulia, where the land was controlled by a handful of latifundists who kept it under "extensive" rather than "intensive" cultivation, leaving a very large number of workless peasants to "own absolutely nothing and live by stealing." On the other hand, where relations between the proprietor and the peasant were better, brigandage did not have deep roots (Massari in Villari, 1963, 93).

Brigandage naturally fed on the general moral and legal chaos produced by the Bourbon dynasty. According to Massari,

Those men who in the period of only sixty years were butchered at the gallows by the Bourbon Government, or sent suffering in prison or in exile, were not the unhappiest victims. The executioner's axe and the hangman's rope were neither the major nor the most cruel instruments of torture used by the Bourbons, who set about with might and main to commit the most nefarious of parricides, namely, that of destroying in an entire people any notion of right and just (in Villari, 1963, 95).

The Church, too, often supported brigandage. Its basic interest was in the development of a guerrilla band that supported the papacy. In a monastery near Salerno, for instance, brigands were recruited. In a city near Bari, leaflets were distributed which announced that "brigands were blessed by the pope." Many monasteries were the headquarters and supply depots of the brigands (Massari in Villari, 1963, 98–99).

Brigandage was eventually eliminated, at least in its most virulent form, but the southern peasants were left with a hatred and disgust for their society and its leaders, the real intensity of which became apparent only at the turn of the century, when the peasants began fleeing their country in a veritable human flood. Massari was correct when he stated in 1863 that "the greatest ill afflicting the southern populations is their lack of faith in legality and justice" (in Villari, 1963, 101).

The policy of divide and rule practiced by the Bourbons,

together with the most squalid poverty and most cruel injustices had, by 1861, produced enormous problems. These were not strictly economic, but were more fundamentally problems of social disorder, rampant suspiciousness, and uncontrollable conflicts. Men lived in a society that was not a society at all in any real sense. He who in a given village had reached the dignity of mayor had also the unlimited powers of a king. Unquestioned, he distributed positions and lands; he alone distributed the weight of taxes; he administered the public-improvement projects in his own favor and to the advantage of his followers. The tenacity with which he held onto the reins of power was in direct proportion to the knowledge of what would happen to him and to his followers should his opponent win. This conduct, these now common usurpations, robberies, and abuses, had inflicted hard blows to the sense of justice. As Vöchting puts it, the individual without scruples came to be considered a hero; violence was an index of energy, whose only proof was success; the situation encouraged any means of self-defense (Vöchting, 1955, 70–71). The kind of Italian that developed as a result was a good candidate to enter the modern world of rational organization and development as a chronic misfit and alienated citizen.

The Years since the National Unification

Southern Italy thus reached 1861, the year of Italian unification, in an indescribable state of economic and social poverty. The region was inhabited by a large number of impoverished, sickly, and demoralized workers living in strange entanglements of hovels and caverns built on hills and mountain tops with little connection with one another, often quite inaccessible and entirely cut off from the external world in the rainy months. Despite the fact that in 1839 King Ferdinand II had been the first in Italy to open a railroad, one going from Naples to Portici, the unification of Italy found the South with a total of only 184 kilometers of track, almost all of it in the neighborhood of Naples. In contrast, the North could boast of a total of 2336 kilometers, distributed rather widely throughout that region (SVIMEZ, 1961, Table 252, 477).

When the soldiers of the Italian army and the Italian administrators entered such classical southern regions as Basilicata and Calabria, they found the population divided into three main classes of people: a small number of very powerful landlords; a group of lawyers too numerous for the needs of a land with very little industry and commerce; and a vast mass of landless peasants living in economic dependence and semislavery. Very few peasants owned land of their own. Still fewer were the merchants, the artisans, and the intelligentsia capable of influencing the socioeconomic conditions of the times (Franchetti, 1950, 55–56). Speaking of the differences between North and South at this period, Neufeld points out that the acquisition of industrial and commercial wealth in the North carried no stigma and thus drew investments from noble families; but in the South,

. . . the owners of extensive real property continued the attitudes of the old landed nobility and disdained any form of commerce or manufacturing. They either turned back into farming, profits garnered from the soil, or used these savings to pay the costs of leading lives of wealthy leisure. The other classes had little capital to invest in anything; nevertheless they absorbed the mannerisms of their economic betters. They too opposed fresh approaches and new methods in business and industry (Neufeld, 1961, 147).

For a while, hopes had been high that Italy would soon enter the community of modern nations as a vigorous and united society. Time demonstrated, however, that the political unification of Italy in the period from 1859 to 1870 brought with it neither economic nor cultural unity. North and South continued to be like two separate worlds. In fact, the already underprivileged economy of the South was gravely damaged by national unification. Although prior to 1861 the South was predominantly an agricultural region, at least Naples and its immediate surroundings had become the seat of considerable industrial activity. This area, in fact, could boast a number of factories producing consumer goods, machine shops, and even a heavy industry which, under a reasonable customs protection, enjoyed relative prosperity. With unification, the protection was dropped, and the competition of northern industry became overwhelming. While the North profited from the extension of its products to the national market (Saraceno, 1961, 704), many of the previously prospering southern firms had to be shut down, while others succeeded in surviving only at the cost of further exploitation of the worker (Vöchting, 1955, 84). The impact of national unification on the Italian South is best realized in Giustino Fortunato's statement of 1890 that "we were still on the threshold of the Middle Ages when we were all at once hurled into the modern era" (1926, 204). The ensuing loss of work and the disbanding of the Bourbon army and police combined to swell the ranks of the unemployed, the vagabonds, and the brigands.

As if all this were not enough, the new Italian state imposed new and higher taxes on the population. The heavy debts contracted during the wars of unification had to be paid. New debts were necessary in order to bear the financial burdens of the new administration, the organization of the schools, the system of communications, and the army. United Italy, moreover, soon developed the tastes of a "major power," engaging in foreign adventures which involved newer and greater debts for the masses to bear. The impoverished South naturally felt the brunt of the new taxes most bitterly. So crippling was the new tax burden on the southern masses, and so angered were they, that the southern populations sometimes massacred entire units of the newly arrived Piedmontese soldiers as a form of protest (Russo, 1958, 285–286).

The original disadvantage of the South was further aggravated by the economic policy of united Italy, a policy that was dominated by northern interests. Nitti contended, for instance, that after the political unification of 1861 both the tax burden and public expenditures were inequitably distributed between North and South. The South contributed more to government revenues in proportion to its wealth, while at the same time benefiting less from government disbursements in proportion to what it paid (Nitti, 1958). Nitti attributed great weight to this factor as a source of progressive impoverishment of the South, and although other scholars have questioned the accuracy of his argument, few probably would deny that the tax burden borne by the South was too high in relation to its share of the national income (Lutz, 1962, 96).

In the 1880's, the new Italian state embarked on a protectionist policy, with respect to foreign trade, that was particularly deleterious to the South. Thus in 1886–1887 Italy made a revision of its tariff, which France, her chief customer, immediately countered, precipitating the grave Italian economic depression of 1887–1890. The increased duties on French goods provoked such retaliation that 40 percent of Italian exports were dammed up. The volume of annual exports to France dropped precipitously from a total value of 500 million lire to one of 167 million. The South was hit particularly hard. At that time Italy exported mostly agricultural goods, with the result that exportation of the southern products came almost to a standstill. The agricultural depression that ensued in the South shook the very foundations of that region's economy. The price of wheat fell first to 22 lire a quintal in 1888, and then to 13.5 in 1894. Yet Sonnino, then minister of the treasury, chose this moment to increase the tax on grain and to raise the price of certain basic consumer goods, among them salt. As a result of measures such as these, capital was drained from the South at precisely the time that it was so badly needed.[7]

The die of national political unity, however, had been cast, and it was only a matter of time before the Italian government realized that a country could not be truly united unless it were economically united. Accordingly, it soon began to address itself to the economic problems of the southern regions, so that in 1961, Pasquale Saraceno (1961, 694), then vice president of Associazione per lo Sviluppo Dell'Industria nel Mezzogiorno (SVIMEZ, Association for the Development of Industry in the South), a government-sponsored association specifically concerned with industrial development in the South, could state that it was alto-

---

[7] For a brief discussion of these questions, see Smith, 1959, especially pages 157–162 and 230–242.

gether correct to say that we can today "remember at one and the same time a century of political unity and a century of political intervention for the South."

As early as 1861, the new Italian state began to show an appreciable interest in the construction of roads and waterworks, in the repair and construction of ports, in the installation of telegraphs, in subsidies to the merchant marine, and above all, in the extension of the railroad network. Thus, whereas in 1861 the railroads in the South comprised only about 7 percent of the total national network, fifteen years later about one-third of the national network was located in this region (Saraceno, 1961, 695).

Similarly, the new state did not fail to address itself to the solution of the old problems carried over from the days of feudalism. Thus, between 1860 and 1885 appeared a variety of laws such as the law for the enfranchisement of the land on the famous Tavoliere in Apulia; numerous laws dealing with the liquidation of municipal rights, the assessment of municipal demesnes, the abolition of primogeniture rules; and above all the law, enacted in 1867, for the confiscation of Church property (Saraceno, 1961, 695). Such measures were intended to give the southern regions an opportunity to compete with those of the North from a base of comparable economic and legal structures. Underlying them was the erroneous assumption that, given analogous social and legal structures, the South would soon catch up with the North in the economic sphere. Furthermore, until the last quarter of the century, the lack of serious study concerning southern problems allowed for yet another assumption deleterious to the South, namely, that this region was a naturally rich area impoverished by Bourbon misrule and the laziness and corruption of its inhabitants (Smith, 1959, 230). Ultimately, it was realized that the economic chasm existing between North and South was not bridgeable by such devices. Starting from an initially superior position, with superior natural resources, the North actually increased its advantages over the South, so that from year to year the economic gap between the northern and the southern regions widened rather than narrowed.

It was not until the end of the nineteenth century that,

largely owing to the influence of a handful of profound scholars
of the Italian South, attempts were initiated to rectify this situation by giving the South a head start, as it were. Thus between
1897 and 1906 special laws were enacted for the southern regions.
One law for the city of Naples in 1904 sought to give a boost to
the industry of the South by giving the industrial zone around
Naples special fiscal and customs privileges. Such industrial privileges were then extended to the entire South in 1906.

The roots of the southern economic difficulties, however,
were very deep. They included not only the natural poverty of
the South, but also those historical and social circumstances, previously mentioned, which weakened the will and the ability of
the people to engage effectively in any form of communal or
collective undertaking. If the southern regions failed to respond
to the national attempts to create an economic and cultural rapprochement between North and South, it was not alone due to
the fact of having a smaller economic dowry. It was also a matter
of not having sufficient resolution to support these attempts, nor
sufficient faith in their efficacy. Cooperation, conduct directed to
the public good, and faith in one's fellow men, particularly the
political elite, had long ago disappeared from the cultural endow-
ment of the southern people. The southern bourgeoisie and nobility had long exploited the masses for personal advantage; the masses
were only too aware of this fact. Any public intervention, however honest and well meant, was defined only in this light. As a
result of these circumstances, and no doubt also as a result of the
rapidity of economic expansion in northern regions, which were
by then in the midst of the Industrial Revolution, the Italian
nation reached the dawn of World War I with North and South
further apart than ever.

Despite the new problems and expenditures created by the
war, the government did not cease in its attempts to solve the
southern problems. Thus—partly as an attempt to harness the
support of agricultural workers to the war effort as the country
was preparing to enter the war—all kinds of solemn promises,
particularly favorable to the southern peasantry, were officially
proclaimed by representatives of the government. After the war

had already begun, for instance, Salandra, then president of the Council of Ministers, made the following declaration in the Chamber of Deputies, subsequently read and explained to the soldiers at the front:

After the victorious end of the war, Italy shall accomplish a great act of social justice. Italy will give to the peasants the land and every-thing else that is required, so that each hero, returning from the front, after having valorously fought in the trenches, can achieve economic independence. This will be the reward offered by the homeland to her courageous sons (Di Vittorio in Villari, 1963, 572).

This lofty promise was never honored. Nevertheless, at the end of the war, the sharecroppers and other dependent peasants were the recipients of numerous advantages—more so in the North than in the South, but even in the South some benefits were felt. First and perhaps foremost among these benefits was the replacement of individual by collective contracts, whereby the landowners could no longer impose their will on the individ-ual, hence defenseless, peasants. With the advent of the collective contract, the peasant organizations dealt with the landowners, or with the organizations representing them, concluding a single contract for all the peasants of a given zone; this zone very often comprised an entire province. Many of the most hideous forms of exploitation which had remained since feudal times were now abolished. The following examples will give a good idea of the magnitude of peasant achievements in the period between the close of World War I and the advent of Fascism in 1922.

In all sharecropping contracts, seeds, chemical fertilizers, and other products necessary to agricultural production had pre-viously been entirely the responsibility of the peasant. Similarly, the peasant had been subject to the so-called *appendici,* a complex set of taxes which the landowners levied against the sharecroppers and other dependent agricultural workers. For instance, each year the peasants were obliged to contribute a certain number of workdays on the landowner's farm without receiving any com-pensation. They also had to give gratuitously a certain number of chickens per year and perhaps a fixed number of eggs per week.

Again, they paid a yearly sum for the rental of the farmhouse, and they even had to pay a special tax if they wished to raise a pig.

With the advent of peasant organizations and the phenomenon of collective contracts, many of the landowners' special privileges were abolished. According to the new contracts, the owners were compelled to pay half of all expenses for seeds, insecticides, fertilizers, and the like. Furthermore, it was now established that even after the contract between the landowner and peasant was terminated, the landowner could not evict the peasant except for such reasons as were considered valid by a local commission of experts, of whom half were representatives of the peasantry. And through the so-called Visocchi Decree on September 2, 1919, the Italian government recognized the right of those organized into cooperatives to occupy the uncultivated or poorly cultivated lands of latifundists. In fact, the measures taken in favor of the peasantry were truly impressive. Farmhands received an appreciable increase in wages, a reduction in working hours, and various other benefits. According to one law, agricultural cooperatives and poor peasants were granted long-term loans at favorable rates of interest, while another law prohibited increases in rent.

A number of active peasant organizations strengthened the resolution of the government to do away with those aspects of the feudal system which still lingered on. A few of these deserve special attention. The socialist National Federation of Agricultural Workers had, by 1920, a membership of 1,145,000. It was among the first peasant organizations to demand and fight for collective contracts. The Italian Confederation of Workers had a membership of around 945,000, and was sponsored by the Catholic Partito Popolare, headed by the sociologist-priest, Don Luigi Sturzo. Among the various other peasant organizations which might be mentioned, the National Association of War Veterans, though not specifically a peasant association, was in rural localities composed almost exclusively of peasants. And the Peasant Party, though small in membership, was active and on the whole successful in its demands (Di Vittorio in Villari, 1963, 581–582).

When in 1922 Fascism came on the public scene, the Italian peasantry in general and the southern peasants in particular suffered a severe setback in their efforts. Not only did the new regime discontinue the measures of the previous years, but in many very important respects it took steps that were intended to undo the little that had been previously achieved.

Of the numerous ways in which Fascism was detrimental to the cause of the Italian peasantry in general and the southern peasantry in particular, three are outstanding. In the first place, the Fascists failed to recognize that, although they are an agricultural area, the southern regions, as we shall see in the next chapter, are not at all well adapted to the cultivation of wheat. Early in their drive toward autarky they hastily instituted and encouraged the so-called *battaglia del grano*, whereby the peasants of the South were exhorted to engage in wheat cultivation, the most irrational type of agriculture for that region. Not only are the southern regions unfavorable to wheat cultivation, but the emphasis on wheat production further encouraged the existing tendency against diversification—against industrial activity, among other things. Of all agricultural products, wheat lends itself least to the rise of related industrial undertakings.

In the second place, the Fascists, by and large representing the interests of the bourgeoisie and landowners, hastened to wreck the various peasant organizations and to undo the concessions that had been granted the peasantry in the wake of World War I. In 1920, even before they had achieved national control, the Fascists had engaged in sustained terrorist activities against the peasant organizations. The first such organization to be attacked was the National Federation of Agricultural Workers, the representatives of so-called "red peasants." For a while, the Catholic organizations were spared. However, after solidifying their national power in 1922, the Fascists began a second wave of attacks and now the agricultural cooperatives of the Catholic peasants were sacked, devastated, and finally, as had been the case with the socialist organization, utterly destroyed.

The crushing of the peasant organizations was accompanied by the disappearance of many of the benefits and rights that had been acquired during the preceding few years. For instance, Law Number 252, promulgated on January 11, 1923, annulled the aforementioned Visocchi Decree of 1919 by declaring illegal the occupancy, already effected, of untended lands belonging to latifundists (Di Vittorio in Villari, 1963, 587–588). The unfortunate peasants thus began by gaining tracts of weeds and woods, and ended by losing producing farms developed by assiduous labor and great sacrifice.

With Law Number 1583, promulgated on December 3, 1922, only thirty-four days after its ascension to power, the Fascist government for all practical effect restored to the latifundists the right to evict at will the peasants working their lands. This same law reinstated the landowners' right to increase rents if they so desired.

Of the numerous other actions and laws deleterious to the peasantry, one more deserves specific mention. Upon assuming control of the government, the Fascists liquidated the so-called municipal councils elected by the people, substituting in their place the *podestà*. This official, designated by the national government rather than elected by the people, was responsible only to the government for the local administration. The podestà was granted extensive power and great freedom of action with respect to the population. It was within his power to levy taxes, and he alone decided on school and health questions. He was solely responsible for municipal lands. The general population had one single duty, that of submission and obedience. Moreover, in many agricultural towns the podestà was also a large landowner. The peasant was often entirely at his mercy for a livelihood.

In still a third major way the Fascist regime engaged in conduct detrimental to the southern peasantry. Up to 1925, the demographic pressure and the resulting unemployment in the southern regions were somewhat alleviated by the migration of southern peoples to countries overseas. Beginning with that year, such movement was largely limited. At the same time the Italian government began restricting internal migration. Given the economic and demographic conditions of the South, the series of Fascist laws enacted against the rural exodus were in effect discriminatory restrictions imposed upon the entire southern population. For instance, a law enacted in 1931 decreed that "the movement of groups of workers and of agricultural families for purposes of work from one province to another shall at all times require authorization by the commissariat for migrations and internal colonization" (Compagna, 1959, 128).

In 1939, another law was enacted whereby the restrictions on internal migration were expanded to include not merely movements from one province to another but also those from smaller to larger localities within the same province. Known popularly as the law "against urbanization," it decreed that

. . . no one may transfer his residence to capital cities of the kingdom's provinces, or to other localities with a population exceeding 25,000 inhabitants, or to cities of notable industrial importance, even if of smaller population, if he cannot show that he is compelled to make such a movement by his particular occupation, or if he has not previously found a profitable and stable occupation in the place of immigration, or if he has not been induced by other justifiable motives, and at all times only on the condition that the immigrant can show that he will not become a public charge in the place of immigration (Compagna, 1959, 129).

With this law, the Fascist regime practically compelled the overpopulated and underemployed masses of the South to remain in a state of overpopulation and underemployment. At the same time, and more injuriously, it indirectly instituted perhaps the most effective obstacle against the industrialization of the nation, for industrialization is traditionally dependent in part upon the migration of rural people to urban centers. The failure of the Italian state to industrialize more fully, in turn, was perhaps the main cause of the continuing economic underdevelopment in the southern regions, a situation not aided by the prolonged depression of the late twenties and early thirties.

Perhaps the one truly constructive agricultural policy that the Fascist regime pursued was to continue the work, begun earlier, of developing irrigation and reclaiming various malaria-ridden lands. However, these efforts were concentrated in the central regions, and in some cases only northern agricultural workers profited from them. For instance, several areas outside of the city of Rome, where some of the reclamation was carried out by the Fascists, are worked by farmers brought down for that purpose from the Venetian regions.

To conclude this part of our discussion, we can state simply that Fascist policy did little good and much damage to Italian society as a whole and to the South in particular. There is little cause for amazement in this conclusion since, as Clough puts it:

The goals which they [the Fascists] decided upon were progressively more military, imperialistic, and vainglorious, and were not aimed at economic development in order to improve the economic well-being of the Italian people (Clough, 1964, 238).

Moreover, World War II, in which the Fascist regime involved Italy, proved to be particularly damaging to the South since much of the fighting after the Allied invasion in 1943 was concentrated in that region. By the end of the war, southern Italy was in a state of total economic and political chaos. The task of looking seriously into the tremendous depth of "the southern question," reserved, as it had been by Fascist default, for the postwar years, became yet more pressing.

With the advent of the democratic regime in Italy after World War II, a set of measures much more favorable to the South was undertaken. First of all, the harmful and unfair restrictions on migration were for all practical purposes abolished; a policy precisely the opposite of that of the Fascists was pursued in this matter. For instance, the so-called *Schema Vanoni*, embodying the realization on the part of Italian scholars and politicians that the industrialization of a nation depends to a large extent on a vast reservoir of workers, made provisions for a migration to the city of 1,050,000 agricultural workers during the period from 1954 to 1964. Of these, 350,000 were to be from the northern regions and 700,000 from the southern ones. In addition, the Schema Vanoni provided for migration from the South to the North of 600,000 workers of all occupational categories, and set out to encourage as well a total migration of 800,000 to foreign nations (Di Vittorio in Villari, 1963, 140).

In addition to this migration policy, two other major measures were taken by the government after World War II.[8] The first measure deals with agrarian reform. Attempts at passing effective land-reform legislation were revived with the 1945 laws affecting agricultural contracts. Under these laws the farm tenant profited from a general 30-percent reduction in land rents. Furthermore, landlords were compelled to retain previous tenants even after the expiration of their contracts.

But land-reform laws in the strict sense did not come into being until 1950. Three laws in that year provided for land expropriation in certain areas where there were concentrations of large holdings. These were the *Legge Sila* of June 12, the *Stralcio* or "Extract" law of October 21, and the Sicilian Regional Law of December 27, all of which are drawn up on similar lines, though the Stralcio and Sicilian laws have rather different provisions from the Sila Law in regard to expropriation.

As a broad generalization, it may be said that according to these laws all properties exceeding a market value of 20,000,000 lire, corresponding roughly to $32,000 in United States currency, were subject to at least partial expropriation. The amount of property holding above which expropriation began, however, varied with the region. In Apulia it averaged 100 hectares, while in the Calabrian mountains it began at 300 hectares (Gaetani D'Aragona, 1954, 15).

The agrarian reform embodied in these laws was not simply a matter of expropriation and redistribution of land to landless peasants. The redistribution of land was only part of a more far-reaching policy which aimed at the creation of an improved

---

[8] In fact, the period since the end of World War II has witnessed intense legislative activity in favor of the South, the institution of a large number of agencies, and the allocation of quite substantial amounts of government funds. A volume compiled by SVIMEZ (1957, II) contains nearly 350 laws enacted by either the regional or national government during the period 1947 to 1957. Since then the number has grown steadily. In this chapter, only the main lines of the policy can be mentioned.

system of agriculture throughout the South and, consequently, at a reasonable standard of living and a new social structure. It involved, in other words, land reclamation on a grand scale, mountain conservation, reforestation, control of torrential mountain streams, drainage and irrigation, and construction of roads, aqueducts, power stations, and the like (Carlyle, 1962, 46).

Almost all the land available for distribution has by now been allocated. The area expropriated so far, together with land otherwise acquired by the reform agencies, amounts to a little less than 800,000 hectares, of which roughly two-thirds have been expropriated in the South. The plots of land distributed are of two types. In about half of the cases, peasant families have been established on allegedly self-supporting farms. The second type, distributed to the other half of the families, consists of allotments of small pieces of land, or *quote*. These assigned properties have been sold by the government to landless peasants under a thirty-year, long-payment arrangement, the first payment not due until three years after the date of assignment. Building facilities, including farm buildings, have been contributed by the government.

Unfortunately, it may now be said that today, many years after the initiation of the land reform, this government attempt has been nothing short of a total failure. The goal was to accommodate as many landless peasants as possible. The result was that the units of land were often as small as a mere five or six acres, which soon turned out to be totally inadequate for the needs of a family, and were in a great many cases quickly abandoned. The reform failed for a variety of additional reasons, one of them being of extreme importance. Very often land was distributed to individuals or families that either had no agricultural training at all, or had no intention, from the very beginning, of cultivating the assigned plot. Thus, an inquiry concerning the recipients of the land expropriated by the Agrarian Reform in Apulia, Basilicata, and Molise revealed that a large proportion were people who lived elsewhere and let their land to peasants under varying forms of lease (Ramadoro, 1956, 181–190).

The other major activity in favor of the Italian South had

been incorporated by the *Cassa per il Mezzogiorno*, founded in 1950. This fund for the financing of public works in southern Italy concentrates most of its investment program on the provision of funds for agriculture and certain essential ancillary services, extending credit facilities not merely to cooperatives and public agencies, but to farmers on small and medium-sized farms as well. In addition, the Cassa also has industrial interests, and has provided some of the initial funds for three industrial-credit institutions, one each for the continental South, Sicily, and Sardinia. The objective of these credit institutions has been to finance industry at reasonable rates of interest.

Originally, the Cassa had a twelve-year program; later the program was extended to cover the fifteen-year period from 1951 to 1965, during which time it could dispose of about 2040 billion lire, for an average yearly expenditure of about 136 billion lire. Again, after several weeks of wrangling, early in October, 1963, the Italian Parliament decided to extend the Cassa's charter for another fifteen years, until 1980.

While, as we have noted, the Cassa is primarily directed toward agricultural improvement, we find that especially since 1957 great stress has been laid on the importance of increased industrialization in the South. By general agreement, it is felt that the basis of a new agriculture has already been formed in that region and that what is required now is a great deal more work on the infrastructure—transportation, communications, water supply, and the like. What this amounts to is a recognition of the need for occupational alternatives to agriculture, which would indeed seem to be the only practical way out of the historical difficulties of the Italian South. But even this may not in the long run be the most effective answer to southern problems. As Lutz argues, there is an ultimate limitation on industrialization in the South, which lies in the slowness of market expansion for industrial produce, resulting in turn from the poor natural resources, an unfavorable geographical location, and a high population density (Lutz, 1962, 131).

Perhaps for this reason, in the words of Lutz, "The results achieved by more than ten years of southern policy have, by fairly general admission, fallen short of expectations." The infra-structure of industry that was built has failed to attract an industrial "superstructure" on the scale originally anticipated, with the result that little or no progress has been made toward closing the income gap between the North and the South (Lutz, 1962, 130). Writing in 1961, Pasquale Saraceno felt justified in stating that "the two Italies continue to remain profoundly diverse and distant from each other" (Saraceno, 1961, 714) although he held high hopes for the future of the South.

In large measure, as will be discussed in detail in later chapters, these hopes rest in fact on the phenomenon of large-scale emigration. It may safely be said that of all events that have occurred in the history of the Italian South in recent centuries, the most important, both in an economic and a social sense, has been the emigration of southern peoples to countries abroad and to cities in the North of Italy itself. Southern emigration has occurred in two major waves. The first one began shortly before the turn of the present century and reached its peak in 1913. The second began immediately after World War II and is still going on in full strength at the present. The social dynamics involved in this movement form, in the remainder of this book, the core of analysis of the changing conditions in southern Italy today.

REFERENCES

Anderson, M. S. 1962. *Europe in the Eighteenth Century*. New York: Holt, Rinehart, and Winston, Inc.

Arias, Gino. 1919. *La Questione Meridionale*. Bologna.

Artz, Frederick B. 1934. *Reaction and Revolution*. New York: Harper and Brothers.

Blanch, Luigi. 1945. "Il Regno di Napoli dal 1801 al 1806," in Benedetto Croce, ed., *Scritti Storici*. Bari: Editori Laterza.

Burckhardt, Jacob. 1961. *The Civilization of the Renaissance in Italy*. Irene Gordon, ed. New York: The New American Library. [Original publication 1867]

Carlyle, Margaret. 1962. *The Awakening of Southern Italy*. New York: Oxford University Press.

Clough, Shepard B. 1964. *The Economic History of Modern Italy*. New York: Columbia University Press.

Compagna, Francesco. 1959. *I Terroni in Città*. Bari: Editori Laterza.

Dal Pane, Luigi. 1932. *La Questione del Commercio dei Grani nel Settecento in Italia*. Milan.

Di Vittorio, Giuseppe. 1963. "Il Fascismo contro i Contadini," in Rosario Villari, ed., *Il Sud Nella Storia d'Italia*. Bari: Editori Laterza.

Fortunato, Giustino. 1911. "La Questione Demaniale nell'Italia Meridionale, 1879," in *Il Mezzogiorno e lo Stato Italiano*. Bari: Editori Laterza.

Fortunato, Giustino. 1926. *Il Mezzogiorno e lo Stato Italiano, Discorsi Politici (1880–1910)*. Florence.

Fortunato, Giustino. 1963. "Il Problema Demaniale," in Rosario Villari, ed., *Il Sud Nella Storia d'Italia*. Bari: Editori Laterza.

Franchetti, Leopoldo. 1950. "Relazione della Commissione Reale per i Demani Comunali nelle Provincie del Mezzogiorno," in *Mezzogiorno e Colonie*. Florence.

Gaetani D'Aragona, G. 1954. "A Critical Evaluation of Land Reform in Italy," *Land Economics*, XXX, February.

Genovesi, Antonio. 1963. "Il Problema della Terra," in Rosario Villari, ed., *Il Sud Nella Storia d'Italia*. Bari: Editori Laterza.

Levi, Carlo. 1947. *Christ Stopped at Eboli*. New York: Farrar, Straus & Co.

Lutz, Vera. 1962. *Italy: A Study in Economic Development*. New York: Oxford University Press.

Massari, Giuseppe. 1963. "Il Brigantaggio," in Rosario Villari, ed., *Il Sud Nella Storia d'Italia*. Bari: Editori Laterza.

Mumford, Lewis. 1938. *The Culture of Cities*. New York: Harcourt, Brace and Company, Inc.

Neufeld, Maurice F. 1961. *Italy: School for Awakening Countries*. Ithaca, N.Y.: New York State School of Industrial and Labor Relations, Cornell University.

Nitti, Francesco S. 1958. *Scritti sulla Questione Meridionale*. Bari: Editori Laterza.

Pareto, Vilfredo. 1935. *The Mind and Society*. New York: Harcourt, Brace and Company, Inc.

Pino-Branca, Alfredo. 1938. *La Vita Economica negli Stati Italiani nei Secoli XVI, XVII, XVIII (Secondo le Relazioni degli Ambasciatori Veneti)*. Catania: Studio Editoriale Moderno.

Ramadoro, A. 1956. "Le Riforme Strutturali nell'Agricoltura," in *Problemi di Sviluppo nell'Agricoltura Italiana*. Rome: C.I.S.L.

Ricchioni, Vincenzo. 1946. "Cenni Sulla Proprietà Fondiaria nel Mezzogiorno avanti le Riforme Francesi," *Rivista di Economia Agraria*, I, September.

Russo, Giovanni. 1958. *L'Italia dei Poveri*. Milan: Longanesi and Company.

Saraceno, Pasquale. 1961. "La Mancata Unificazione Economica Italiana a Cento Anni dall'Unificazione Politica," in Biblioteca della Rivista "Economia e Storia," *L'Economia Italiana dal 1861 al 1961*. Milan: Dott. A. Giuffrè Editore.

Schachter, Gustav. 1965. *The Italian South: Economic Development in Mediterranean Europe*. New York: Random House.

Smith, Dennis Mack. 1959. *Italy: A Modern History*. Ann Arbor: The University of Michigan Press.

SVIMEZ. 1957. *Legislazione per il Mezzogiorno*. Rome.

SVIMEZ. 1961. *Un Secolo di Statistiche Italiane, Nord e Sud, 1861–1961*. Rome.

Vöchting, Friedrich. 1955. *La Questione Meridionale*. Naples: Istituto Editoriale del Mezzogiorno.

Yvers, Georges. 1902. *Le Commerce et les Marchands dans l'Italie Méridionale au XIIIe—et au XIVe—Siècle*. Paris.

II THE PHYSICAL CONDITIONS

We shall now explore the present social and economic conditions in the Italian South.[1] Certain factors singled out for particular emphasis can make a special contribution to a more nearly complete understanding of the general life conditions of the peasant in that region of the world. Among these factors are (1) the nature of interpersonal relations; (2) the class and prestige structures, both within the community and beyond, as they operate in the consciousness of the individual and create for him special problems of social adjustment; and (3) the phenomenon of emigration together with its consequences, especially within the context of the emigrant's home community.

Preliminary Considerations

In this chapter and the next, certain circumstances of the peasant's life experience shall be examined which, though strongly

---

[1] The island of Sardinia will be largely excluded from the analysis.

indicative of the cultural transformations now going on in his society, vividly reflect at the same time the lingering reality of his past, as briefly sketched in the previous chapter. First, however, two preliminary considerations are in order.

THE PEASANT DEFINED

A peasant is any worker engaged in *direct* agricultural activity as his major occupation or way of making a living. Because of the peculiar circumstance whereby agricultural activity in southern Italy is sharply distinguished from other occupational activities, the basic unit of analysis is the individual rather than his family group. For all practical purposes, a peasant father and his student son (or for that matter his seamstress daughter) belong to two distinct social worlds. Indeed, they often speak differently, at least in public. They play differently, dress differently, even partake of different meals, whose preparation generally follows the criterion of quantity for the peasant and that of quality for the nonpeasant member of the family.

In using the term "direct" in the definition of the peasant, only those agricultural workers whose major occupational role involves manual labor, whether they work their own land or that of others, can be subsumed under this category. "Absentee" farm owners, managers, and such others whose activity, though fundamentally agricultural, is only of a supervisory nature are excluded. This definition rejects as incomplete Kroeber's classic definition of peasants as people constituting "part-societies with part cultures" and forming "a class segment of a larger population which usually contains also urban centers" (Kroeber, 1948, 284). This characterization is tempting to those who are concerned with city-village relations and with an analysis of social structure and change in peasant villages viewed in relation to the surrounding civilization. It is, however, too general and diffuse to help the appreciation of those social and occupational circumstances that require explanation if the peasant's status is to be understood *within* the social structure of his own particular community.

Robert Redfield's widely cited definition presents one additional major difficulty when it represents peasants as "rural people who *control* and cultivate *their land* for subsistence and as a part of a traditional way of life and who look to and are influenced by gentry or townspeople whose way of life is like theirs but in a more civilized form" (Redfield, 1960, 20).[2] The definition is vague and omits from consideration a very large portion, if not the majority, of agricultural workers throughout the world, for in areas too numerous to count, most agricultural workers neither own nor control the land they work on; they merely cultivate it under the direct or indirect control of landlords and supervisors.

Many a southern Italian agricultural worker is still today, although to a decreasing exent, a landless farmhand, a sharecropper, or a petty owner engaged in the use of biblical farming techniques to derive a precarious subsistence.[3] To this extent, Firth's simple definition of the peasant comes much closer to the mark than the others so far mentioned. According to this scholar,

The term peasant has primarily an economic referent. By a peasant economy one means a system of small-scale producers, with a simple technology and equipment, often relying primarily for their subsistence on what they themselves produce. The primary means of livelihood of the peasant is cultivation of the soil (Firth, 1956, 87).

THE PROBLEM OF SOCIAL CHANGE

The other problem to be mentioned before turning to the main task of the present chapter concerns the question of social

---

[2] Italics added.

[3] According to the 1961 census on agriculture, a total of 1,562,071 farms in southern Italy were under the "direct" cultivation of peasants, as against only 350,299 farms under other forms of cultivation. However, when we consider the number of hectares involved, the former category accounted for 4,777,444 hectares, while the latter comprised the almost equal number of 4,253,083 hectares. These figures in effect indicate that farms directly under the control of peasants as *coltivatori diretti*, are relatively small in size. This case is also suggested by a comparison of the total agricultural labor force to the total number of hectares. Rounding off the number of agricultural workers to a very reasonable 2,500,000, we find that on the average each worker controls a maximum of 3.6 hectares. This figure is certainly small by any standards, and suggests a level of living that leaves much to be desired. But the situation is not even this good. The majority of farm owners possess at best two or three acres of land, and the coltivatore diretto himself is *not* always the owner of the land he cultivates. (See Istituto Centrale di Statistica, 1962, Table 32, 39.)

change. It is unfortunate but true that of all the properties of
social systems, that of change is among the most neglected in
social science. So much is this the case that a few years ago, when
"functional analysis" was in the process of advancing toward a
position of sociological predominance, many scholars attacked it
on the basis, among other things, that it was predicated on a status
quo metaphysics. In recent years, the theoretical bases of this
criticism have been effectively undermined.[4] Just the same, a
tendency still prevails in sociology and anthropology to focus on
the statics of social structure to the neglect of studies of social
change.

An explanation of this unfortunate fact need not necessarily
lead us into a consideration of the ideological idiosyncrasies of
social scientists, as is sometimes assumed. Their deemphasis of
social change is to a very large extent a by-product of their
heavily philosophical tradition, which tends to emphasize the
universal and the timeless and, correlatively, of their relative
independence from the historical disciplines, which tend to focus
on series of specific events in specific times and places.

Studies of peasant peoples are not immune to the charge of a
static orientation. Often various properties of peasant societies are
focused on as if they were immobile entities. Indeed, these
properties are occassionally described on the basis of statements
made by other scholars and by peasants who themselves belong
to past generations. Small wonder that in the literature the expression "traditional society" is very widely, but erroneously, used
as a synonym for "peasant society."

It is symptomatic of this state of affairs that, in discussing
peasant society and culture, as keen and masterful a student of

---

[4] For two statements in this connection, see (1) Merton, 1957, especially
Chapter 1, where it is argued that the concept of "dysfunction," which implies the concepts of strain, stress, and tension, provides an analytical approach to the study of social change; and (2) Lopreato, 1965, 1–35, where
attention is drawn to Pareto's keen sensitivity to the matter of social dynamics as expressed especially in Pareto's treatment of "cycles of inter-
dependence" and in his very definition of "social system" in terms of a
tendency toward a given state of equilibrium, which, however, is constantly
changing.

peasants as Redfield himself first presented a totally static view of peasant society and then, in passing, warned the reader, in his conclusions, that "many peasants are changing very rapidly," that "what was stable is no longer so," and finally that "peasants now want to be something other than peasants" (Redfield, 1960, 77).

Aware of the necessity of taking the process of social change into account if a more nearly adequate understanding of the subject of this study is to be achieved, a special effort shall be made in this book to look at the peasant and his society and culture as continuously changing entities. The chief interest will be not so much in what the peasant has been or even what he is today, but in what he is becoming and in the factors that underlie his transformation.

Let us begin in this chapter with a discussion of some of the major material characteristics of the Italian South which, by their severity, have long afflicted the peasant, and are indirectly instrumental in his current transformation.

The Volume of Emigration

For more than three-quarters of a century, the peasantry of southern Italy has been a major source of immigrants for many foreign countries as well as for the Italian North. Excluding internal migration, it is estimated that from 1871 to 1951 the southern regions had a combined net emigration of 4,414,000 (SVIMEZ, 1961, Table 107, 122). This figure, of course, does not represent the total flow of southerners but only those who, within this period, were permanently subtracted from the total population. It says nothing about the widespread practice of repatriation and reexpatriation among southern Italians. To appreciate the total flow, the following information might be considered. The wave of emigration in the decade from 1906 to 1915 was so large that, excluding the returned emigrants, the combined region of Abruzzi-Molise had a net loss from emigration of 43 percent of its inhabitants; Calabria, 40 percent; and Basilicata, 38.5 percent (Vannutelli, 1961, 572).

There is no adequate way of estimating the total number of

expatriates. If, however, we bear in mind the fact that traditionally only about one-half of the Italian emigrants settle permanently abroad (Unione Italiana delle Camere di Commercio, 1959,
572), it is possible to estimate that roughly 9,000,000 southern
Italians went abroad between 1871 and 1951.

An estimate of migration from the South is more difficult for
the period since 1951, for during this period the bulk of the
emigrants have gone to other regions of Italy and have more
easily escaped official bookkeeping. Various unofficial estimates
indicate, however, that in the period from 1952 to 1963 at least
2,500,000 persons migrated from the southern regions. Most of
these have been individuals in the 20- to 50-year age bracket
(Istituto Centrale di Statistica, 1963, *Annuario di Statistiche*,
Table III, 146). To a very large extent, they have also been male
agricultural workers. The massive nature of this male agricultural
emigration is well attested to by the fact that from November,
1951, to October, 1963, the number of employed male agricultural workers decreased from 2,479,898 to 1,542,000, while that of
female agricultural workers increased from 925,912 to 953,000.[5]

Such figures explain why, given present work habits and
technology, the land supply in many parts of southern Italy now
by far exceeds the demand for it. Yet, until only a few years ago
the insufficiency of tillable land was one of the most critical
problems of that region, and in the words of the agricultural
economist Rossi Doria, "land hunger" (Rossi Doria in Caizzi,
1955, 139) was one of its saddest characteristics. The flow from
the farms has in recent years assumed the dimensions of a veritable exodus, the people departing as if a scourge were relentlessly
pursuing them from the country. Thus, throughout the South,
the population of numerous towns and villages has been more
than halved by emigration since the end of World War II. Many
towns and villages have been almost totally abandoned or reduced
to waiting colonies of the aged, women, and children.

[5] See and compare (1) Istituto Centrale di Statistica, 1957, Table 6,
603–605, and (2) Istituto Centrale di Statistica, 1964, Table 11, 28. The figures
for 1963 include the southern part of the Latium region; the real difference
between the two years is, therefore, actually greater.

A basic assumption of this book is that this massive wave of emigration is symptomatic of certain social and economic problems particular to the area. These problems can, therefore, be analyzed through an attempt to explain the phenomenon of emigration itself. Such a task involves answering this query: Why do peasants emigrate? The question is a crucial one for both theoretical and practical reasons. Practically speaking, an answer to it should be helpful to those in Italy who are engaged in large-scale economic planning. Italian authorities are so preoccupied with the rural exodus that many provincial governments are seeking ways to solve what to them seems a problem of great proportions impinging on the very development of their economy. The Italian government itself has in recent years instituted a law for the *ricomposizione fondiaria*, according to which agricultural workers would be encouraged to continue working the land by consolidating the infinitesimal and scattered holdings characteristic of the Italian countryside. The underlying rationale is that the agricultural worker would be happier to remain in his occupation if he had one relatively large tract of land to farm. The thinking of the Italian authorities, therefore, runs largely along purely economic lines. And this brings us to the second consideration, the theoretical one.

In the literature on causes of human migration, one critical factor has received little systematic attention, namely, the psychocultural rejection by the emigrants of their own particular society. Probably, this neglect is at least in part a result of a rigid and long-standing theoretical commitment to the Sumnerian conceptions of the "ingroup" and the "outgroup" as two largely closed and exclusive units whose real or hypothetical mutual relations are characterized by hostility at both the communal and individual levels. The possibility that an individual would feel negative about his own group *at the same time* that he felt positive about an alien group was not entertained in Sumner's conceptualization (Sumner, 1906, Chap. 1). In recent years, however, certain advances in social theory have provided systematically formulated conceptual tools which will help to fill the theoretical gap still remaining in the etiology of human migration.

The theoretical advances have come from two major directions. On the one hand, anthropological studies of peasant societies and cultures have revealed the necessity and theoretical fruit-
fulness of assessing the cultural channels that link peasant society
and culture to its "surrounding civilization." Thus Redfield en-
joins students of peasant societies to consider that:

> The culture of a peasant community . . . is not autonomous. It is an
> aspect or dimension of the civilization of which it is a part. . . . the
> peasant village invites us to attend to the long course of interaction
> between that community and centers of civilization (Redfield, 1960,
> 40–41).

On the other hand, sociologists concerned with urban groups
have discovered processes of interaction in which a given individual takes the values of other individuals and groups as a "comparative frame of reference." "Nonmembership" groups are often
taken by an individual as models for the evaluation of his "membership groups" (Merton, 1957, Chaps. VIII–IX).

Why Peasants Emigrate: Material Conditions

In the next chapter, these advances in social theory will be
used to bring into focus various causes of emigration in the
particular case of southern Italian peasants. For the present, the
causes of this phenomenon will be discussed.

NATIONAL ECONOMIC DEVELOPMENT

Causes of emigration have conventionally been analyzed in
terms of "pull factors" and "push factors." Pull factors refer to
those conditions present in receiving societies which constitute an
attraction to the potential migrant; push factors concern those
conditions existing in the migrant's own society that tend to
discourage him from staying there. Among the pull factors, economic opportunity constitutes perhaps the major cause of human
emigration. In our case, if consideration is limited to internal
migration, it is possible to argue that perhaps the chief cause of
migration from the South has been the accelerating industrializa-

tion and economic expansion of the Italian society. It may be noted, for instance, that as a result of external economic aid, involvement within a rapidly expanding European economic market, and a more rational utilization of natural resources, in recent years Italy has been providing an additional 200,000 jobs per year. Most of these new jobs have become available in "the industrial triangle" of the North—Milan, Turin, Genoa—thus providing a formidable pull factor for the unemployed and underemployed workers of the South.

As Forte argues, the Italian internal migration can, therefore, be partly expressed in terms of the development of "an economy of well-being" (Forte in Autori Vari, 1962, 77–105). This is to say that, given the national expansion of the economy during the past fifteen years, the relatively idle and unproductive southern labor could not but be transferred to places where it could produce more and contribute more effectively to the progress of the economic system.

POVERTY OF LIFE CONDITIONS IN THE SOUTH

Pull factors do not operate independently of push factors. The migrants do not merely respond to enticements from the outside. Pull factors operate effectively only when local factors do not apply a counterbalancing force. The fact of emigration itself generally indicates that economic and other conditions are by and large inadequate in the emigrant's community, or are judged to be so by him.

Overpopulation and Poverty

Of key importance among the southern difficulties is the combination of overpopulation and natural poverty. Southern Italy is an exceedingly poor region characterized by a decreasing but still high birthrate. In 1957, when emigration was at a peak after World War II, the birthrate for Italy as a whole stood at 17.8 per 1000 inhabitants, one of the lowest in Europe. This rate was due mostly to the exceedingly low fertility in such northern regions as Piedmont, Friuli-Julian Venetia, and Liguria, which had birthrates of 12.0, 11.7, and 11.1, respectively. On the other hand, the birthrate attained its maximum of 24.5 in the southern region of Calabria, closely followed by other southern regions at rates of 24.1 for Campania, 23.9 for Basilicata, and 23.8 for Apulia. It was to a large extent due to this high birthrate in the South that the excess of births over deaths in Italy as a whole amounted in that year to 8.1 per thousand, that is, a total of 399,268 persons (Unione Italiana delle Camere di Commercio, 1959, 34–35).

Fertility rates in themselves, however, say little about the economic conditions of an area. Some of the most economically developed countries in the world have higher fertility rates than some underdeveloped areas. Moreover, it is worth noting that the South of Italy comprises 40 percent of the total geographic area of the country, but only 37 percent of the entire Italian population.[6] The demographic question is meaningful, therefore, only when related to the level of employment opportunities.

Economic Development: Some Contrasts with the North

Increasingly today, economic well-being is everywhere becoming synonymous with industrialization and economic expansion, or, in the case of farm areas, mechanization. The extent to which the South of Italy is underdeveloped in these respects can best be appreciated through a series of comparisons between this region and the rest of the nation. As Rossi Doria states, strictly speaking, there are two Italies, not one (Rossi Doria, 1958, 320). Focusing on industrialization, for instance, it may be pointed out that, while in the North thirty-five provinces out of a total of fifty-eight had, in 1958, more than 50 percent of their working population engaged in nonagricultural activities, the corresponding figure for the South was only four provinces out of a total of thirty-two (Istituto Centrale di Statistica, 1959, 17). Stated otherwise, in October, 1963, as in the previous decade of "the economic miracle," southern industry employed only about 25 percent of the total Italian industrial labor force (Istituto Centrale di Statistica, 1964, Table 11, 28).

What passes for "industry" in the South, however, often

---

[6] Sardinia has been included in the South in this case.

refers to small household enterprises and artisan shops which are typically family-run and rarely employ more than two or three family members. Thus, in the South artisans constitute 70 percent of the industrial labor force as compared to 35 percent in the North (Schachter, 1965, 24). This peculiarity inherent in the industrial statistics for southern Italy is best exemplified by focusing attention on a single southern region. For instance, in 1957, 44 percent of the money income in Calabria was produced by agricultural activities; 17.5 percent of it was earned in public administration; and 38.5 percent was allegedly produced in what are broadly termed "commercial and industrial activities." However, when only strictly industrial concerns are considered, it is estimated that the percentage of 38.5 shrinks to a mere 12.0 percent, while the residual 26.5 percent is divided between small commercial, craft, and hotel activities (Centro di Analisi di Opinione Pubblica e Mercato, 1958, 16). This is to say that about 70 percent of all Calabrian concerns classified as "industrial or commercial" are in fact small barber shops, shoemaker shops, carpenter shops, hotels, and the like.

The economically backward nature of the South can be further illustrated by considering the state of public facilities and utilities. Differences between North and South in the development of these obviously affect the economic growth pattern of these regions, and in this case at least, clearly reveal the depressed status of the South in the development of the Italian nation. The first item that comes to mind is road development. In 1904, the North had 62 kilometers of highway per 100 square kilometers of territory; nearly sixty years later, in 1961, this figure had increased to 80. Development in the South, during this same period, was comparable to that in the North, increasing from 30 to 43 kilometers (SVIMEZ, 1961, Table 259, 488). However, much of what passes for highway in the South consists of narrow and tortuous roads that either wind uselessly around isolated mountain pcaks or meander dangerously along the doorsteps of village hovels. Unlike those in northern Italy, roadways in southern Italy are badly in need of repair.

No country or region can reach its goals of industrialization and economic development unless it first develops its means of communication and transportation. Highway construction is an essential ingredient of this development. Yet it is a sad commentary on public attempts to develop the South that the famed *Autostrada del Sole* (Highway of the Sun), the main road artery that was to link Milan to the island of Sicily, was completed by 1965 in the North, but had still in 1966 gone only a few miles south of Naples.

The story concerning railroads presents an equally unbalanced situation. The South now has only about one-third of the nation's total kilometers of railroad tracks; of these only about 20 percent are electrified, while the remainder depend on coal, which is imported and expensive. Only about 400 kilometers are double tracks. In the North, on the other hand, over 50 percent of the tracks are electrified, and more than 4000 kilometers of them are double (Istituto Centrale di Statistica, 1962, *Compendio*, 200). Needless to say, transportation in the North is speedy, effective, and relatively inexpensive, while in the South it is difficult, expensive, and slow, impeding the movement of both goods and population.

Differences in investment between North and South are also an excellent index of general economic differences between the two regions. In 1954, when the reconstruction of Italy was reaching a steady pace, about 3 billion dollars were invested in the North (a little more than one-fourth in public funds and the rest in private undertakings), as against roughly 880 million dollars in the South (about half in public funds and half in private undertakings). Thus 77.4 percent of all national investment took place in the North, and only 22.6 percent in the South. And again, of all private investment in the country, 84 percent took place in the North, as against 16 percent in the South (SVIMEZ, survey, 1956). Such figures clearly indicate not only the relative poverty of the South, or at least the lack of economic enterprise among the wealthy classes there, but also the heavy economic dependence of the region on the initiative of the national government.

While the above regional variations already indicate the magnitude of the economic differences between North and South, estimates of per capita income, which provide more comprehensive indices of economic development, reflect still more effectively the economic discrepancies between "the two Italies." Thus, per capita income for the *active* population in the South in the 1950's was about 50 percent of that in the North. If further correction is made for the fact that in 1951 the South's ratio of "active" to "resident" population was 39 percent, compared with 46 percent for the North, then per capita income of the whole southern population was in the 1950's only about 45 percent of that in the North (Lutz, 1962, 91). In dollars, this means that, by 1961, while per capita income for Italy as a whole was roughly $452 per year, it was about $550 in the North and about $290 in the South. What is even more revealing is that, despite all attempts to achieve the economic unification of Italy, the economic gap between the two Italies has in fact widened. Thus, in 1951, the North received 75.8 percent of Italy's national income, and the South accounted for the remaining 24.2 percent. By 1961, they received, respectively, 76.3 and 23.7 percent (Tagliacarne, 1962, 339–419; Schachter, 1965, Table II, 98).

In presenting the above facts, reference to population has been general, without regard to possible differences within the South itself between the peasantry and the rest of the population. Unfortunately, official statistics of this nature are hard to come by. However, the findings from a national sample survey of 1569 family heads, carried out under my direction by DOXA of Milan (Institute of Statistical Research and Public Opinion Analysis) from December, 1963, to January, 1964, can throw considerable light on this question.[7]

Table 1, which shows the declared income of the peasants in comparison to all other southerners in the sample, indicates that the income of this group is substantially below that of the rest of the sample. The most striking finding in this table is that while over half of the peasants earn $80 or less per month, the comparable proportion among the nonagricultural portion of the sample is

---

[7] The findings from this survey will be discussed in more detail in a future volume on social classes and social change in Italy.

TABLE 1. Monthly Income of Peasant and Nonpeasant Families, 1963–1964

Income per Month, U.S. Dollars	Peasant Families		Nonpeasant Families	
	N	%	N	%
Up to $40	27	15.2	16	5.2
$ 41–80	71	39.9	51	16.6
$ 81–120	43	24.2	87	28.2
$121–160	20	11.2	66	21.4
$161–240	6	3.4	46	14.9
Over $240	6	3.4	37	12.0
No information	5	2.8	5	1.6
Total	178	100.1	308	99.9

Source: Lopreato Sample Survey, 1963–1964.

only a little over 1 in 5. It should be noted, however, that at least a few peasants are to be found in the higher income brackets, a fact which, as will be seen later, may be largely attributed to the changes which are today occurring throughout the South, of which emigration stands out as one of the chief causes.

Other evidence of this same nature is given by the findings of a parliamentary committee of inquiry on poverty in Italy (Table 2). Focusing on the traditionally more affluent coltivatore diretto

TABLE 2. Families Classified as Wretched and as Needy per 100 Families with Family Head as Coltivatore Diretto,* by Region

Region	A, Percent Wretched	B, Percent Needy	A + B, Total
Northern Italy	1.0	3.5	4.5
Central Italy	6.9	12.3	19.2
Southern Italy	25.4	24.2	49.6
Islands	17.2	22.7	39.9
Italy	11.7	13.5	25.2

* Includes most agricultural workers except farmhands.

Source: *Atti della Commissione Parlamentare d'Inchiesta sulla Miseria in Italia* (Rome, 1953), Vol. 1, Tomo II. Reported in Gabriele Gaetani D'Aragona, "Situazione Demografica ed Agricoltura nel Mezzogiorno," *Nord e Sud*, Anno II, No. 8 (July, 1955), p. 25.

alone, who is either the owner of his land or a tenant paying a fixed rent, the committee found in 1951 that in the continental South 25.4 percent of the family units headed by a coltivatore diretto could be classified as "wretched." An additional 24.2 percent could be classified as "needy," for a total of 50 percent who were classifiable as economically underprivileged. By contrast, the 4.5 percent of economically underprivileged in the North and the 19.2 percent of Central Italy (treated elsewhere in this book as part of the North) seem like goals—unfortunate though they may be—that the regions of the South were likely to find too optimistic to strive for.

The Land

The state of agriculture in the South leaves much to be desired. At least since 1951, the active southern population engaged in agriculture has represented 44 percent of the farming population of the entire nation. The gross value of the saleable output of southern agriculture has, however, averaged only about 33 percent of the national total, while the net value (after deduction of expenses) has averaged an estimated 36 percent (Lutz, 1962, 91–93).

One of the most striking facts about the agricultural South is the paucity of arable land. Although Italy as a whole has the rugged topography that is characteristic of all Mediterranean countries, the South is exceptionally rough. The territorial surface of Italy covers about 30 million hectares, or about 75 million acres, of which 75 percent are mountains and hills. Less than 25 percent of the total, specifically 7 million hectares, are plains; of these, only about 2 million hectares are in the South. In other words, the farming population in the South represents about 44 percent of the entire farming population in Italy, but it has at its disposal less than 29 percent of the Italian plains. The remaining 10 million hectares of southern Italy consist of barren hills and mountains of a geological composition which grossly limits their agricultural value (Istituto Centrale di Statistica, 1963, *Annuario Statistico*, Table 2, 2–3). What is most ironic is that the southern mountains, unlike many of those in the North, are high enough to be useless for agricultural purposes but not sufficiently high to provide the peasant with a continuous supply of the precious water from melting snows in the spring and summer.

Looking at a geological map of Italy, two features stand out all along the entire Apennines, from the Ligurian Sea to the Ionic Sea. The central band consists of limestone, while the two sides are made up largely of clay and loam that go back to the tertiary epoch. There is one enormous difference in the South; the clays and the loams, in their extraordinary variety of forms, prevail much less in the northern regions than in the South, where in some places they cover entire provinces (Fortunato in Caizzi, 1955, 159–160). The terrain is markedly impermeable, so that the 2 million hectares of plains in the South are extremely subject to erosion, being constantly washed away by the torrential seasonal rains, another scourge of the Italian South. As Kayser points out, everywhere in the South—on the plains, on the hills, and on the mountains—landslips are ever present or are a constant threat (Kayser, 1964, 66).

Under these circumstances, it would almost seem that whatever little the southern peasant has been able to accomplish has been largely due to centuries of heroic tenacity and shrewdness that defy the imagination of modern farmers and the laboratory know-how of agronomists alike. Moreover, given the nature of the southern terrain, it is not at all surprising that the peasant's achievements have been made through the application of what are generally considered biblical farming techniques and implements, with the ancient hoe the major tool. Little else would have allowed the peasant to climb the steep shoulders of his hills and mountains and build, in spite of all obstacles, truly marvelous gardens of farming: almost spiteful georgics to a stingy nature. Nor is it surprising, therefore, that in 1959 the North had more than ten tractors per 1000 hectares of farming land, compared to less than three in the South (Presidency of the Council of Ministers, 1960, 206).

The Climate and the Weather

The particular topography and the impermeability of the southern terrain would in themselves constitute tremendous ob-

stacles for the southern peasant. But these difficulties are associated with another factor, the aridity of the southern regions.
Southern Italy has an abundance of sunshine, which, when it is
rarely accompanied by rain, can be an unmitigated evil. On the
whole, temperatures are more favorable to the South than to the
North, being about equally warm in both regions in the summer,
but warmer in the winter months in the South. In the average
year, however, the South receives an average of about fifty days
of rain a year, about two-fifths less than the North, which has an
average of about ninety days. The North, moreover, gets much
of its rain in the fall and summer, in the periods of rapid growth,
whereas in the South the rainy season coincides with the late fall
and winter, when most vegetation has slowed down or stopped
growing altogether. In some years, the summer drought may last
for six months or more.

According to the botanist Cuboni, the aridity or drought of
the southern regions must be considered the fundamental cause of
all difficulties which maintain the southern agriculture in a state
inferior to that of the North. All other causes that are frequently
spoken of, such as the phenomenon of the latifundia, the lack of
farmhouses and barns, and even the lack of capital are only
derivatives of the first real cause, the poor productivity of the soil
due to the drought.[8]

Whatever the merits of this argument, one fact remains
hardly disputable: Under the conditions described, the range of
possible products to cultivate is very limited, and even the most
potentially fertile land normally refuses to yield according to the

---

[8] (Cuboni in Caizzi, 1955, 98.) Writing in 1907, Maranelli, a geographer,
disagreed with this type of argument, maintaining that the importance of
the drought had been exaggerated. For him the fundamental obstacle to a
more rational development of southern agriculture lay in the lack of capital
which, together with less fundamental factors, prevented southern peasants
from taking advantage of the abundance of rain in the winter. Specifically,
he blamed the widespread practice of "extensive" cultivation, arguing in
favor of a more "intensive" cultivation with winter leguminous forage, which
would encourage cattle raising, and with cereals and other plants that reach
maturity before the advent of the summer drought (Maranelli in Caizzi,
1955, 113–114).

needs of those who depend on it for their livelihood. Matters are made still worse by the fact that when the rains finally come in the late fall, they assume a torrential character from which only the ocean can profit. The problem of rainfall in southern Italy can be readily appreciated when one travels the tortuous roads of that rocky region. In certain places, every few hundred feet, a small bridge is met, bearing the name of the stream which passes under it. By and large the rocky bed is either dry or a torrent of muddy water, which often overflows and carries seeds, plants, topsoil, and everything on its way to the sea.

It is revealing to note that no major rivers can be found in southern Italy. In an average year, eight Italian rivers average a discharge of more than 100 cubic meters of water per second, and they are all in the North. The relative capacity of the southern rivers may be illustrated by pointing out that their total capacity put together is less than that of the river Arno, which flows in the northern regions of Emilia and Tuscany (Istituto Centrale di Statistica, 1963, *Annuario Statistico*, Table 5, 7). Again, no major water basins are found in southern Italy, except for the Varano and Lesina Lakes in Apulia, which comprise 60 and 51 square kilometers, respectively. The North, on the other hand, is endowed with large reservoirs of water such as Lakes Garda, Maggiore, and Como, comprising 370, 212, and 146 square kilometers, respectively (Istituto Centrale di Statistica, 1963, *Annuario Statistico*, Table 6, 7).

It may be easily surmised that irrigation, too, leaves something to be desired in the South. Thus, in 1958, the South accounted for only 10 percent of all irrigated land in the country. Fertilizers, too, is less widely used than it might be, largely due to the nature of the terrain and the paucity of the water required to dissolve it. Thus in 1958, the South used only about 25 percent of all fertilizers consumer by the country as a whole (Presidency of the Council of Ministers of the Italian Republic, 1960, 32).

To recapitulate, the following appear to be the basic causes of what some have referred to as the "natural poverty" of the

South: (1) the small ratio of plains to the entire geographic area; (2) the absence of mountains high enough to guarantee the continuous presence of snow and, therefore, of a regular flow of water; (3) the large area of hilly land which is constitutionally infertile and subject to easy erosion; and (4) the small amount of rainfall together with its concentration in the winter months (SVIMEZ, 1956, *Notizie*, 21ff.). Finally, the historical isolation of the South, the relative lack of commerce, the peasant's continual struggle for survival, the necessity of self-reliance for his subsistence, and the ignorance of his gentry and leaders[9] have induced the peasant to seek from the land only those products necessary to his own survival. This practice has meant an emphasis on the cultivation of grains, which are ill-adapted to the southern terrain.

Speaking about this problem, Rossi Doria has argued that a tragic contradiction has dominated the history of the South, a region largely fit for a pastoral economy, yet unable to devote itself to this. To eke out a living, the peasant has had to turn to the most absurd of all cultivations, wheat. Wheat grows best under typical Northern European farming conditions, since in order to give a good yield, it needs the long winter inactivity after sowing, the slow growth during bloom and ripening time, and the moderate and prolonged sunshine peculiar to the cool temperate zones (Rossi Doria, 1953, 148).

In concluding this section on the natural poverty of the South, it may be finally noted that a representative of SVIMEZ recently divided the South into "economically homogeneous zones" and estimated that more than seven million persons, or 42 percent of the total southern population which resided in 59 percent of the total southern area, lived in zones without "consistent possibilities of development." Therefore, even without considering the highly unbalanced man–land ratio existing in other

---

[9] The most recent example of this is given by the "*battaglia del grano*" (campaign for wheat) organized and carried out by the Fascist government, whereby the preexisting southern monoculture was further intensified.

zones more capable of further economic development, given the new needs and values that are being nationally developed and reinforced, for a very large number of southern Italians there was little or no place in the economy of their region (Novacco, 1959, 3–18).

Since the hope of development for his region in the near future is certainly not very good, what else is left for the southern peasant to do but emigrate? As Giorgio Bocca suggests in his amusingly journalistic, yet somber, exposé entitled *The Discovery of Italy*, despite all recent public attempts to develop the South, little of any consequence has changed that is attributable to those endeavors. "It is the old face under the new mask." And "everything changes in the South, one might say, in order to reproduce itself" (Bocca, 1963, 358–359). This view is no doubt more caricature than truth. Nevertheless, my own observations are at least partly in agreement with it. Most peasants who have, for one reason or another, been unable or unwilling to seek amelioration outside of the South still feel today the formidable brunt of a forbidding legacy.

Arduous Leisure

The general life conditions of many of these individuals are still truly penurious. After more than a decade of "miraculous economic boom" in his nation, many a peasant's home is still a one- or two-room hovel which he shares with his wife, three or four children, and very often a donkey, a goat, or a pig.[10] But the whims of history and terrain, as well as the peasant's peculiar type of relation to the land, involving excessive fractionalization, are such that his hovel generally is located not on the land he works but in a village built far away from the land, and sometimes high

---

[10] The quality of the peasant's dwelling is indicated by the findings of the 1963 survey. On a list of ten consumer items (refrigerator, stove, radio, television, automobile, running water, telephone, toilet with bath, washing machine, and vacuum cleaner and/or buffer), we found that two-thirds of the peasants owned less than three items, while nearly one in five possessed none. Only 3 percent claimed more than six. By contrast, the corresponding figures for the rest of the population taken together were 17, 4, and 27 percent, respectively.

on a hill peak.[11] Not infrequently, therefore, he spends several hours a day walking to and from his tiny strips of land, carrying his ancient hoe, a water receptacle, and a lunch bag containing bread, a piece of cheese, an onion, some olives, and dried fruit. When he arrives on the land, his body, already weakened by burden, disease, and starvation, is exhausted by the long march in the mud or the dust. No wonder that, when asked in the survey mentioned above whether they preferred some other kind of job and why, southern peasants, more than any other occupational category, singled out such reasons as the regularity, ease, security, and cleanness of work as factors that recommended the preferred occupation. Almost 3 in 10 cited these factors, only the desire for a higher income receiving more peasant choices. Thus, the very nature of his work provides a painful burden for the peasant.

What is worse is that if by a supreme act of will and pride he succeeds in accomplishing a little work, too often it comes to nought. After paying an exorbitant share to his landlord and losing much of his produce to thieves, birds, diseases, landslides, or drought, the unfortunate peasant usually manages to store enough grain, fruit, or beans to keep him and his family barely alive until early spring, months before the new harvest. At such time, then, he frequently finds it unavoidable to incur debts which keep him in continuous bondage. Writing about Butera, a Sicilian community of about 10,000 population, Sciortino Gugino has said:

Woe to those who find it necessary to be in debt, be it with private persons or with banks. From then on the family has lost its peace.

---

[11] Rossi Doria justifiably ridicules the numerous explanations for the agricultural village, such as defense from pirates and brigands, escape from malaria, and the peasant's distaste for solitary living. According to Rossi Doria, the southern peasant lives in villages, rather than in scattered homesteads, because the villages are natural centers of the scattered plots of land that he sometimes cultivates (Rossi Doria in Caizzi, 1955, 134–136). To this we would add that, assuming land fractionalization to be, in the last analysis, due to the scarcity of land, the southern peasantry has chosen to live in villages, which are usually built on land totally unfit for cultivation, at least in part to preserve the available arable land.

With banks, when all is counted, the interest rate amounts to 13 percent. Very rarely, however, is a peasant judged a good risk by the director of the local bank. With usurers, interest rates are always higher than 20 percent and often reach 50 percent for a six-month loan, or even for a two-month period in the spring (Sciortino Gugino, 1960, 44).

These may be extreme cases, but in the logic of southern Italian affairs, "extreme" is not always equal to "rare." Among many others, Ferrarotti and his associates, in their study of Castellammare, a town of 63,000 in Campania, found the phenomenon of usury, with interest rates of 20 or even 30 percent per month, anything but unusual (Ferrarotti, 1959, 80).

This unhappy state of chronic insolvency frequently induces a peasant to purchase a donkey, a goat, a pig, or sometimes even one or two calves. In his desperate estimate, the profit on the future sale of any of these may, and indeed sometimes does, permit him to make ends meet at the end of the year. But all too often the ends do not meet. Here is a case, apparently extreme but not atypical. In December, 1962, a Calabrian sharecropper succeeds in inducing his landlord to buy a calf at the cost of about $116. Four months later, in April, 1963, the calf is sold for $158. Total gross profit: $42. Sharecropper's share: $21. Daily gross profit: 16 cents. Major expenses: hay and straw for a total market value of $10. The labor factor: inestimable. Suffice it to say that in order to be kept fed and safe from thieves, the calf required constant attention, whether it was on a Sunday, on Christmas, or on Easter. Total net profit? In the colorful words of the peasant himself: "the hen's udders."

No wonder that in many southern dialects the word for "to work" is *fatigari* (to drudge or make oneself tired) and that, as Moss and Cappannari report, for many a southern peasant " 'Life is hell and work is a beast.' The economic struggle occupies many of the waking hours of the peasantry" (Moss and Cappannari, 1960, 28–29). One may wonder, under these circumstances, why the peasant engages in this kind of enterprise in the first place. The reasons are complex. His desperate hope for a lucky twist of fate has already been mentioned. One other explanation may now be added to this. In the peasant's eyes, this type of "arduous leisure," as it may be called, is also the source of a little prestige. *Fare buona figura* (to project the proper image) is an important characteristic to the southern Italian in general. One may be poor, but must never show himself totally subdued by his poverty.

Economic profit is possible. At times, after a few months' assiduous care of an animal, a peasant clears a net profit of from $60 to $80; some years, nature is generous, and he brings in a fair harvest. Assuming now that he has no rapidly multiplying debts to be paid, there is often a daughter to marry off, a lawyer to consult, an illness to be cured, or a funeral to pay. It is no accident that many a peasant is an inveterate pessimist. Ask him in a good year, "How is the harvest?" The answer is likely to be "poor." Ask the healthiest one about his health, and the answer is almost surely "not very good." To answer otherwise would amount to disturbing that precarious and mysterious equilibrium that some-times results in a moment of peace, or even to inviting the *iettatura* (evil eye).

Rare is the peasant family in which there is not at least one person who suffers from illness. If it is not heart disease, it is a liver condition; if not anemia, it is kidney trouble; if not the eyes, then the teeth; if it is not arthritis, it is a hernia. Despite a relative abundance of medical doctors, such disorders have a peculiar way of being persistent. *"Tanti medicini, ma simu sempi malati"* ("De-spite so many medicines, ills are ours to the tomb"), a disheart-ened peasant complained.

The peasant's sickness is understandably a source of constant worry for him, and for more reasons than one. Given as he is to occasional arduous labor, not infrequently he breaks a bone or suffers a heart attack. At such times, he has urgent need of medical care. Each town has a medical doctor appointed by the High Commissioner for Health, but all too often the doctor is nowhere to be found. His residence may be in another town, several miles away, where he usually has a private practice. Or he may travel daily to his native town many miles away to visit his parents or to eat his mother's food. Not infrequently, when he returns to his official place of work, often late at night, he finds someone who asks him to write a death certificate, and a large number of suffering patients who have been waiting many hours for medical attention. As a well-informed Roman doctor said recently in a personal conversation, "then prescriptions for patent medicines start flying." By then it may happen, however, that the pharmacies nearby are closed—legally or otherwise—and there is nothing that the peasant can do short of cursing under his breath against his God, his ill fate, his fellowmen, or his poverty. Or in the hours of resigned and meditative protest, he may merely create a stanza such as the following:

> *L'inferno è pieno*
> *di notari e giudici,*
> *uomini approbi,*
> *speziali e medici.*
> (Hell is full
> of notaries and judges,
> upright men,
> druggists and doctors.)

REFERENCES

Bocca, Giorgio. 1963. *La Scoperta dell'Italia*. Bari: Editori Laterza.

Centro di Analisi di Opinione Pubblica e Mercato. 1958. *La Calabria*. Milan: Franco Angeli Editore.

Cuboni, Giuseppe. 1955. "I Problemi dell'Agricoltura Meridionale," in Bruno Caizzi, ed., *Antologia della Questione Meridionale*. Milan: Edizioni di Comunità.

Ferrarotti, Franco, *et al.* 1959. *La Piccola Città*. Milan: Edizioni di Comunità.

Firth, Raymond. 1956. *Elements of Social Organization*, 2nd ed. London: Watts & Co.

Forte, Francesco. 1962. "Le Migrazioni Interne come Problema di Economia del Benessere," in Autori Vari, *Immigrazione e Industria*. Milan: Edizioni di Comunità.

Fortunato, Giustino. 1955. "Povertà Naturale del Mezzogiorno," in Bruno Caizzi, ed., *Antologia della Questione Meridionale*. Milan: Edizioni di Comunità.

Istituto Centrale di Statistica. 1957. IX Censimento Generale della Popolazione, 4 Novembre 1951. Vol. IV, *Professioni*. Rome.

Istituto Centrale di Statistica. 1959. *Compendio Statistico Italiano 1958*. Rome.

Istituto Centrale di Statistica. 1962. *Annuario di Statistica Agraria*. Rome.

Istituto Centrale di Statistica. 1962. *Compendio Statistico Italiano 1961*. Rome.

Istituto Centrale di Statistica. 1963. *Annuario di Statistiche del Lavoro e dell'Emigrazione*, Vol. IV, 1962. Rome.

Istituto Centrale di Statistica. 1963. *Annuario Statistico Italiano 1962*. Rome.

Istituto Centrale di Statistica. 1964. *Rilevazione Nazionale delle Forze di Lavoro, 20 ottobre, 1963*. Rome.

Kayser, Bernard. 1964. "L'Erosione del Suolo nell'Italia Meridionale," *Nord e Sud*, XI—Nuova Serie—No. 49, January.

Kroeber, A. L. 1948. *Anthropology*. New York: Harcourt.

Lopreato, Joseph, ed. 1965. *Vilfredo Pareto*. New York: Thomas Y. Crowell Co.

Lutz, Vera. 1962. *Italy: A Study in Economic Development*. New York: Oxford University Press.

Maranelli, Carlo. 1955. "Considerazioni Geografiche sulla Questione Meridionale," in Bruno Caizzi, ed., *Antologia della Questione Meridionale*. Milan: Edizioni di Comunità.

Merton, Robert K. 1957. *Social Theory and Social Structure*. Glencoe, Ill.: The Free Press.

Moss, Leonard W., and Stephen C. Cappannari. 1960. "Patterns of Kinship, Comparaggio and Community in a South Italian Village," *Anthropological Quarterly*, 33, January.

Novacco, Nino. 1959. "Zone 'Omogenee' e Sviluppo Economico Regionale," *Nord e Sud*, Anno VI, No. 51, Vecchia Serie.

Presidency of the Council of Ministers of the Italian Republic. 1960. *Italian Affairs: Documents and Notes*, Vol. IX, No. 3. Rome.

Redfield, Robert. 1960. *The Little Community* and *Peasant Society and Culture*. Chicago: University of Chicago Press (Phoenix Books). (Reference will be at all times to the second of these combined works, unless otherwise specified.)

Rossi Doria, Manlio. 1953. "La Struttura e i Problemi Fondamentali dell'Agricoltura Meridionale," in Cassa per il Mezzogiorno, *Problemi dell'Agricoltura Meridionale*. Naples: Istituto Meridionale del Mezzogiorno.

Rossi Doria, Manlio. 1955. "Cos'è il Mezzogiorno Agrario," in Bruno Caizzi, ed., *Antologia della Questione Meridionale*. Milan: Edizioni di Comunità.

Rossi Doria, Manlio. 1958. *Dieci Anni di Politica Agraria nel Mezzogiorno*. Bari: Editori Laterza.

Schachter, Gustav. 1965. *The Italian South: Economic Development in Mediterranean Europe*. New York: Random House.

Sciortino Gugino, Carola. 1960. *Coscienza Collettiva e Giudizio Individuale nella Cultura Contadina*. Palermo: U. Manfredi Editore.

Sumner, William G. 1940. *Folkways*. Boston: Ginn and Company. [Original publication 1906]

SVIMEZ. 1956. *Notizie sull'Economia del Mezzogiorno*. Rome.

SVIMEZ. 1956. "The Under-developed Areas of the South of Italy and Their Industrialization: Economic and Social Aspects," survey undertaken for the Eighth International Social Service Conference. Munich.

SVIMEZ. 1961. *Un Secolo di Statistiche Italiane: Nord e Sud, 1861–1961*. Rome.

Tagliacarne, Guglielmo. 1962. "Calcolo del Reddito Prodotto dal Settore Privato e dalla Pubblica Amministrazione nelle Provincie e Regioni d'Italia nel 1961 e Confronti con gil Anni 1960 e 1951. Indici di Alcuni Consumi e del Risparmio," in *Moneta e Credito*, Vol. XV, No. 59, September.

Unione Italiana delle Camere di Commercio, Industria e Agricoltura. 1959. *Economic Survey of Italy*, 5th ed. Rome.

Vannutelli, Cesare. 1961. "Occupazione e Salari dal 1861 al 1961," in Biblioteca della Rivista "Economia e Storia," *L'Economia Italiana dal 1861 al 1961*. Milan: Dott. A. Giuffrè Editore.

III  THE SOCIAL SETTING

In the preceding chapter, the harsh nature of the peasant's physical environment was the concern. In this chapter and the next, interest will center upon certain major social conditions which constitute the traditional matrix of the peasant's cultural existence. These, like the material conditions, have worked as push factors in determining the emigration of the peasant. Discussion continues about the basic question raised in the preceding chapter: Why do peasants emigrate?

Interpersonal Relations

The precariousness of the peasant's situation, together with other factors to be discussed later, often gives rise to certain other conditions that keep him in a constant state of insecurity, fear, distrust, animosity, and conflict with his fellowmen. His life is in continual anguish. A former peasant, who had returned from

Canada to visit his parents and to satisfy his nostalgia for his birthplace, complained:

The village is too small a world to live in. It is impossible to breathe freely in it. It is dirty; you must always hide something, or from someone; everyone lies about everything: money, food, friendship, love, God. You are always under the eyes of someone who scrutinizes you, judges you, envies you, spies on you, throws curses against you, but smiles his ugly, toothless mouth out whenever he sees you.

The conflict-laden nature of interpersonal relations among southern Italian people in general has been well documented by many observers. Referring to the people of a small Basilicata village, yet confident that his remarks are applicable to much of the South, Banfield argues that they are characterized by "amoral familism." This type of behavior tends to proceed on this assumption: "Maximize the material, short-run advantage of the nuclear family; assume that all others will do likewise." The Southerner's "conditions of life" are often "brutal and senseless." "In so fearful a world," each individual is motivated by self-interest and by suspicion of all who stand outside of the small family circle, for these are "potential competitors and therefore also potential enemies" (Banfield, 1958, 11, 85, 115–116).

In this connection a Calabrian peasant who had never left his province expressed himself as follows:

Italy is a stinking place. We are all like cats and dogs, constantly at each other's throats. I don't know why, but one can't trust even the Lord God himself. If you don't look after your own things twenty-four hours a day, people will spit on you, steal everything you have, and then will say that you did it to them.

Suspicion of one's fellowmen is rampant among southern Italians. Writing about the Sicilian town of Ragusa, Anfossi and associates argue that the Ragusan lacks the notion of sociality as an aspect of his collective life. Indeed, it would seem that "his first instinct" is a defense from all others, a form of suspicion which in its pure state "can isolate the individual even within his family," the only nucleus recognized by him as a social organism, and which in any case "makes difficult any relations that go beyond mere formalism and convention" (Anfossi *et al.*, 1959, 200).

Among peasants suspiciousness may even be greater. As has been repeatedly suggested, southern Italian peasants have traditionally occupied the position of economic and social underdog. Typically, they have until recently worked every day between sunrise and sunset on other people's land. The stinginess of this land and the peasant's high expenses for taxes, disasters, and payments due to the landlord have combined to maintain him in a state of continuous insolvency, insecurity, and servility. The peasantry has traditionally been the most exploited and persecuted class in southern Italy. While the gentry have for centuries institutionalized the sweet life of leisure as the chief pastime of their life, and while they have grown long fingernails as evidence that their hands never engage in manual labor, the peasant has shed blood and sweat to wrench from a hostile soil enough for his minimal needs and much more for the luxuries of his gentry. For the peasant, making a living has been, as have many other aspects of his existence such as the very emotions of love and compassion, in the words of Foster, a "limited good." Not only, continues Foster in speaking of peasant society in general, do " 'good things' exist in finite and limited quantities, but in addition *there is no way directly or indirectly within peasant power to increase the available quantities*" (Foster, 1965, 296, 311 footnote 5).

In the last analysis, stress and conflict in peasant southern Italy, as in peasant society in general, are rooted in the precariousness of its economy. In such an economy, not only are the sources of the peasant's livelihood quite meager, but for a long time they tended to be unchanging as well. "The pie is constant in size" (Foster, 1960–1961, 174–178; Lopreato, 1962, 24). Consequently, while the past evokes memories of painful hardships, and the present is a tense and uncertain struggle for survival, the future constitutes for many a threat of hunger, sickness, humiliations, and futile toil. Under these circumstances, the peasant becomes a wolf preying on his fellowmen. He is constantly on guard against possible impingements on his meager share of the local "economic pie." At the same time, he is maneuvering against all but his own dependents to enlarge his own share so as to achieve a higher degree of comfort and security. Such facts as these explain such widely diffused maxims in southern Italy as: "Do not trust even your brother," "Friends with all, loyal to no one," "Even your best friend is a traitor."

Stress and conflict do not arise only in economically insecure societies. They may equally well arise in more affluent societies, to say nothing of the fact that, like many other social states, poverty has the peculiar property of being widely definable. What, among other things, distinguishes the peasant economy from other types of economy today is its presently expanding linkage to industrial society, with the radical transformation that this entails for the social structures and value systems inherited from the past. Whether it be in southern Italy or in South America, in Africa, or in Asia, strong elements of transformation are active in peasant society. The ensuing economic improvement is not, however, equally distributed. It follows that the traditional power and prestige structures are radically disturbed, resulting in an intensification of the preexisting, economically derived conflict.

The peasant is often so insecure about his economy, and so wary of any planned alterations in the existing partition of the economic pie, that, depending on the extent of his resources and power, he may veto all public attempts at local economic development. From the perspective of the observer, or the politician, it is not difficult to envision a future state of affairs in which the traditional pie has been vastly enlarged to provide for each person a much larger share than has been available in the past. But the destitute peasant himself can see the future only from the perspective of the past. From this vantage point, any change or any differential improvement is likely to suggest to him a diminution of his own share of the pie.

Foster proposes, as a corollary to his principle of "limited good," that if "good" exists in limited and unalterable amounts, and if the system is a closed one, then *an individual or a family can improve a position only at the expense of others.* Like many others writing about peasant society, however, he fails to appreciate fully the very real social inequalities in peasant society, arguing rather that "an apparent relative improvement in someone's position with respect to any 'Good' is viewed as a threat to the entire community. . . . to *all* individuals and families" (Foster, 1965, 296–297).

If peasants are seen, as they should be, in relation to others in their society—other peasants and other classes, too—it is not hard to draw certain unmistakable conclusions. First, the "limited good" must appear more limited to some than to others. Second, and relatedly, some are more opposed to change than others. And finally, it is likely that the individual is motivated more by self-interest and self-seeking than by a commitment to a status quo per se.

Change of any type never affects the members of a population in precisely the same way and to exactly the same extent. The destitute peasant must surely know that probability favors the more privileged and the more powerful—whether other peasants or gentry—when the economic pie is altered. The pie may be constant over time, but the economic values are not equally distributed among all those who partake of it. Some have larger shares of pie than others, which is to say that some are wealthier and more powerful than others. An old adage is valid still: Wealth begets wealth. And this the peasant knows. His opposition to change, therefore, is not determined only by his image of a limited good, but also, and perhaps above all, by his knowledge of the gross inequalities existing in his society and, therefore, by his assessment of his own chances of improvement when and if change occurs. By and large, such chances are not very good while he remains in the community. Hence, change—real or potential—induces further stress among the relatively deprived peasants and, as a consequence, greater conflict in his social milieu.

Social Inequalities

The economic realities of life quite naturally have repercussions for the peasant's position in the status system of his society. *"Chi non ha, non è"* ("He who has nothing is nobody"), states a

Calabrian proverb. The peasant's economic poverty is translated into social insignificance, subordination, contemptibility. Where the economic pie is pitiably small and the future is, therefore, dreadfully uncertain, the least economically secure are also the most manifest failures. The peasant who is unable to demonstrate his ability to insure his future is also deemed useless and unworthy of respect. As a sharecropper or farmhand, he is completely

TABLE 3. Level of Education among Adult Peasants and Nonpeasants, Southern Italy, 1963–1964

Level of Education	Peasants		Nonpeasants	
	N	%	N	%
No education	39	21.9	17	5.5
Elementary, without diploma	74	41.6	63	20.5
Elementary, with diploma	57	32.0	114	37.0
More than elementary	4	2.2	108	35.1
No information	4	2.2	6	1.9
Total	178	99.9	308	100.0

Source: Lopreato Sample Survey, 1963–1964.

dependent on the capital of others for his livelihood. Even as a petty owner, he disposes of little wealth with which to exercise influence beyond his own family dependents in a society that lays an enormous stress on social differences. Lacking the support and the leadership to organize a protest, the impoverished peasant has traditionally sought to insure his continued subsistence by practicing an abject servility. But such social response has become through the centuries the focus of general derision.

To make matters worse, the peasant has little or no schooling. Once again turning to the survey data, Table 3 strikingly reveals the extent to which the educational level of the peasantry falls below that of the rest of the population in the southern regions. Close to two-thirds of the peasants, as compared to only about one-fourth of all other occupational categories combined, have not completed elementary school and may thus be assumed to be functionally illiterate, or semiliterate at best. The peasants, moreover, are almost totally unrepresented among those who went beyond the elementary level. Their poor or nonexistent education naturally hampers their chances for emigration. It forestalls a more rational cultivation of the land. It discourages more determined attempts to inform themselves about and participate in public affairs. It represents a handicap in relation to their children's opportunities for higher education and occupational achievement. Not least of all, in the "country of the thousand dialects" and "scintillating rhetoric," the educationally deprived peasants lack the speech refinement of the prestigeful mother tongue.

Again, in a society which has recently raised fashion to a national institution, the impoverished peasant lacks the most manifest of all symbols of social importance: correct dress. All these disadvantages and the cruel fate of centuries of suffering stamped clearly on his face and on his back render him easily identifiable from a distance and reduce him nearly to the level of a pariah. So, it may happen that a young high-school student, proud of his talcum powder and hair tonic, prefers to walk two or three miles to a nearby town rather than to take a bus "crowded with fetid *contadini* (peasants)."

If by social status is meant, as C. Wright Mills put it, "the amounts of deference received" (1959, 36), then very many peasants in southern Italy have little or none—at least outside of their own class. Sciortino Gugino observes that Sicilian peasants "continue to make up the lowest stratum." Nonfarming workers treat them with contempt; *"pedi 'ncritati"* ("muddy feet") is their nickname. The peasant is credited with feeding everybody, and yet he is everybody's laughingstock. *"Viddanu si e di viddanu ti trattu"* ("You are rustic, and as such I treat you") (Sciortino Gugino, 1960, 51).

The peasants themselves are only too aware of this grievous situation. When asked in the survey just mentioned to state "how much respect people have for the type of work you do," nearly half of them described it as "little" or "very little," and fewer than 10 percent claimed that their occupation received "much respect." The corresponding figures for the rest of the population were 21 and 28 percent, respectively.

The novelist Silone offers more dramatic evidence of the lowly status of southern Italian peasants and of their awareness of this fact. Speaking of the social hierarchy of his famed Fontamara in the Abruzzi, Silone lets the peasant Michele inform us on the status of the likes of himself as follows:

God is at the head of everything. He commands in Heaven. Everybody knows that.
Then comes Prince Torlonia, ruler of the earth.
Then come his guards.
Then come his guards' dogs.
Then nothing.
Then more nothing.
Then still more nothing.
Then come the peasants.
That's all. (Silone, 1961, 37)

It is, therefore, no surprise to learn that in 1948, according to a national survey, only 14 percent of Italian parents wished their male children to become agricultural workers. The actual percentage of such workers was no less than 48 (Luzzatto Fegiz, 1956, 1037). When in another such survey, carried out in 1950, the respondents were divided into the four regional categories of North, Center, South, and Islands, the percentages were, respectively, 25, 12, 8, and 19 (Luzzatto Fegiz, 1956, Table 1.6, 1050).

In a nation where it is generally recognized that "you need pull to be able to live," the life chances of the poor and unpolished peasant are very low indeed. In the shops, at the market place, in the hospital, in legal offices, in the army, in court, in the pharmacy, in church, in the post office, everywhere but in his own smoky and malodorous hut, the peasant is either neglected or altogether ridiculed and humiliated.

The government, the provincial church, the lawyers, the petty bourgeois referred to by Salvemini as "the most ruinous scourge of the South," the "passive snobs" brilliantly studied by the novelists di Lampedusa and Silone, townsmen in general, and especially the aristocracy ("the most stupid aristocracy of the world," according to Fortunato), have combined to perpetrate against the peasant the most indescribable social cruelty of all European peoples. Through the centuries, a mercilessly harsh relationship has developed between the peasant and those above him. It has been said that aristocratic pride is especially significant when it turns into an arrogance of status that has an effect on the strata below (Toennies in Bendix and Lipset, 1953, 50). In southern Italy, the stressful behavior that obtains among the peasants themselves is one very important effect of such arrogance. To a considerable extent it is a form of displaced hostility. Unable to hit back at the real cause of their misery, they have learned to vent their anger and humiliations on one another. Rats may be conditioned to attack one another with tremendous brutality; so can humans. What such anger amounts to is a particularly sad class expression of the old principle: "*A nuju pozzu, ma a mugghjerima pozzu*" ("If I can't beat anyone else, I can beat my wife").

In their discussion of the social classes of Ragusa, a Sicilian town of about 50,000 population, Anna Anfossi and her associates cogently argue that the century-old contrast between *signori* (gentlemen) and the common people has given rise to a peculiar chain of invidious class comparisons. Each group tends to distinguish itself from the groups that it considers inferior and to imitate the attitudes and style of life of superior groups in the degree to which finances permit, and very often even beyond. This phenomenon, of course, is typical of all societies, as many scholars have reported.[1] But it may be particularly marked in southern Italy, where, as Anfossi and associates report, "the theme of the lower class recurs with an almost obsessive frequency." Everyone tries to distinguish himself, which explains the importance that certain formal facts assume: to dress with affectation

---

[1] See, for instance, (1) Hollingshead, 1949; (2) West, 1945; and (3) Kahl, 1953, Chap. VII, where he summarizes the findings on the value orientations of the classes from various studies.

becomes a symbol of social position, whereby, in the words of an interviewee, "many prefer not to eat but to spend almost all that they have in clothing." The display of jewelry and gold objects, on the part of men as well as women, has the same emulative meaning, while, despite aspirations declared by almost all, little is spent for the home, where few ever enter.

As may be expected, the social class that is most often used as a reference point for purposes of claiming self-superiority is the peasantry. Within this class, further subdivisions are readily made. Thus, a sharecropper complains about farmhands because they "are never content; of course, if they have to go to the movies and eat even fruit, one must pay them 10,000 lire a day" (Anfossi et al., 1959, 171–172).

In public offices, the poor peasant may stay in line for long hours only to discover at the end that it was the wrong line. Yet no one would have told him which was the right line. Fellow citizens cannot be bothered, and in any case they are not very compassionate. The clerk? Well, as a minimum, he will react to an inquiry of this sort in such a way as to make the peasant feel that he is sunstruck. When all is done, the confused peasant usually has lost time, money, and confidence in humanity, his government, democracy, justice.

An apposite case took place in Rome at Christmastime in 1963. A Calabrian migrant felt the need to visit his family in his old village, but had been seriously ill and was very weak. So, he made a remarkable sacrifice and reserved a first-class seat on the train many days ahead of departure time. On that day, however, the railroad station was the scene of a mob of thousands of other desperate and exhausted human beings who, after months or years of heavy and often humiliating toil away from the family, also wanted to return home for Christmas. The trains had been promised in abundance, but as usual they were not adequate to the needs.

As a consequence, the former Calabrian peasant could not even get close to the train for which he had expensive reservations. After hopelessly waiting around for a few hours, he, therefore, decided to call off his trip. He began looking for the appropriate ticket window in order to have his money refunded. Italian public announcements and instructions do not exactly take the many millions of semiliterate citizens into consideration. So, Signor Sebastiano went to the nearest window and inquired in his rustic Italian: "I have paid for a reserved seat but cannot get to my train." "Why are you telling me?" the busy clerk replied. "Go to some other window. Can't you see I am busy?" After visiting two more windows, he was finally sent to the right one. He was refunded his money, minus a 20 percent service charge. "But it is not my fault if I could not get on the train," complained Signor Sebastiano. The logic in the clerk's answer was as incredible as its rudeness: "Well, whose is it—mine?"

In his relations with those above himself, the peasant has been, and to a large extent is still now, placed in the role of the cicada in the well-known Calabrian tale "The Fox and the Cicada." Once upon a time, the story goes, a fox and a cicada decided to join efforts in order to cultivate a farm. When it was time to sow, the fox said to the cicada, "Why don't you sow, and then I'll hoe?" And the cicada sowed. Then it was time to hoe, and the fox proposed to the cicada: "You hoe, and then I'll reap." And the cicada hoed. And the cicada alone also threshed. Finally, the fox said to the cicada: "Partner, let's now divide the crop: you take the straw, and I shall take the wheat." The cicada protested; whereupon the fox ate him (Lombardi Satriani, 1963, 27–28).

Discussing the treatment received by peasants in their society, an informant recently put the matter succinctly thus: "Well, what can I say? We are *cornuti e bastuniati* (first made cuckolds and then beaten up)." This type of treatment is apparent every day. In the spring of 1963, in the post office of a southern market town, among the endless crowd of waiting clients was a visibly exhausted peasant woman who had most likely left her little village at sunrise that morning to come and sell her score of eggs at the market. One by one, many fellow customers went ahead of her, oftentimes by their own initiative, sometimes because invited to do so by the postal clerk. When she could tolerate it no longer, she whispered to the clerk in a meek tone that could have aroused general shame and compassion: "Be charitable. I have been waiting an hour."

She must have wished she had never opened her mouth. The clerk's immediate, violent reaction was to order her to hold her tongue until he was good and ready to listen. Then he had a clever afterthought. "But what do you wish?" he jested. "A special-delivery stamp," she begged. "But why, my good woman? Can you write?" That question was indeed clever. It had the effect of a clown act in a children's circus: the spectators exploded in laughter. One of them, who until then had been merrily conversing with the clerk at the nearby window about the exploits of an Italian soccer team, appeared to be a member of the local police. He could not help but volunteer a bit of his own wisdom for the occasion. "And what do you know about the difficulty of dealing with these blessed peasants?"

The tired and outraged lady retreated without the stamp. Picking up her wicker basket from the floor, and using the only form of protest open to her, she exclaimed: "May you die with rabies, arrogant cowards!" Given her lowly social position, the whole thing ended there, for all but her. When she returned home that day and heard her young son mention the possibility of going to seek work in Milan or Lausanne, it is not very likely that she discouragd him.

City people amuse themselves at the mere appearance of the peasant. Recently, a poor woman was mocked, vilified, and pushed to the ground on the main street of a southern town by a group of teenagers. Adults looked on with keen enjoyment. Her only crime was to have attempted to protect her pretty young daughter who had come to town probably to buy part of her dowry, but who looked like a *pacchiana* (a cad or hick). "Wow, what a sexy beauty! May I touch your hair?" the senseless youngsters had jeered.

"To tell you all the jokes they [the city people] played on us would take a week," report the peasants of Fontamara to Silone. It also takes the patience of the most humble to endure. Thus, when the people of Fontamara, who for about forty years had not had a curate, sent in a final plea to the bishop for a permanent priest, word got to them from the nearby town that, contrary to their expectations, their petition had been granted by the bishop. They proceeded to get ready for the arrival of their priest. The church was cleaned and decorated. At the entrance to the village a triumphal arch with curtains and flowers was erected. House doors were decorated. On the day the priest was expected to arrive, all the village went out to meet him. *"Viva Gesù!"* *"Viva Maria!"* *"Viva la Chiesa!"* ("Long live Jesus!" "Long live Mary!" "Long live the Church!") the pathetic people of Fontamara chanted upon seeing what looked like the new priest's group. "Just then the funny group from the city opened up and, urged on by kicks and stones, out ran the new curate—in the form of an old donkey covered with paper colored like priestly vestments." (Silone, 1961, 40–41).

When the peasants of Fontamara on another occasion went from their hamlet to the town hall in order to protest the diversion of the stream from their land to that of a local speculator, they received more of the same treatment. The constable shouted from a window of the town hall, "Don't let them in! They'll fill the town hall with lice!" Everyone laughed and jeered. The town clerks looked at one another, astounded. "What do you want?" they asked. "We want to speak to the mayor," the peasants of Fontamara replied. Then the clerks began laughing "like madmen." They began repeating the peasants' request at the top of their lungs. "Guess what? They've come to talk with the mayor!" (Silone, 1961, 41–46).

In the meantime, the sun and the dust had made the peasants' throats dry. So, they went to the nearby public fountain to drink. Some of them managed to drink, "but suddenly there wasn't any more water." Then, when they were about to go away, the water "came back all of a sudden." The poor people were flustered, anxious, and frustrated. An argument about drinking priorities ensued. "A couple of girls grabbed each other by the hair. Finally order was restored. But the water stopped again."

It was like this: when there wasn't any water we went away from the fountain, and when we were away the water came back. This happened three or four times. When we returned, the water dried up; when we left, the fountain started up again. We were dying of thirst and we couldn't drink. We could only look at the water from far away. If we went closer the water disappeared. After the water had disappeared once more as we came up, about ten policemen approached, surrounded us and asked us in a nasty tone of voice what we wanted. . . . "O Jesus!" we said. "What sins have we committed more than the others that you punish us in this way?" With the two policemen in front and back, we were like a captured herd (Silone, 1961, 47–49).

The snobbery and obduracy that the southern peasant must tolerate from townsmen and local authorities are proverbial and need not be documented further. It might be briefly pointed out at this point that often the peasant receives analogous treatment from higher authorities as well. In the winter of 1963–1964, several peasant villages and hamlets in the Calabrian province of Catanzaro were hit by a storm. When the local electric system went out of order, the authorities did nothing about it, and the people were left without electricity for several days. More frequently still, street lamps burn out, and the people must wait many months for a "roaming team" with a high ladder to come and replace them.

Until recently the indescribable poverty of the southern peasant and the heartaches that accompanied it had rarely been the serious concern of their government. The end of World War II witnessed the beginning of a new era for "the southern question." Nevertheless, ill-conceived policies administered by a bungling bureaucracy have easily been blocked by old interests and ideas; or else they have favored those who were at the start relatively affluent and influential. Such has been the case, for instance, with farm-improvement projects, which as a rule have benefited only the economically solvent or those who could produce a guarantee of such solvency. As a peasant put it recently, "if you want to improve your little plot, you must have money and pull. Otherwise, the government doesn't know you."

But that is not all. In recent years, a few roads have been built to replace or supplement the old farm trails. To build them, the government necessarily has had to cut across farms. One cannot

complain about this unavoidable practice. But many peasants find
it difficult to understand why in a number of cases, a decade and
more after the expropriation of their land, they have not yet been
remunerated for their loss. Nor can the poor people turn to
anyone to find out what has gone wrong. "No one knows. Lawyers and notaries keep trying to find out for impossible fees."
And the things they find out are very often of a most peculiar
sort. They remind one of Don Circostanza, that colorful lawyer
so vividly described again by Silone. Don Circostanza was known
among the people of Fontamara as "the People's Friend." When
the people succeeded, after repeated trials, in seeing the mayor, a
local schemer known as "the Trader," to protest about the stream
water that he had illegally diverted into his own land, Don
Circostanza presented the solution.

> "These women are right," the People's Friend went on. "I have
> always defended them and will continue to do so. Basically, what is
> it that these women want? They want to be respected—"
> "That's right!" interrupted Marietta, and she ran up to kiss his
> hands. . . .
> "These women claim that half the stream isn't enough to irrigate
> the land. They want more than half, as I interpret their needs.
> Therefore there is only one possible solution. We must give *three-
> quarters* of the water to the podestà [the mayor] and *the other
> three-quarters* to Fontamara. Thus *both will have three-quarters*, a
> little more than half. I am sure that my proposal will be very
> detrimental to the podestà, but I appeal to his sentiments as a
> philanthropist and public benefactor" (Silone, 1961, Chap. 2; italics
> added).

The closing statement of Silone's novel is fitting for the
substance of our argument:

> What can we do?
> After so much suffering, so many tears, and so many wounds, so
> much hate, injustice, and desperation—WHAT CAN WE DO? (Silone,
> 1961, 224)

The only way out, under the present circumstances, is to get
out—by emigrating. As a peasant put it in 1963, "I have got to get

out, go somewhere, leave this miserable hell. God! My heart is
always under a stone. The very thought of being stuck here
m'accuppa 'u cori" (". . . encases and compresses my heart").

Peasant Restlessness

If the basic question of this and the preceding chapters—Why
do peasants emigrate?—is raised anew, it must be concluded that,
contrary to the view of some scholars,[2] emigration from southern
Italy is not primarily a question of seeking one's fortune. To a
very large extent it has become a question of escaping what a
peasant from Basilicata has recently referred to as "the inferno of
the peasant's life," a culture of tragedy and persecution. This
the peasant no longer tolerates.

Until a few decades ago, southern peasants, like peasants
everywhere, saw themselves as subject to the working of history
but scarcely as makers of it. One of the chief characteristics of
peasant culture was that for them history, as well as the environment, belonged to the realm of the given (Friedmann, 1962, 91).
The cultural evolution of recent years has altered this view in the
southern Italian peasant. He has now taken a step into the stream
of history, and has started to manipulate, though still feebly, the
processes that go into making it. Channels of communication,
linking his society to the larger national society and to the world
at large, have opened up to an extent previously inconceivable,
and have become crucial factors in fostering a new perspective in
the peasant.

POLITICAL PARTIES

One of the most important factors has been the continuing
political struggle in his nation. In the wake of World War II, a
multitude of political parties came into being in Italy, varying
from the extreme left to the extreme right. Today, three rather

---

[2] See, for example, Hempel, 1959, 125, where he states that "There is
no doubt whatsoever, that the Italian immigrant to Australia is more than
any other, 'homo oeconomicus.'"

homogeneous political blocks may be distinguished as having an influence in southern affairs: the Left, composed of Communists and Socialists, with the latter increasingly polarizing toward the Communists or toward the Center; the predominant Center, consisting mostly of Christian Democrats; and the Right, composed mostly of Monarchists and neo-Fascists.

All parties and coalitions have naturally been jockeying for power, each on the basis of its own definition of national and regional needs and its own notion of what constitutes the best solution of such needs. Some goals, however, the political blocks have held in common, with varying degrees of seriousness: certain alleged goals involving especially a step-up in the industrialization of the country, particularly of the agricultural South; employment and a decent income for all; reorganization and improvement of agriculture; and more adequate welfare measures.

The parties of the Left in particular have been outspoken in pointing to the chronic poverty of the South in general, and of the southern peasant in particular, calling for "more land for the peasant and more work for everybody." All parties, however, have, to a greater extent than ever before, recognized the miserable conditions of the peasant's situation. They have vied for his vote, for his recognition of their efforts on his behalf, and for his own greater awareness of the problem. In so doing, they have emphasized and publicized his pervasive poverty and invited the peasant to a future mode of life that excites his self-esteem, his achievement ideology, and his imagination.

The power of the landlord and the traditional aristocracy also has come under attack from many political directions, with the result that, as the peasant learns of better opportunities elsewhere, he sheds his traditional habits and servility, and moves away.

MODERN MEDIA OF COMMUNICATION

A second major factor in the new peasant awareness is the increasing operation of the modern media of communication. Focusing on television alone, which is perhaps the most important of them, we find that those few times that the peasant watches it, whether it be at home, at the village café, or frequently merely by peeking in the house of a neighbor while standing outside on the road, he is left with incipient wants and a heightened discontent with his life situation. Television discloses a world which in comparison to his own is utterly fantastic: all light and color, wealth and comfort, beauty and joy. Such a world is as different from the peasant's as day is from night. Television intensifies his dissatisfaction with his present status and helps create a new, and a more realistic, image of the good life.

At the heart of this view, so easily promoted by extravagant television producers, lies a vision of unlimited good, coupled with an absence of incessant toil. In our observations in southern Italy, the peasants' most striking reaction to television was perhaps their notion that life could be so pleasant and yet so devoid of exertion. Upon hearing that Mike Bongiorno, a popular television star, probably earned scores of thousands of dollars per year, a group of peasants in a mountain village in the Abruzzi responded almost in unison: "That's what I call living. They call that work!"

Studying the influence of television on a small group of Basilicata peasants, de Rita reports that the most frequent term used by them to designate the world represented by television is "modernity" (de Rita, 1964, 223). And modernity is what, with few exceptions, the peasants of South Italy strive for. "The young ladies [of the South] seek to imitate the young ladies from the other Italy [the modern Italy], but their mothers are not displeased because that is modernity" (de Rita, 1964, 225).

Television creates a new awareness of still another sort. As Pitkin has stated, "peasants, by and large, have existence only in relation to cities" (Pitkin, 1959, 161). Until recently, this city-dominated relationship presented itself in a way that was unknown or mysterious to the peasant. He vaguely recognized that there was a "command center" somewhere far away in Rome. From here came the orders for those agencies and persons in his village who in turn articulated and regulated most of his social activities: the *Segretario*, or the effective executive of his town and an official of the Ministry of the Interior; the federal police chief; the teachers assigned by the Ministry of Education; the priest appointed by the bishop, in turn responsible to the Vatican; the tax collector responsible to the Ministry of Finance; the state-designated medical officer; the postmaster; and others. The peasant has very few opportunities for making decisions affecting the life of the community to say nothing of the nation. However, as the peasant moves from being a passive recipient of history to assuming a more active role in its making, a new kind of dynamic begins to underly the relationship between city and peasant, namely, "a more symmetrical distribution of social responsibility" (Pitkin, 1959, 165–167).

In disclosing the mechanisms of national decision making, and in revealing the broader matrix of his social existence, television is accentuating for the peasant the need to partake of the decision-making processes and the distribution of social responsibility. There is reason to believe that an individual's tendency in relation to the sources of power and decision making in his society is generally centripetal in nature. The attempt to "get close to the leader" is a fairly well-known phenomenon in small-group research (Whyte, 1943). In larger social structures it does not seem unlikely that the individual will at least seek to learn about, and get close to, the proximate context of decision making and public action. The possibility of doing so is missing in the peasant's restrictive community, whereas television suggests that outside it is possible.

EMIGRATION

Perhaps the most important factor underlying the peasant's new awareness has been emigration itself, particularly the first wave of it at the turn of the present century. Emigration begets emigration. Whatever the original causes of departure, after some profitable years abroad, some of the old emigrants returned to their old communities to enjoy at leisure the fruits of their labor. And here they have, by their improved style of life, displayed to the less fortunate previously unimagined possibilities of economic and social betterment. The impulse to throw away the hoe becomes progressively stronger and more general. Indeed the perception of even a small improvement in former peers increases the level of aspirations and accentuates the awareness that they cannot be realized at home.

Despite the innumerable hardships often suffered abroad—whether in New York, Milan, or Toronto—the peasant has experiences that reinforce his disaffection with his old society and his position in it. Or at home he hears about them. Particularly critical has been the migration to English-speaking countries, where the former peasant has earned amounts of money which by his old standards are extraordinary, and has discovered a form of social relations which, despite the well-documented handicaps of the immigrant, he has found to be greatly more "democratic" and "humane" than those from which he escaped. The difference has been so impressive that the peasant very often idealizes the new well beyond recognizable proportions. In comparison, the old becomes altogether despicable. A few years ago an emigrant wrote from Canada:

The beauty of it is that here, when five o'clock comes around, I clean my fingernails, dress like a king, and I am a king, like everyone else. I am not the son of So-and-So; I am not a hodman; I am just Mr. [name deleted], and I feel a hundred times better than those *vagabondi* [lazy do-nothings—persons of leisure in his old community].

A returnee from Australia said in the anteroom of a radiologist in Messina, Sicily:

In Australia you never have to wait very long in the office of a doctor. You have an appointment with him, and when it's time for you to go in, you go in. If you don't have an appointment, it's first-come-first-served. Here it is first-come-last-served, unless you come accompanied by a *commendatore* [honorific title].

He then proceeded to relate an experience he had had with a notary public in a town near his village. It was the sort of story which in southern Italy has been heard many times before. One day, shortly after temporarily returning from Australia, the enterprising fellow had left his village very early in the morning to arrange a transfer of property with the notary. He had waited six or seven hours in the notary's waiting room while many other clients had gone in and out of the office. On those few occasions in which he had the courage to inquire about his own status in the obviously arbitrary procession of services, he was told in brisk terms by the notary's maid that when his turn came he would be informed of it. And he waited. Finally, late that afternoon the maid approached and lashed him with the information that there was no reason to wait any longer, for the "*professore*" had gone out two hours previously. "What are you waiting for? Can't you see he is not here? Return tomorrow." And so it was for several additional days.

The working of foreign bureaucracies has very favorably impressed many peasant emigrants. One of them expressed his admiration for the Canadian officialdom as follows:

In Canada you can often settle the most difficult official business with a single telephone call. In Italy you must take your hat off to hundreds of good-for-nothings throughout the country in order to solve the simplest problem. After many months or years, after having filled scores of officially stamped and expensive sheets of paper, and after having wasted large sums of money which end up in the pockets of thieves, you are told that you may not have the document because the law has changed.

Aside from the fact that emigrants send remittances or bring back sums of money that by local standards are quite large and permit the recipients to buy many cultural symbols of social importance and superiority, they are also important agents in the diffusion of customs and beliefs that feed the most cherished of the peasants' newly developing values. This point will be discussed in more detail in a later chapter. For the present, it may suffice to note that, upon returning to his old village—permanently or temporarily—after a few years abroad, the previously deprived magnifies the better reality of foreign cultures and titillates the imagination of those who have not yet left. Stories are told of "the complete equality of Americans"; of houses luxuriously equipped in which one can go about in shirt sleeves when the streets outside are covered with snow; of stores

where one can buy most of his necessities in a few minutes and
for little money; of beefsteaks and milk that are fed to the pigs; of
public officials who serve with kindness and loyalty; of public
notaries who notarize a document for an insignificant fee from
behind a drug counter; of doctors who correct an old-standing
disturbance with a single pill; of beautiful women who pursue
"the passionate Italian." [3]

Three important clarifications are necessary at this point of
the discussion. First, the peasant's rising social resoluteness must
be viewed as a process that is at least a half-century old. The
considerations discussed so far would suggest only that the process has become more intensive recently.

Second, the recent wave of emigration from southern Italy is
qualitatively different from that which reached its peak around
1913. A large number of the peasants who went to the United
States five and more decades ago had to tolerate conditions which
were not much better (if indeed they were not worse) than those
they had left at home. Many lived in unheated shanties, isolated
and lonely. Nor was their economic avail very high. The lucky
ones earned $1.50 for ten hours of work, while a pair of work
shoes cost $1.75, and eggs sold for ten cents a dozen. These facts
may explain the large percentage of migrants who returned home
after only a year or two abroad. Only those who persevered for
many years profited from the building of America. Of these,
some never went back to their community of origin; others
returned and spread the word about "the land of opportunities
and equality."

The situation today is radically different. Until the end of
World War II, life conditions in southern Italian villages had
changed but little; the world that peasants now see in Milan, in
other parts of Europe, or in one of the English-speaking countries
overseas often verges on the phantasmagoric. The migrant earns

---

[3] These findings would suggest an affirmative answer to Merton's question as to whether there is "a tendency for outsiders to develop unrealistic
images of nonmembership groups which, if they are positive reference
groups, lead toward unqualified idealization (as the official norms are taken
at face value). . . ." (Merton, 1957, 351).

more money in real value; on the whole he finds a better recep-
tion by the native population; he lives a fuller cultural life; and,
partly as a result of the first wave of emigration, present-day
emigrants have fairly clear ideas as to what they can expect and
accomplish abroad.

Third, no suggestion is here being made that current conditions are about to bring peasant life to an end in southern Italy.
The historical circumstances to which the peasant is anchored
are very complex and deep-rooted. Furthermore, human values
often change less than appearances would lead us to believe. What
is happening in southern Italy at the present merely indicates that
peasants desire a change, that they wish to help in bringing it
about, and that in any case, barring a major setback, they will
keep departing until the remaining few will be literally compelled
to farm rationally whatever land will prove itself tillable. As a
result, clear evidence already shows that the ancient poverty,
fatalism, and hopelessness are for many today becoming mere
memories that render the present all the more enjoyable.

A general theoretical statement may now be hazarded for a
better understanding of the recent massive movement of southern
peasants from their land as well as of the nature of their general
situation. Because of various historical, demographic, and geographic factors, the peasant lived for a long time in a world of
abject poverty and precarious life conditions. Concomitant with
his dire economic position has been a low social position that has
inspired contempt and derision from those more fortunate than
he. But for various reasons his peasant society has gradually been
increasing its contact with the surrounding world. In displaying
before his eyes the conditions and possibility of a more commodious, secure, and just life, this new world has also intensified his
sense of poverty and strengthened his wish to escape it. As
Banfield remarks:

Unlike the primitive, the peasant feels himself part of a large society
which he is "in" but not altogether "of." He lives in a culture in
which it is very important to be admired, and he sees that by its
standards he cannot be admired in the least; by these standards he

and everything about him are contemptible or ridiculous. Knowing this, he is filled with loathing for his lot and with anger for the fates which assigned him to it (Banfield, 1958, 65).

It would seem that the peasant's enduring poverty, the afflicting interpersonal relations that ensue therefrom, and the subservient, handicapped social status, which also follows from his poverty and from his work conditions, constitute the objective preconditions of his decision to escape his traditional situation. Once, for whatever reason, the communication channels linking his peasant world to national and extranational societies have opened up and become objects of his awareness, the peasant sees in the outside world a mode of life and standards of conduct that intensify the discomfort and discontent inherent in the objective preconditions. In his observation of this new world an intense feeling of relative deprivation emerges, and the need for achievement is greatly intensified.

What has happened is that the peasant is now in a position to evaluate the social values and opportunities of "nonmembership groups," and to refer to these for an appraisal of the values and opportunities of his own society. Within this "comparative frame of reference" (Merton, 1957, Chaps. VIII, IX), his society receives a negative judgment, and the need to escape that society is heightened.[4] It may be said, therefore, that when an individual's self-image feeds on stimuli deriving from his own cultural milieu

---

[4] Alberoni, too, recognizes that the peasants' desire to emigrate is not exclusively of an economic nature, but "is founded on a rejection of their own community and of the social world in which they have lived and live." He errs, however, in asserting that extranational, in contrast to internal, migration offers "a phenomenon of this sort only in a very small measure" (Alberoni, 1963, 25). As we shall have further occasion to see in a later chapter, migration to foreign countries and especially English-speaking countries is at the base of a new egalitarianism and a greater social resoluteness among southern peasants. The fact that many of them still prefer to undertake the hardship of long and very expensive trips to and from Australia, where they sometimes earn a lower income than they would in Turin or Milan, clearly attests to the heavy role of extranational emigration in the peasant's rejection of his peasant and national society alike.

which tend to denigrate it, he is likely to reject his cultural milieu and to search for nonmembership groups that will provide stimuli to restore his self-respect. He is likely to refer positively to nonmembership groups for attitude formation and for the rationale that bears on the pursuit of his future life chances. The evolution of personal goals then follows an itinerary that frequently concludes with geographic mobility and usually with an improvement in economic and social position as well as in self-evaluation.

Until recent decades, peasants turned aside from active comparison of themselves with others not of their own kind. In their forbidding contact with the local gentry lording a basically static society, they had learned not to question the system of evaluation which publicly symbolized them as socially inferior by the basic tokens of social importance. In the near impossibility of escaping their own estate, they turned to creating various gradations of social worth within the stratum itself.

The evidence from southern Italy would contradict Tumin and Feldman's categorical proposition that "lower caste or class members [do not] accept the criteria of ranking by which they are deemed functionally and morally inferior" (Tumin with Feldman, 1961, 480). Lacking in southern Italy was, and still is, any notion of the spirit of *dignidad* that Tumin and Feldman report for Puerto Rico in the form of a

. . . belief that all men are ultimately equal and equally worthy of respect, regardless of temporary or even enduring differences in their material standard of living, in the formal power they exercise, or in the prestige which their occupations and educations evoke (Tumin with Feldman, 1961, 18).

The southern Italian peasant, unlike the Puerto Rican *jibaro*, has never been "romantically honored." May it suffice to say that in the Italian language all terms (*contadino, villano, terrone, bifolco,* or the like) used to designate the peasant are also synonymous with such words as "stupid," "ill-bred," "uncouth," and the like.

In the local dialects, a much vaster array of terms exists (such as *zulu, tamarru, zammaru, picuni, pedi 'ncritati, viddanu*, and the like) which render even more obnoxious meanings.

In the absence of opportunities for change and of an extralo-cal source of positive self-appraisal, the peasant accepted his lower position. The peasant, however, did not think, as Hagen asserts, that "the concept of his trying to change it [is] ridiculous, shocking, a little indecent, and immoral" (Hagen, 1962, 71). If their society appeared to them as an immutable system, the peas-ants' attitude was more likely to be, as Pitkin cogently supports, one of resignation to their destiny, which saw fit to so divide the world and place them among the lower orders of it (Pitkin, 1954, 153).

It is, however, important to keep in mind the fact that destiny, like other things, does change, and that at any given time a peasant knows that it has changed for at least a handful of his fellow peasants. Peasant society is never totally static, and the peasant knows it. Otherwise, he would not be constantly on guard against its disturbance, a circumstance which partly ex-plains stress and tension in peasant society.

As long as his chances of improvement appear to him to be nil, he accepts his lowly status. He concurs with the public denigration of it. And he believes that as a peasant he is indeed functionally and morally inferior. As one such peasant put it recently,

Well, what can one say? We peasants are poor earthworms. We live with the animals, eat with them, talk to them, smell like them. So, we are a great deal like them. How would you like to be a peasant?

But could the peasant's acceptance of a low status for himself bring any comfort to his personal integrity? There is no reason to believe that he of all people would be forever a total stranger to the "wish for recognition." In his case, however, this basic wish could only mean a cessation of agricultural activities. Emigration is patently suited to achieve this goal; with few exceptions it involves also occupational mobility and social betterment.

In short, the peasant is leaving the land on which he has worked for many reasons, but foremost among them seems to be a desire to regain, or to earn, his self-esteem, his dignity, and his personal integrity. To a large extent, the stimulus to leave has come from the outside, and particularly from various groups within the surrounding civilization whose economic and ideologic forms have proven to be uncommonly benevolent.

In displaying before his eyes the conditions and possibilities of a more commodious, secure, and just life, the outside world has also intensified his sense of poverty, his despair, and his discontent with his society,[5] thus strengthening his wish to escape it. As Barnett might say, today's peasants in southern Italy are "resentful." They are not resigned have-nots; rather they are dissatisfied because they are denied the opportunities and the values that in their larger society are esteemed the most. They "are markedly receptive to the suggeston of a change which will at least equalize opportunities or, perhaps even better, put them on top and their smug superiors on the bottom" (Barnett, 1953, 401).

Basically, what appears to be happening is that out of the old feudal mass of deprived and unhappy workers, cruelly subject to the whims of a stingy land and a hostile society, is emerging a self-conscious class of workers who, because of their excessive poverty, their total lack of social power, and their negative self-

---

[5] The transformation in the emigrant's psychology as he goes from one country to another is a different question and would be the object of very interesting study. There is reason to believe that initially many an immigrant becomes demoralized and for some time oscillates between nostalgia for the old society and thwarted hopes for the new in an uncomfortable succession of ambivalent feelings. In an interesting study carried out in Perth, Western Australia, Heiss found that immigrants from southern Italy displayed a significantly higher level of satisfaction with their life in Australia than migrants from northern Italy, where conditions are initially more favorable than in the South. A detailed analysis of the data led Heiss to suggest that the level of satisfaction was directly related to the degree to which actual achievement was consonant with the expectations that immigrants had brought to the new country. It would seem to us, in other words, that the particularly unfavorable circumstances prevailing in southern Italy made adjustment in the new society all the more easy. Heiss has a more complex explanation for his findings, but no more cogent. See Heiss, 1966, 165–177.

image, are seeking to lose their class identity. They are doing so by emigrating.

REFERENCES

Alberoni, Francesco. 1963. "Caratteristiche e Tendenze delle Migrazioni Interne in Italia," *Studi di Sociologia,* Anno I, January–March.

Anfossi, Anna, Magda Talamo, and Francesco Indovina. 1959. *Ragusa.* Torino: Taylor Editore.

Banfield, Edward C. 1958. *The Moral Basis of a Backward Society.* Glencoe, Ill.: The Free Press.

Barnett, H. G. 1953. *Innovation.* New York: McGraw-Hill Book Co.

De Rita, Lidia. 1964. *I Contadini e la Televisione.* Bologna: Società Editrice il Mulino.

Foster, George M. 1960–1961. "Interpersonal Relations in Peasant Society," *Human Organization,* 19, Winter.

Foster, George M. 1965. "Peasant Society and the Image of Limited Good," *American Anthropologist,* 67, April.

Friedmann, F. G. 1962. "The World of '*La Misera,*'" *Community Development Review,* VII, June.

Hagen, Everett E. 1962. *On the Theory of Social Change.* Homewood, Ill.: The Dorsey Press.

Heiss, Jerold. 1966. "Sources of Satisfaction and Assimilation among Italian Immigrants," *Human Relations,* 19, No. 2.

Hempel, J. A. 1959. *Italians in Queensland.* Canberra: The Australian National University.

Hollingshead, August B. 1949. *Elmtown's Youth.* New York: John Wiley.

Kahl, Joseph A. 1953. *The American Class Structure.* New York: Rinehart & Company, Inc.

Lombardi Satriani, Raffaele. 1963. *Racconti Popolari Calabresi,* Vol. IV. Cosenza: Editrice "Casa del Libro."

Lopreato, Joseph. 1962. "Interpersonal Relations in Peasant Society: The Peasant's View," *Human Organization,* 21, Spring.

Luzzatto Fegiz, Pierpaolo. 1956. *Il Volto Sconosciuto dell'Italia.* Milan: Dott. A. Giuffrè Editore.

Merton, Robert K. 1957. *Social Theory and Social Structure.* Glencoe, Ill.: The Free Press.

Mills, C. Wright. 1959. "On Intellectual Craftsmanship," in Llewellyn Gross, ed., *Symposium on Sociological Theory.* Evanston, Ill.: Row, Peterson and Company.

Pitkin, Donald S. 1954. *Land Tenure and Family Organization in an Italian Village.* Unpublished Ph.D. dissertation, Harvard University.

Pitkin, Donald S. 1959. "A Consideration of Asymmetry in the Peasant-City Relationship," *Anthropological Quarterly,* 32, January.

Sciortino Gugino, Carola. 1960. *Coscienza Collettiva e Giudizio Individuale nella Cultura Contadina.* Palermo: U. Manfredi Editore.

Silone, Ignazio. 1961. *Fontamara.* New York: Dell Publishing Co., Inc.

Toennies, Ferdinand. 1953. "Estates and Classes," in Reinhard Bendix and Seymour M. Lipset, eds., *Class, Status and Power.* Glencoe, Ill.: The Free Press.

Tumin, Melvin M., with Arnold S. Feldman. 1961. *Social Class and Social Change in Puerto Rico.* Princeton: Princeton University Press.

West, James. 1945. *Plainville, U.S.A.* New York: Columbia University Press.

Whyte, William F. 1943. *Street Corner Society.* Chicago: University of Chicago Press.

IV INTERPERSONAL RELATIONS: A Theoretical Issue

In the preceding two chapters, some of the factors underlying the heavy migration from southern Italy were pointed out and explained. The chief interest in the discussion was not the phenomenon of emigration per se, but an examination of the foundations—geographic, economic, and social—on which the evolving peasant society of that region rests at the present time. The picture drawn reveals the peasant as an individual who has had to exist in a prohibitively hostile environment. On the one hand, nature has been stingy; on the other, society has evolved systems of inequality and interpersonal relations that have continuously and brutally chastened the peasant. The result has been a deep sense of dissatisfaction, which he has sought to alleviate by emigrating. It has been suggested that, given the fundamental fact of the precarious character of peasant economies everywhere, stress and dissatisfaction are very probably universal characteristics of peasant people.

This generalization is not unique, as we shall presently see, nor is it unopposed. The dispute concerning the relation of peasant peoples to their environment and their particular experiences in it is long-standing in social science. Indeed, the controversy is growing at a rate equal with the growth of the literature on peasant peoples. No wonder, for the question bears great relevance to the task of explaining and predicting the uneasy course of the vast portion of human society which is represented by preindustrial peoples.

Discussion might begin with a broad generalization by noting a tendency among social scientists to describe peasants throughout the globe as a homogeneous category, holding in common a basic value system and certain very marked characteristics, regardless of differences in language, religion, and geographical area. Whatever theoretical disagreements exist concern the particular nature of such characteristics.

The quarrel among interested scholars does not extend to all aspects of peasant society and culture. It is generally agreed that, given the precarious nature of the peasant economy, peasants everywhere emphasize hard work and frugality as necessities, though not necessarily as moral qualities. Similarly, given the fact that they are often totally dependent on others for the source of their very livelihood, peasants everywhere may be expected to be relatively submissive. Again, due to their generally low social status and high degree of isolation from matters political, they are probably everywhere suspicious of those above themselves and of city people in general. It is interesting to note that even novelists who have dramatized the essential misery of their own nation's peasants have not failed to see basic similarities among peasants everywhere. Thus, one of Silone's characters informs us that

I was in the Argentine pampas when I was young, and there I talked with peasants of all races from Spanish to Indian, and we understood one another as if we all came from Fontamara. But we spoke with an Italian who came to us every Sunday from the consulate without understanding him. . . . On our farm there was a Portuguese deaf-mute and we understood each other even without speaking. But we didn't understand this Italian (Silone, 1961, 30–31).

Approaches to the Study of Peasant Society

Some observers of peasant people have gone further than real conditions would seem to warrant and argued, in a Hesiodic key, that peasants everywhere tend to live a relatively contented and well-adjusted life. As can well be imagined, this position has produced some controversy that may be worth a brief summary. At issue here is, basically, the nature of interpersonal relations in peasant society.

THE CONSENSUS MODEL

The controversy was touched off, it appears, by Robert Redfield, who, though presenting rather conflicting evidence from his various studies, held on the whole that peasant society represents a stable and well-integrated structure based on consensus of values and harmonious relations among its members (Redfield, 1930; 1960). Oscar Lewis accurately summarized the viewpoint first developed in Redfield's study of Tepoztlán, Mexico, in the following statement from his own restudy of this same community:

The impression given by Redfield's study of Tepoztlán is that of a relatively homogeneous, isolated, smoothly functioning, and well-integrated society made up of a contented and well-adjusted people (Lewis, 1951, 428).

Redfield, in short, belongs to a school of thought which emphasizes "consensus" or "general agreement" as the basic mechanism of social order. He therefore belongs to that school of thought which the German sociologist Dahrendorf has recently represented as "the integration theory of society" (Dahrendorf, 1959, 157–165).

THE COERCION MODEL

The major point of view opposed to the consensus model is one which represents peasant society as being characterized by disagreements, conflict, coercion, and disintegration. Thus, in restudying Tepoztlán, Oscar Lewis stressed "the poor quality of interpersonal relations," specifying the attributes of constraint, detachment, lack of affectionateness, suspicion and distrust of others, malice, hidden and indirect hostility, absence of altruism, envy, and harsh and unrelenting gossip (1951, Chap. 12).[1] Indeed, Lewis has gone further than most related observers and emphasized suspicion, tension, and conflict even within the nuclear family itself (Lewis, 1951, Chap. 14; 1959, 23–57).

Foster, as previously noted, takes a position similar to that of Lewis, characterizing interpersonal relations by such terms as envy, suspicion, conflict, and "violent reactions." However, he takes a major step in the direction of theory construction and explains this type of behavior in terms of his principle of the "Image of Limited Good" (Foster, 1965),[2] which we have already had occasion to appreciate.

Scholars like Lewis and Foster belong to a school of thought which stresses disagreement, coercion, and constraint as the basic mechanism of social order. Again following Dahrendorf, these could be classified under what he terms "the coercion theory of society" (1959, 157–165).

THE HUMAN-COST MODEL

The strong position of this second group has caused at least a partial revision of the first viewpoint, as represented by Redfield, along the lines of a methodological afterthought. Thus, Redfield, in an attempt to salvage at least a portion of his original viewpoint, in later years argued that the first two viewpoints heretofore mentioned may differ in the basic premises upon which they are based. For instance, what has been called the "integration" model is supposed by Redfield to answer the question, "What do these people enjoy?" The "conflict" model, on the other hand, answers the question, "What do these people suffer from?" In

---

[1] The reader is reminded also of Banfield's work on southern Italian peasants (1958).

[2] See also Foster, 1948, and Foster, 1960–1961. For an informative exchange of views, see also, in the same issue, *Comments* to above by Oscar Lewis and J. A. Pitt-Rivers, and *Rejoinder*.

brief, Redfield argued that differences among scholars as to their view of the peasant's social situation are due, in part, to "choices made by observers and writers as to an aspect of a social situation to be stressed" (1960). Redfield suggested that, in order to achieve the needed comparability, any investigation of the values of a people should answer at least three critical questions: (1) What do such people desire? (2) What qualities do they try to develop in their children? and (3) To what kind of life do they attach highest esteem—whether or not they consider it possible for themselves or their children, and whether or not it is what they in fact desire?

A point analogous to the above is made by Pitt-Rivers, who maintains that it is futile to argue about similarities or differences in value systems between particular peasant societies as long as an objective cross-cultural method of analysis is lacking. What a given cultural behavior means to the peasant in a given society, Pitt-Rivers seems to argue, may or may not correspond to what it means to the observing social scientist, who may be ignorant of analogous behaviors elsewhere. As a result, comparable evaluations of that phenomenon are difficult if not altogether impossible. Pitt-Rivers goes on to say, however, in a somewhat startling fashion, that

One cannot evaluate a value, one can only concur or dissent, and for an author to state his attitude towards the standards of another society is of interest only insofar as it throws light on his own personality and method of working. It cannot provide a basis for the classification of societies (in Foster, 1960–1961, 182).

It would almost seem that Pitt-Rivers would deny altogether the possibility of a comparative sociology, but in fact he does not. He proceeds to make a very important observation which may reveal the possibility of passing judgment, say, on the nature of interpersonal relations in a given society, even in the absence of an objective cross-cultural method of analysis. The individual members of a society, he points out, judge the social events occurring therein as "degrees of success or failure" with respect to their "expectations" of them (Pitt-Rivers in Foster, 1960–1961, 182–183). To say this is tantamount to saying with Oscar Lewis that "The success of a social form must also be evaluated in terms of its human costs" (in Foster, 1960–1961, 179). The question may be solved more easily than Pitt-Rivers gives reason to believe, without resort, in any given study, to a cross-cultural method of analysis. There are two complementary solutions.

The first may be labeled the "basic needs" approach. On the basis of detailed analyses of wide ranges of human behavior both in time and space, certain scholars have hypothesized the existence of what are severally known as values, needs, wishes, interests, forces, or sentiments which tend to be fundamental to all men everywhere and at all times. Among these scholars, to mention but a few, are Ratzenhofer, Thomas, Small, and Pareto.

Ratzenhofer argued in his theory of conflict that society is produced by individuals seeking self-fulfillment on the basis of certain "interests" (Ratzenhofer, 1907, 17; 1898, 244–250). According to Martindale (1960, 348), W. I. Thomas was later influenced by Ratzenhofer and Albion Small, from whom he borrowed the basis of his famed typology of "the four wishes." According to Thomas, every individual has a vast variety of wishes which can be satisfied only by his incorporation in society, but four are fundamental: (1) the desire for new experience, (2) the desire for security, (3) the desire for response, and (4) the desire for recognition. Basically, such wishes provide the basis for the formation of "attitudes" that enter into what he terms the "definition of the situation," which is "preliminary to any self-determined act of behavior" in any person. Thomas then goes on to make a statement that is particularly useful to those who have noted the excessive dominance of the gentry in relation to the peasant masses. He contends that there is "always a rivalry between the spontaneous definitions of the situation made by the member of an organized society and the definitions which his society has provided for him" (Thomas, 1923, 42).

The argument presented by Vilfredo Pareto said that human behavior is founded upon "sentiments," that is, certain premotivational forces that are the basic causes of human conduct.

He enumerated and classified fifty-two such sentiments, or "residues," among which perhaps most important are the residues of "persistence" or traditionalism; "combination" or innovation; "integrity of the individual"; and "sociality," such as a "need of uniformity," "sharing one's property with others," and a "need of group approbation" (Pareto, 1935, Chaps. VI, VII, VIII).

The point to be made here is that many profound observers of human behavior have found reason to believe that certain forces, whether they be termed interests, wishes, needs, sentiments, or something else, are on the whole basic to human beings everywhere. The universality of some of these is probably open to question. About others, however, it is very difficult, if not altogether impossible, to argue, as appears to be the case with such needs as new experience, uniformity, and especially security and recognition or approbation. The need for security is the primordial and fundamental cause of human society. Similarly, the need for recognition is one of the fundamental precipitants of systems of social stratification, which may be found everywhere in human society.

My contention is, accordingly, that a social scientist studying a peasant society can, in a scientifically valid sense, analyze the nature of interpersonal relations in that society by examining the extent to which the basic needs of the people are satisfied by the particular type of social relations existing in their group. Similarly, the quality of interpersonal relations can be studied by examining the degree of rivalry existing between an individual's spontaneous definition of his situation and the definitions that others may impose upon him. There is in this mode of thinking no particular need for a cross-cultural method of analysis, for the scholar has at his disposal a universal tool of analysis, namely, some classification of basic human needs or values.

A second approach is available if the social scientist finds it difficult to accept as given the existence of "basic needs." Again, it is possible to make explanatory statements about the nature of interpersonal relations as they exist in a given society, and thereby go beyond merely throwing light on the observer's own personality and method of working. Specifically, he can inquire directly of the people in a given society about their needs, goals, and values as well as the degree to which their social forms allow them to satisfy these. The people so observed and questioned will tell us what is significant to them, and how it is significant. They will tell us, in other words, about "the human cost" of their social forms, their "degrees of success or failure," and their own level of satisfaction with them. In following this approach, the social scientist minimizes the danger of misinterpreting the substance of his subjects' experiences and the accompanying danger of imposing on them his own personal and cultural standard of behavior. In the next section, where I shall again turn to evidence concerning the nature of interpersonal relations in southern Italy, I shall rely very heavily on this human-cost model. For the present, however, the fourth of the general models mentioned earlier will be discussed.

THE HISTORICAL MODEL

The historical approach is characterized by an inclination to look at peasant society through what might be called a dynamic and historical perspective. In the over-all discussion of social relations in peasant society, this fourth approach provides an element of scientific prudence that is particularly welcome in view of the fact that peasant societies everywhere are now in the process of transformation. In brief, the present point of view suggests that variations in the nature of the cultural contact and the communication channels existing between peasant communities and their larger societies may explain contrasting views of the peasant societies among social observers. Thus, Wolf suggests that both Redfield and Lewis may have been correct in their contrasting characterizations of interpersonal relations in the same peasant society, Tepoztlán. He feels that the difference between the two may have been due to the changes in the character of the village's relationship to the national Mexican society which occurred during the period between the two studies (Wolf in Leslie, 1959, 1).

Similarly, two social scientists might present two antithetical descriptions of social relations in two different peasant communities because the two communities differ greatly in the dynamic character of one or more of their institutions. Redfield himself recognized the fact that today many peasants are changing very rapidly, and that indeed they "now want to be something other than peasants" (1960, 77). It seems reasonable, therefore, to assume that there are, in this respect, marked differences between one peasant society and another, and that such differences are reflected in the relative level of satisfaction that may be expected when moving from one society to another.

Interpersonal Relations in a Calabrian Town

Which one of the above four approaches is the most adequate? The question is a most difficult one to answer. No doubt, all have an element of validity, depending on the particular peasantry examined, the point in time at which it is examined, and the thoroughness of the examination. My own information highlights the importance of the human-cost model in providing support for the Lewis-Foster school in the controversy with the Redfield school.

My evidence comes from "Franza," a Calabrian village of about 2300 population.[3] Subsequent chapters will focus in more detail on this village, which is fairly typical of aggregates of up to 10,000 throughout agricultural southern Italy. For the moment, we are interested only in making direct inquiries into the peasants' evaluation of social relations in their own community. In the controversy about the nature of interpersonal relations among peasants, something should be gained if the peasant is heard, if he is brought directly into the controversy.

The peasants of Franza are on the whole given to suspicion, quarrels, vituperation, violence, and conflicts of all sorts. But what is more important for our purposes is that they are cognizant of

---

[3] Franza will be described in more detail in Chapter V. In an attempt to avoid any embarrassment or inconvenience to myself or to my informants and friends, I am using a pseudonym for the actual community studied. This decision is further justified by the fact that much of what is said is not specific to any particular village, but is generally applicable to hundreds of small communities scattered throughout the Italian South.

this fact, and in moments of reflection they condemn themselves for it. They point out with horror, as well as exaggeration, that there is "a murder a year." They inform with anger that theft, both in the village and in the country, is a disastrously common occurrence. They point, with a mixture of shame and fear, to the fact that it is virtually impossible to find an extended family free from animosities that often last an adult lifetime. As the Franzini frequently say, "*Si sparanu pe' lupi*" (local dialect for "They kill each other as if they were wolves"). The land, which keeps them in the peasant state they intensely hate, is nevertheless a source of iniquitous quarrels between close relatives almost every time that it comes up for division or revision, which is indeed quite often. By their own standards and admission, the people of Franza are a wretched people.

A few years ago an "ultramodern" flour mill was installed in the village by an enterprising young man. As a form of competition, the owners of an already existing mill are said to have more than halved their grinding charge. The new mill immediately did a thriving business because, as an informant wrote in a letter, "Who knows what the others are doing behind the curtains?" Yet, in the same breath he suggested: "Perhaps we are fools, and are the losers for it in not trusting even *Domine Iddio*" (". . . the Lord God").

Many peasants are obviously distressed by their life conditions. Frequently they refer to themselves as living in hell. Ask them if they believe in God, and the answer is a timid yes; ask them further if they believe in hell, and the answer is very probably, "If you don't, look around yourself. All you see is mud, hunger, and venom."

Malicious gossip is unrelenting. At present, much of it is directed against the wives of emigrants (young and old alike) and their husbands, the *cornuti* (cuckolds), who presumably "know and forget—and all for the sake of the dollar." An artisan, a peasant man, and a peasant woman were interviewed about "the rumors concerning local morals." Among the three of them, they accused nearly a hundred women of adultery or fornication, a number which I consider totally extravagant. Interestingly enough, the two male informants counted themselves among the male partners to the alleged illicit sexual behavior, although the principal partners were reputed to be several *signori* (members of the gentry) and a number of distant relatives of the accused women themselves. It was revealing, however, that at a certain point in the interview, the female informant volunteered:

Of course, how can one be sure about such matters? Perhaps even now others are talking about my own family. *Mala Pasca chi simu brutti!* (Confound us, how ugly we are!)

Ample evidence suggests that the people of Franza tend to reject their own culture, both the local and the national, as they see it. For instance, they readily make invidious comparisons between Italy and "America," a generalized reference group including most countries of immigration but referring especially to the United States of America. Thus, they like to point out that

In America everyone is a mister, and all give each other the *voi* [polite *you*]; only in Italy some people think that Christians [human beings] are animals. . . . In America . . . Christians are more humane and just.

An emigrant wrote from Canada:

One thing about these people is certain. They respect each other and give each other a friendly hand when it's necessary; they do not keep each other down the way we Italians do.

This informant then went on to point out an interesting phenomenon that I have since observed often in many parts of southern Italy: in a card game, the loser, especially if he plays for money, never receives the sympathy of the winners or of the spectators. Rather, he is the butt of jokes "and crucified without mercy." Similarly, in Franza, persons outside of the strict family circle often take pleasure when a young person is kept back in school.

The Franzini unfavorably compare southern Italy to northern Italy, too. The Northerners are admired and thought to be rich, "civilized," and "peaceful." Southerners are thought to be *affamati* (starving), "barbarous," and "sanguinary." They believe that life conditions are difficult in southern Italy, and, when asked what they think the Italian government should do, they suggest that it should get rid of

. . . the public thieves (public officials) who suck the blood of the poor Christian . . . civilize us . . . and make just laws so that we won't be easily fooled by the charlatans (lawyers), (and especially) create more jobs so that we won't have to eat each other like dogs.

The Franzini link social conflict to the conditions of their existence and judge their own behavior, in part at least, by positively referring to the real or imagined cultural standards of nonmembership groups. Many of their cultural goals are not functions of their own objective life conditions but of their conception of the conditions prevailing in nonmembership groups, especially "America." It is also interesting to note that, when asked why things "are so bad here," they quickly point to the economy as the basis of their social strains and tensions. As one informant explained,

Simu abbramati, e chi boliti? Ndi mangiamu comu 'i cani. (Local dialect for "What can you expect? We are starving; hence we eat one another like dogs.")

What has been said must be understood in the light of an important consideration. Franza's economy today is much less precarious than it was until just after the end of World War II. In view of recent events, and especially of both the direct and indirect consequences of emigration, to be discussed later, it seems almost irrelevant to speak of "starvation" today. Some, of course, are still hungry in Franza. Most are no longer so. The people's insistence on their poverty and starvation should, therefore, be understood to indicate that they properly understand and evaluate their social situation in an historical perspective. When they say today that they are starving, some of them are stretching a fact that was real until recent years, before their men went away and started sending money, or before they found themselves recipients of a government pension or of unemployment compensation, or again before it became relatively easy to find good land to rent and cultivate or relatively well-paying employment under the supervision of others.

Interpersonal Relations in the Folklore

Further evidence in favor of the human-cost and coercion models can be adduced from still another aspect of peasant culture. Among the infinity of phenomena to be observed in any society, one is extraordinarily important and interesting: not only do human beings live and act in society, it is also the case that, as Simmel so brilliantly argued, they "play society" (Wolff, 1950, 50). They play society by creating and acting within certain social forms, or "models," which, in addition to reflecting their perception of social reality, often assume through time the character of moral and explanatory principles. Such forms are social games, rituals, songs, proverbs, fables, and the like. No society can do without these. The sociocultural system is so complex a phenomenon that most, if not all, of its members would under normal circumstances be unable to interpret it and to live reasonably orderly lives within the specifications of its boundaries. Social sensitivity and control would be seriously impaired. The problem is partly solved through the emergence of social models which represent larger social realities in a nutshell by reducing complex phenomena to often simple exercises in entertaining activity. Anyone who will stop to think about a football game will not fail to be struck by the teachings and the principles which it represents. Among these, for instance, are the principles of group organization and solidarity, controlled competition, fair play, and leadership. In playing the game, the individual understands automatically the meaning of these principles and honors the normative messages that underlie them.

Social models, of course, are not all of one type. Some appear to discharge mostly practical functions, such as helping to train the young for certain social positions or providing them with an idea of basic rules of interaction. Social games appear to be largely of this type. Others more directly indicate ideal systems of values toward which a people ought to reach. Religious models fall by and large into this category. Another species may constitute warnings to individuals about certain problematic aspects of their society. And still another type may merely express a protest against those aspects. Many of the proverbs, songs, and tales known to the peasants of southern Italy seem to correspond to a combination of warning and protest. An intensive analysis of hundreds of such cultural items indicates that this theme is most basic to their folklore.

In the remainder of this section, a few samples of that folklore shall be presented. The reader will recognize in them ample evidence of a way of life in which, as Lombardi Satriani has put it, "miseria and ruthlessness are the dominant characteristics" (L. Lombardi Satriani, 1964).

E Va Fa Beni, Va! (Never Do Good!)

Once upon a time, a peasant at work heard a voice calling for help. Going in the direction of the voice, he noticed a huge snake trapped under a rock.

"Oh, Mr. Peasant," implored the snake, "please help me out of here, and you will be handsomely rewarded." The poor peasant fetched his hoe and lifted the rock, so that the snake could get out from under it. Once free, the snake, who was as large as a house, said to the peasant:

"You have freed me, and now I will eat you."

"But," the startled peasant protested, "you promised that if I freed you I would be well rewarded, and now you want to eat me?"

"Ah, my dear fellow, I have to eat you."

"If that's the way you feel about it," the peasant argued, "before you eat me, we must go to ask a judge if it is right for you to do this after I did such a great favor for you."

"Very well, let's go," agreed the snake.

Some distance down the road, they met a horse so old and hungry that his bones were sticking out.

"Mr. Horse," inquired the peasant, "tell me if it's right that this snake should eat me. He was trapped and helpless under a rock, and I toiled half a day to free him. Now, as a reward he wants to eat me."

"Certainly, he must eat you," immediately replied the horse, "for I worked hard all my life for my master, and now that I am old he lets me loose on this wasteland where I am dying from hunger and, worse still, from thirst. You see, then, how one is rewarded in this world?"

"You won't do for me," the peasant said, and turning to the snake he suggested they proceed to see another judge. On the way, they met a rooster, to whom they told the same story. Like the horse, the rooster answered:

"Yes, it is right that he should eat you, because I sang and sang for my master, and yet the other evening I heard him saying, 'Now it's Christmas, and I will eat the rooster.' You see, then, why it's right that the snake should eat you!"

The desperate peasant proposed to consult still another judge. Further down the road, they finally saw Comare Rosa, the fox, and they told her the entire story.

"What can I tell you?" Comare Rosa argued. "This is a question that can be answered only on the spot, where the whole thing happened."

While returning in that direction, the snake crawled ahead, while the peasant and the fox walked closely together.

"Mr. Peasant," Comare Rosa proposed, "I am going to save you, but you must let me into your hen coop for a bellyful of chickens."

"Anything you wish," the peasant replied. "Save me from this damned snake, and you shall have anything you desire."

Having arrived at the place where the peasant had saved the snake, Comare Rosa proposed:

"Before I decide whether the snake should eat you or not, I wish to satisfy my curiosity. The snake is so huge that I don't believe he could have been trapped under this rock. Therefore, Mr. Snake, crawl under it and take the position you were in when Mr. Peasant saved your life."

And the snake did so, while the fox and the peasant turned the huge rock back on top of him.

"Have you seen?" the snake asked from his original position of distress.

"Yes," replied the other two. "Now you stay there as you were, and we shall return safely home."

And so they did. On the way, the peasant and Comare Rosa talked again about the bellyful of chickens.

"By all means," said the peasant, "we'll go home now and speak to my wife about it, so that this evening you may come and eat all the chickens you want."

In fact, upon arriving at home, the peasant said to his wife:

"Comare Rosa saved my life, and I promised to let her have a bellyful of chickens."

"Not my chickens!" screamed the wife. "There is a sickly little chicken, and she may have that one only!"

The fox, who was just outside, heard this, and when the peasant came out, she said to him:

"I want your wife to know that I don't eat sick chickens. I am accustomed to the best chickens."

"Patience, patience," the peasant comforted her. "Don't pay attention to the words of a woman. Come this evening, and you will find the hen-coop door open. Go in and eat all you want. I shall never forget that you saved my life."

The appeased fox returned to her den and waited until dark. In the meantime, the peasant and his wife started thinking.

"But, why don't we set a trap at the entrance to the coop, so we can catch the fox and eat her up?"

And so they set the trap. In the meantime, it had gotten dark. Comare Rosa came to the coop. She stuck her head in and saw all the chickens settled. She rejoiced. She started to enter. Bang! The snare went off. The fox was trapped.

"*E va fa beni, va!*" she lamented. Never do good! (R. Lombardi Satriani, 1963, 49–53)

THE BAREFOOTED SHOEMAKER

Once upon a time, there was a very rich man, richer than a duke, even richer than a king; at the end he was richer than the sea. One day, he said to his servant:

"Go and find a courier to dispatch a very important letter."

The servant went to the home of a poor shoemaker by the name of Testa, who often worked as a courier.

"Master Testa, come. My lord wants to send you with a letter. In this way you will earn a little money."

The shoemaker went to the rich gentleman. "What do you wish, Excellency?"

"Listen, you must go to the top of that mountain; on it you will find a little meadow. Do you see it?" asked the rich man, pointing out the mountain to the shoemaker. "When you arrive at the place where there are many boulders, call out: 'Oh Fortune of Don Filomeno, oh Fortune of Don Filomeno.' She will come out, and you will give her this letter, telling her not to send me any more riches, because I have no place to put them, and I don't know what to do if she keeps sending me money every day. Have you understood?"

"Yes, Sir, I have understood."

"Well then, now that you have understood, let us see how much I owe you."

"Excellency, you see that it is cold and the mountain is covered with snow. Give me twelve *carlini*."

"Oh how demanding you are! I'll give you ten."

"Excellency, don't you see that I am barefooted, and in this cold weather, I might die from cold on the road?"

"Go for ten carlini, or I will call someone else."

"I shall not go."

"Very well, goodbye."

While descending the staircase, poor Testa said to himself: "It is better if I go, because ten carlini is more than sufficient." Therefore, he climbed the stairs again and said: "Excellency, give me the letter; I have decided to go."

"No," said the rich man; "now if you wish to go, I will give you only eight carlini."

Testa went away again and then returned.

"Give me the letter, and I shall go."

"Now I shall give you seven carlini."

Testa went again, and again returned.

"Now if you wish to go, I shall give you only six."

When poor Testa saw that each time he went back to the rich man, the latter sliced off a carlino, he said to himself: "It is better if I go." So, he took the letter and left.

Having reached the top of the mountain, he looked around and called out for Don Filomeno's Fortune. After calling several times, an exhausted woman came out and asked:

"What is it that you wish?"

"I have been sent by Don Filomeno to give you this letter and to tell you not to send him any more riches, because he is tired and does not know where to put them."

"Very well, wait a while."

All at once, there was a hailstorm that covered the entire meadow with white. "Have you seen this hailstorm?" asked Don Filomeno's Fortune. "Tell Don Filomeno that I must send him just as many golden coins. Give him my regards, and goodbye."

"Please, Mrs. Fortune, could you tell me where my own Fortune is? I would like to see her."

"Go in that ravine and call her."

Testa went to the ravine and called out loud:

"Oh Fortune of Testa, oh Fortune of Testa!"

An untidy poor wretch soon came out, cutting the figure of laziness itself. "What is it that you wish?"

"I beg you not to send me any more hunger and to help me a little, because you have caused me to sleep on straw and to be full of lice. I beg of you not to send me any more calamities."

At once there was another hailstorm, even denser than the previous one. "Have you seen all this hail? I must send you just as many lice."

"May the soul of your mother be damned!" poor Testa exclaimed, and he went away.

Having returned to the rich man's house, Testa related to him his experiences on top of the mountain. The rich man listened resignedly and paid Testa the six carlini. Then he brought together all his servants and sent them to the public square with the task of buying all the bacon they could find.

It was an incredible sight: a houseful of bacon! Next, the rich man gave orders to buy all the cats in the village and to let them loose in the midst of all that bacon so that they might eat it.

Eight days later, the rich man sent someone to estimate the damage. But the cats had slept on it without touching it, preferring instead to feed on mice.

"Excellency," he was informed, "the bacon is intact, and the cats are as fat as blind people."

"Oh, the tricks that my Fortune plays on me! Here is what we must do. Go to the port, rent a ship, load aboard all the bacon and the cats, then go to another kingdom and sell everything at a loss."

And so they went. But when they were far at sea, a violent wind erupted, which carried them to a very distant place. They arrived at a city and went to a restaurant to eat. The food was bitter and insipid.

"What kind of food is this? What do you use to season it?" they inquired.

"Well, we have nothing but the oil of wild olives."

So, they took some of the bacon and gave it to the chef, who soon discovered what a great difference it made. The entire city was in an uproar, and before long all of their bacon was sold at the price of its weight in gold.

After they departed from that place, the wind blew them to another faraway city, where they also disembarked in search of a restaurant. In the restaurant they noticed a great number of sticks which, upon inquiring, turned out to be weapons used by the clients to keep the mice away from their food. In fact, they soon saw for themselves that they needed a stick to keep the mice away from their table. Seeing this, one of them went back to the ship, anchored nearby, took a cat, and brought it to the restaurant.

"What a pretty little animal!" exclaimed the host. "What does it do?"

The answer came immediately, as the cat, who was now free, ate all the mice in a matter of seconds. Again the city was in an uproar, and the cats were sold at 100 ducats each, so that, between the bacon and the cats, they filled the ship with silver and gold.

They returned to their country, and everyone thought that they had returned empty-handed. But what a surprise! It took many carts to carry all that money.

After learning of all the events of the trip, Don Filomeno said in resignation: "Well, let my Fortune send me as much money as she wants, and I shall accept it."

And so, he lived a rich and happy life. As for poor Testa, it was only through a miracle that he received his six carlini (R. Lombardi Satriani, 1965, Vol. III, 7–9).

The Two Godfathers and the Pig

Two *cumpari* (godfathers) used to work together. One day, one friend said to the other:

"Cumpari, I would like to butcher my pig, but I am afraid that, since my relatives have no meat, I would have to give much of it away. I don't know what to do."

The other cumpari said. "Go ahead and butcher it, and I will advise you on how to keep all the meat."

"What must I do?" said the other.

"Listen to this," explained the clever friend. "Kill the pig and then in the evening hang it outside by the window so that all may see it. Then get up very early next morning, and taking care not to be seen by anyone, take the meat down and hide it. After that, wait until the neighbors have arisen, open the window, and start screaming: 'Last night I hung the meat next to the window, and now it's not there. Thieves, thieves! You have stolen my meat.' "

The owner of the pig liked his cumpari's advice, and so he followed it. Now, during the night, the clever cumpari stole the meat, so that in looking out of the window next morning, the credulous cumpari saw no meat. He began to shout:

"They have stolen my pig; they have stolen my pig. Last night I hung the meat outside to keep it cool, and they have stolen it."

Sad and angry, he looked for his friend to tell him what had happened.

"Cumpari, they have stolen the butchered pig."

"Good, good. That's the thing to say. In this fashion, you won't have to give any meat to anybody for sure."

"What are you talking about, cumpari?" exclaimed the unfortunate fellow. "Don't joke about it. They have really robbed me."

"Good, very good!" replied the clever cumpari. "That's the way. You play the part very well, and they will believe you."

"Ah, you are making fun of me," said the unlucky cumpari. One word led to another. They argued—cumpari against cumpari—and in the end, neither one could eat any pork. (R. Lombardi Satriani, 1965, Vol. IV, 91–92)

GREETINGS, SIGNORE: THE SONG OF A HUMBLE PEASANT

> Yesterday evening on the square
> I saw someone with a big beard;
> I said to him: Good day, Sir.
> He answered me with a big slap.
> I said to him: But why?
> He answered me with three more slaps.

When I saw it went from bad to worse,
I simply went the other way.
He came and caught up with me,
Four more slaps he let me have.
Run, Vincenzu, or he will kill you! [4]

Proverbs Tell the Truth

It is better to be in the mouth of a snake than on the tongue of people.

From your own relatives, go as far as you can.

He who depends on others will sing but won't eat.

It is a crime to do good to christened flesh.

The tongue has no bone, but it breaks the backbone.

Against my enemies, I'll guard myself; against my friends, may God guard me.

Cold weather always hits the poorly dressed.

The bigger fish always swallow the smaller ones.

The lamb has no defense against the wolf.

Tie the donkey where the master commands.

He who commands does not perspire.

The worker disposes of a salted sardine, and the man of leisure has a chicken.

One humiliation is often worth food for a whole day.

What can be said about the above folklore? Does it reveal anything about the nature of interpersonal relations among the people who have created it or kept it alive? The cultural content

---

[4] From L. Lombardi Satriani, 1965, 3. The literal translation of this song from the Calabrian dialect is mine. The Calabrian text follows:

> *Arzira 'nta la chiazza*
> *Vitti ad uno ccu 'na varvazza;*
> *Jeu nci dissi: Bon giornu, gnuri.*
> *Mi jettau 'nu buffettuni.*
> *Jeu nci dissi: Pecchì?*
> *Mi ndi jettau 'n'atri tri.*
> *Quandu 'a vitti mala pigghiata,*
> *Mutavi strata.*
> *Iju vinni e m'arrivàu,*
> *'N'atri quattru mi ndi jettàu.*
> *Curri, Vincenzu, c'à m'ammazzàu!*

of it can be roughly summarized by the following general principles, which in turn contain certain general rules of conduct.

1. Never do good, except for self-interest, and then never
lower your guard, for good is always repaid with evil. Even a
momentary relaxation from the constant struggle against others
may bring grief and tragedy to the craftiest of all: the fox itself,
which is the very symbol of ruse and cunning. Hence, it is a gross
error to do good to "christened flesh," and one is properly more
kind with animals than with human beings, for while the former
may not repay you at all, the latter will repay you by becoming
your conquerors or altogether endangering your very existence.

2. The above being the case, the best defense against others
will involve going beyond merely keeping up one's guard. In the
most effective instance, it will in fact involve a readiness to punish
him who has done you good, for he has done so out of self-
interest and, anticipating your hostile response, in the end he will
surely punish and destroy you, thereby maximizing his own
self-interest.

3. No moral principles enter the conscience of either the
doer of good or evil, or its recipient. One's judgment of the
human event is always passed on the basis of practical experience.
Hence, it is "right," that is, appropriate, that one who has done
good should be punished, for I too was punished under analogous
circumstances. This law is the basic law of society.

4. Financial success is a result of luck, but not in the sense
that one does nothing to achieve it, for "the bigger fish always
swallow the smaller ones." Success is a result of luck only in the
sense that the merit basis of it is randomly distributed.

5. Again, one does not use his wealth to do other human
beings a good turn. It may be wasted on animals and luxuries, but
never on other persons, against whom the basic law is relentless
exploitation. Thus, barefooted Testa must content himself with a
mere six carlini for the very arduous and dangerous job of seeking
out the good Fortune of the Rich Man and beseeching her not to
burden him with further riches.

6. Wealth begets wealth. Wealth always goes in excessive

measure to the already wealthy, for their Fortune is diligent. Thus he who commands, does not perspire; and cold weather always hits the poorly dressed.

7. Wealth, even when it is excessive and burdensome, is a good to be jealously cherished. Wealth is a powerful instrument of self-defense and, concomitantly, of abuses against others who might advance their claims against you. The poorer, and therefore weaker, man always loses in the bargain. Consequently, despite the fears of the powerful, the best policy on the part of the weak is always to "tie the donkey where the master commands."

8. In fact, the poor and humble man has no defense against any of his superiors, the people with the "big beard." Therefore, within the limits of the possible, it is best to avoid them altogether, for not only do they show no compassion or friendliness, but if the poor and humble chances to get in their way, he will be beaten, given no explanation, pursued, and then beaten some more.

9. Under these circumstances, the individual is a social isolate in his own eyes. Contact with others is always fraught with serious danger. One must never trust others, for in trusting, one is bound to be chastized, as the unfortunate cumpari was, by the very people that one suspects the least. Hence, "Against my enemies I'll guard myself; against my friends, may God guard me."

Do Peasants Constitute a Unique Human Type?

The above materials taken from southern Italian folklore are further and dramatic evidence of a mode of life deeply rooted in the past. Despite the present-day ameliorations to be discussed later, this mode is still basically fraught with tensions, conflicts, and dissatisfaction. Evidence against Redfield's characterization of the world peasantry is consequently multiplied.

This point is of extreme importance. As previously noted, a proper appreciation of the nature of social relations and value systems in peasant, or "underdeveloped," societies bears a great relevance to the task of predicting the likely course of the great number of such societies and, therefore, aiding those who address their economic and political policies to the job of controlling and expediting that course.

Let us return once again to Robert Redfield, dean of peasant studies, and examine in more detail his standpoint concerning peasant society. This procedure will afford not only a chance to attempt a further clarification of some of his arguments but also the opportunity to glance at a fuller range of those basic social phenomena that are pertinent to an understanding of peasant peoples everywhere.

Looking at Redfield's writings, we find that peasants everywhere are alleged to be a unique human type, definable in terms of the following characteristics: social homogeneity; high social integration; personal contentment; an intense attachment to native soil; a love of the land that verges on reverence; a reverent disposition toward ancestral ways; a restraint on self-seeking in favor of family *and* community; a certain suspiciousness of town life; a view of marriage as an economic institution; a patrilocal and patrilineal family; sexual restraint; an emphasis on procreation; an emphasis on land ownership, hard work, and frugality as moral qualities; and a distaste for violence.[5]

About the reality of some of these attributes, little or no doubt exists. Social homogeneity, for example, can be accepted as largely real, by definition. Peasants are after all an occupational category. As such they represent a fairly homogeneous stratum in their community. But even here there are important reservations to be made; for instance, to mention but a few cases, scholars of South American peasant communities have found remarkable social differences between *Ladinos* and *Indios* (Tumin, 1952,

---

[5] See especially Redfield, 1930; 1947, 293–308; 1953, 224–228; 1941; and 1960. For his argument he has also drawn evidence from a great variety of sources, among which the following appear to be of critical importance: (1) Hesiod, *The Works and Days; Theogony; The Shield of Herakles,* translated by Richard Lattimore (Ann Arbor: University of Michigan Press, 1959), and (2) George Bourne, *Change in the Village* (New York: George H. Doran Co., 1912).

59–121) and between Spaniards (or the "civilized") and Indians (Reichel-Dolmatoff and Reichel-Dolmatoff, 1961, Chap. 4). Elsewhere considerable differences are found between plain peasants and *massari* (elite peasants) (Lopreato, 1961, 585–596).

Similarly, with some reservations the following characteristics can be accepted as real: a reverent disposition toward ancestral ways; a certain suspiciousness of town life; marriage as an economic institution; patrilineal, though not patrilocal, family; sexual restraint; and an emphasis on procreation, land ownership, hard work, and frugality.

What are the reservations? As regards the reverent disposition toward ancestral ways, few peoples indeed in human society are not reverent toward their ancestral ways. Such a type of behavior is part of the ethnocentric syndrome so vividly discussed by William G. Sumner. In fact, all people everywhere—whether in nonliterate, peasant, or urban society—tend to idealize their own established folkways. The extent of this phenomenon, however, must be measured with reference to the cultural contact that a people has with the outside world. In Franza, emigration has caused the development of a favorable attitude toward the ways of "America," and at the same time reinforced a negative one toward local culture. Similarly, Tumin found the more socially important *Ladinos* of Guatemala to be, in contrast with the *Indios*, "the outward face of the community" and to be projected toward the cities "far beyond the pueblo and the 'known' luxury, ease, and social reputation of life in those cities" (Tumin, 1952, 120, 270).

A certain suspiciousness of town life is indeed a characteristic of peasants perhaps everywhere, although the same tendency appears also to be a characteristic of rural people elsewhere, for instance, in the United States (Vidich and Bensman, 1960, 103–104).

The contracting of marriage with a view to achieving or consolidating economic security through it is, in fact, widespread in peasant society. It may take the form of "marrying for money" or, more simply, marrying a partner who is healthy, robust, and industrious, disregarding such other qualities as beauty, comeliness, or even agreeableness. Oddly enough, however, this same tendency is widespread among very wealthy urban people everywhere, and, with some modifications, in decaying aristocracies as well. In these cases, the basic cause of economically arranged marriages is usually preoccupation with retaining or improving one's social position. In the case of the peasant, the basic cause has been his excessive economic insecurity together with his attempt to insure, by marrying a pair of strong arms, or into a little property, the minimum base of his livelihood even at the cost of emotional needs.

Similarly, it appears that the patrilocal and patrilineal family has been widely diffused in peasant society, although it probably reached its highest expression among the Chinese peasantry until recent decades (Yang, 1945, 115 and Chap. Six). The patrilocal complex, however, is everywhere disappearing, while the patrilineal complex is a characteristic of most societies, Western industrial society included.

It is probably true that there is a marked degree of sexual restraint in peasant society. In this case, some evidence can be adduced from the Franza findings in support of Redfield's position, despite Tentori's contrary assertion, made through the mouth of a peasant, that "it is the only way that we know how to enjoy life" (Redfield, 1960, 71). This evidence, however, imposes on the term "restraint" a meaning that Redfield most likely did not intend to give it. Thus, one of a score of men, recently consulted about this topic, explained:

Let's put it this way: when you are a young man, making love is a big thing, and whether you do it to yourself, to a goat, or possibly to the local whore, you don't go dry for very long. Then you go in the Army, and whenever you can afford it, you visit the house of prostitution, or you may be lucky and find some ugly thing to have a good time with. But believe me, even then you don't have many chances. But you brag. Oh, you had so many women! A likely story! It is easy to say when you are young. As an old man, however, you don't have to be afraid of losing face, and can speak more openly about these things. Take the period of the *mietitura* (harvest time). During this time, who can make love? You don't even have the energy to stand up, or to open your pants for that matter. Our life is very hard most of the time, and love does not seem as wonderful as when you were in the Army. Besides, you tell me: where is the time ɩd the place to make love when you have five or six children and ɔnly two beds to sleep in? Do you know that my children slept in bed with my wife and me until they were ten years old? What's this nonsense about being like roosters down here? We all know that love breaks your back. Who the hell can lift that big hoe with a broken back?

Here then is an interesting case. Sexual activity seems indeed to be charged with a high value, but the lack of women, money, and energy, the "aching back," and the lack of time and privacy *constrain* the peasant into sexual restraint. Sexual intercourse is indeed a "good," as Tentori suggests, but it is a scarce or "limited good," and for roughly the same reasons for which peasant life is an inferno in southern Italy.

The emphasis on procreation is an especially complex question to handle, and can only be touched upon lightly. Arguments abound in the literature to the effect that children are an economic asset on the farm, and that this fact explains in large measure the peasant's emphasis on large numbers of children. Doubts about this thesis, however, must arise upon considering the mortality rate in peasant societies. It is found, in fact, that while fertility rates are high, at least half of the children begotten die before they reach the age of five (Hagen, 1962, 65). As a result, those who survive may be an economic asset, but the expenses and losses caused by those who die all too often cancel the asset constituted by the survivals. It is difficult to imagine that peasant people have not, through the centuries, learned to appreciate this elementary fact. It is hard, therefore, to speak of an "emphasis on procreation." What is left is merely the observation that in many peasant societies the fertility rate is high. This high rate in turn may result from a combination of the peasant's ignorance of effective birth-control techniques; his desire for some children, a fact which expresses a natural and universal tendency; and finally the fact itself of high infant mortality, which tends to thwart that desire.

How about the alleged emphasis on land ownership, hard work, and frugality? No doubt, they are valid attributes of peasant peoples everywhere. But do they help constitute a special type? Students of social stratification have found that large percentages of urban people from all walks of life express a desire, in any given year, for "a little business of their own," that is, a desire for the private ownership of the sources of their livelihood.[6] Indeed, within the broad context of management-labor relations a desire is sometimes apparent on the part of the workers for coownership of the industrial enterprise. No particular information is, therefore, derived about the peasant as a unique human type from his emphasis on the ownership of the land he works.

Again, given various circumstances, such as the usual scarcity or infertility of the land and the excessive demands made by the landlords, the peasant, like underprivileged workers of other kinds, obviously *must* work hard. The question of the "moral quality" of work, however, remains a moot point. When the impoverished peasant says to his child, "Hard work is a good thing," he very probably has it in mind to say, "Starvation is a bad thing." Or perhaps, hard work is a "good" thing in the sense of the desirability of physical vigor and endurance, as Hanssen finds in his study of Swedish peasants, but not as a "good" in itself, for resting "by the warm stove" is preferable to "any kind of hard work."[7] Similarly, in Franza one may hear a man saying of his son, who does not wield the hoe at a sustained rhythm: "He is a good for nothing." And in the same breath he will add: "It's a rough life—we kill ourselves for nothing." Again, the male peasants of Franza often scorn the townspeople as individuals who tire easily and have little strength. But this is a reaction to suffered humiliations as well as a simple attempt to find something at

---

[6] See, for instance, Lipset and Bendix, 1959, Chap. VI, where these authors find that two-thirds of the manual workers interviewed in Oakland, California, had thought of going into business for themselves, and over one-fifth of them had actually done so. The corresponding percentages for other occupational groups were about as high.

[7] Quoted in Redfield, 1960, 68. The quotation is from Börje Hanssen, Österlen (Stockholm: L. T.'s Förlag, 1952).

which the peasant is better than the townsman. The fact remains, however, that the Franza peasant works hard because "we have got to eat," but he feels that it is better to work little, and better yet not to work at all.

Needless to say, where work is hard and the profit is low, frugality is in the nature of things, with any occupational category. But it is not necessary to rest on this proposition to demonstrate that frugality is not a distinguishing characteristic of peasant society. Max Weber found a most marked type of frugality among ascetic Protestants and attributed to it the rise of capitalism (Weber, 1958)—a phenomenon which, if the American-style large-scale farmer is excluded from the category of peasants, is very far on the horizon of peasant society.

We must now turn to a consideration of the even more problematic and controversial characteristics attributed by Redfield to peasant people: high social integration, personal contentment, an intense attachment to native soil, a love of the land, a restraint on self-secking in favor of family and community, and a distaste for violence. A close look at these attributes will reveal that they can be roughly reduced to the two critical factors of "social cohesion" and "love of the land." A considerable amount of adverse evidence has already been presented in this connection. In the remainder of this section, further information shall be cited from various regions of the globe, omitting southern Italy, however, which has already served amply.

Redfield himself recognized contradictory evidence from the entire Mediterranean basin. Thus, for instance, he was aware that, according to Pitt-Rivers, Andalusian peasants are characterized by the "lack of a mystical attitude towards the land, the value system of a people who dwell in towns from which they go out to cultivate the earth, but who do not love it." According to Pitt-Rivers, such an attitude toward the land is characteristic of the whole Mediterranean area, with the exception of the northwest of the Iberian peninsula (Pitt-Rivers, 1954, 46–47).

Somewhat puzzled by this fact, Redfield was led to recall the emphasis on town dwelling throughout the ancient Mediterranean area and to suggest the possibility that "the prestige of the town, the *polis*, carried with it at an early date the peasant's distaste for agricultural life" (Redfield, 1960, 66). In the light of Hesiod's injunctions as to the virtues of agricultural industry, Redfield, however, rightly questioned his own hunch, even though it is difficult to say whether Hesiod was engaged in describing the peasant life of his time or merely in promoting it.

The reader of Redfield's *Peasant Society and Culture* will notice, however, that in developing his thesis, Redfield gives the impression that the only evidence adverse to his position comes from the Mediterranean basin. Indeed, it is most surprising that Redfield does not refer even once to the book that first and most effectively questioned his view of peasant society—to Oscar Lewis' *restudy* of the very community in which Redfield first developed his thesis (1951).

In restudying the peasants of Tepoztlán, Lewis did not find any particular love of the land among them, although he did find that there was still a remnant of religiosity associated with farming, and that "the ownership of land is one of the basic aspirations of Tepoztlán peasants" (Lewis, 1951, 118, 438). Nor did Lewis discover among these peasants a high degree of social cohesion. Indeed, in this respect he found the very opposite of what had been previously observed by Redfield. Specifically, in referring to Redfield's report of Tepoztlán, Lewis stated:

Throughout his study we find an emphasis upon the cooperative and unifying factors in Tepoztecan society. Our findings, on the other hand, would emphasize the underlying individualism of Tepoztecan institutions and character, the lack of cooperation, the tensions between villages . . . the schisms within the village, and the pervading quality of fear, envy, and distrust in interpersonal relations (Lewis, 1951, 429).

Lewis found a readiness among Tepoztecans to view other people as potentially dangerous, "and the most characteristic initial reaction to others is suspicion and distrust" (Lewis, 1951, 292). Further, the Tepoztecan was lacking in altruism, generosity, charity, and the spirit of sharing. He was "an individualist with faith in his own power alone and with reluctance to seek or give economic aid, to borrow or lend, or to cooperate with others in public and private enterprises" (Lewis, 1951, 296–297).

More recently, through sustained interviews and tape recordings, Lewis has found further evidence of misery, stress, and conflict among Mexican peasants. The stories that unfold are stories of quarrels and feuds, violence and suffering, selfishness and social isolation. The quality of their social world is perhaps best expressed in the words of Sanchez, head of a family, who evaluates his father's contribution to his socialization thus:

"I'm not leaving you anything—says the dying father—but I will give you a piece of advice. Don't get mixed up with friends. It's better to go your way alone." And that's what I've done all my life (Lewis, 1961, 6; see also Lewis, 1959).

Remaining in Latin America, where Redfield had considerable personal experience, further evidence is found which is contradictory of his viewpoint. Thus, Foster's findings in Tzintzuntzan led him to conclude that

An objective appraisal of a peasant village, however fond the ethnologist may be of his people, will in all likelihood reveal basic strains and tensions in interpersonal relations that make it difficult to understand how the community continues to function.[8]

In his study of a Guatemalan community, Melvin Tumin found that skills in "slaughtering others' reputations" through gossip and, in turn, the ability to defend one's self against this practice were of considerable significance. According to Tumin, tension in the community he studied was basically due to the essential clash between the two castes of *Ladinos* and *Indios*, who were oriented to two different cultures: the first to the urban, European culture, and the second to the Indian and traditional. But Tumin found, further, that today many Indians are breaking away from traditional patterns, and "in this group of Indians one

---

[8] Foster, 1960–1961, 175–176. The findings on Tzintzuntzan are found in Foster, 1948.

finds the nub of tension and disequilibrium in Indian social structure. For they do not have the insulation against insult, mockery,
and general social depreciation which the *Ladinos* express with
regard to Indian behavior" (Tumin, 1952, 31, 148).

More data could be cited.[9] The best evidence against Redfield's position, however, is Redfield himself. This section of the
discussion shall be concluded, therefore, by taking a critical
glance at some of Redfield's own findings.

In *The Folk Culture of Yucatan,* which is one of the most
interesting studies in the area of our present inquiry, Redfield
engages his reader in a delightful examination of trends toward
social conflict and disorganization as he moves from the small
Maya hamlet of Tusik through the village of Chan Kom and the
town of Dzitas to the port city of Merida. His basic findings are
that disorganization, secularization, and individualization increase
with increasing urbanization and social change. For instance, the
town of Dzitas, which at the time of the study was primarily an
agricultural community with a population of about 1200, was
"irksome because people are self-conscious and restless and frequently in evident distress" (Redfield, 1941, 153). Similarly,

The observer who also knows the life of the village is impressed in
Dzitas with the relatively greater indications of feelings of personal
insecurity. . . . The older generation frequently lament the changes
that have occurred in their lives and criticize their neighbors and
their children for their impiety and mannerlessness. There are relatively more open quarrels and disputes; vituperation, abuse, and even

---

[9] Evidence which is favorable to Redfield's viewpoint is also available,
although, it seems, in much smaller quantity. Thus, for instance, Wagley
finds peaceful race and family relations in an Amazon community. See
Charles Wagley, *Amazon Town: A Study of Man in the Tropics* (New
York: The Macmillan Co., 1953), especially pp. 263–264. And in a comparison between Mexican peasants and the peasants of Rani Khera in India,
Oscar Lewis himself finds that the villagers of Rani Khera "still love the
land" and "seem psychologically more secure and relate better to each other."
See Oscar Lewis, "Peasant Culture in India and Mexico: A Comparative
Analysis," in "Village India," *American Anthropological Association Mem-
oirs,* 57, No. 83 (Chicago: University of Chicago Press, June, 1955), pp.
165–166.

violence occur in public in Dzitas not uncommonly (Redfield, 1941, 151).

But even in the strictly peasant village of Chan Kom, Redfield found that

The double effects of the invasion of new ideas in bringing about the disorganization of culture and also its reorganization appear from the brief history of Protestantism in Chan Kom (Redfield, 1941, 144).

Continuing, then, with a discussion of this event, Redfield states that "the new cult served to bring into the open a schismatic division of the population which had long been latent" (Redfield, 1941, 145).

Redfield's position with respect to the peasant's attitude toward the land is less vulnerable in terms of his own evidence. In general, his position is consistent with a statement by a Chan Kom peasant to the effect that "one should care for the land as for a wife and family" (Redfield, 1960, 70). Redfield's position, however, remains precarious, for the above statement cannot be construed as clear evidence that the Chan Kom peasant in fact loves his land. Many peasants in Franza share that feeling today, and Silone's peasants too claim that

If someone else takes your land, even if he gives you money for it, it's always a little as if he had taken your wife (1961, 81).

Why? Is a man jealous only of a beautiful and loved wife? The plain fact is that, however despicable it might be, the land, a source of sorrow, is also the only source of livelihood. In this sense, it would seem that "love" and "care" of the land are mere equivalents to a simple interest in one's own precarious survival.[10]

---

[10] A good test of the peasant's alleged love of the land can be found in the occupational orientations of peasants who go abroad to make a living. It is interesting to note here that of the millions of Italian peasants who have migrated to the United States, Canada, Australia, and elsewhere, only an insignificantly small number have continued the pursuit of agricultural activities.

To conclude the present section, I hold that the evidence reveals in Redfield an idealistic and romantic strain, which, though admirable as an ideology, renders little service either to social science or to the peasants themselves in their now obvious attempt to attract attention to a difficult life and to social injustices too long endured. The crux of the question is that peasants everywhere are learning to look around themselves, then look at their situation again, and reject what they see. Redfield's view of the peasant was a beautiful one, part of an artistic imagery that reveals the man's basic admiration for the rural personality. It is hard and somehow embarrassing to dispel it or prove it unreal. The only saving grace in this ungracious work is the thought that, as an old Calabrian proverb goes, " '*U medicu pietusu fa 'a piaga verminusa*" ("The compassionate physician will encourage a verminous wound").

Before this chapter ends, one important observation must be made. In opposition to Redfield's standpoint about the nature of the peasant's adjustment to his society, it has been argued that the peasant of the Italian South, and most likely peasants elsewhere, are poorly adjusted individuals. It has not so far been suggested that the peasant constitutes in this respect a unique type, distinctly separate from other categories of people, such as nonliterate or urban people. Indeed, if anything, the position was taken in discussing the characteristics attributed to peasants by Redfield that many of those same features are easily attributed to social collectives everywhere. May it suffice in this connection to remember the voluminous and long-lasting discussions of "alienation" and related phenomena in relation to the urban world.[11] Foster is most likely correct when he judiciously warns that "the Image of Limited Good," together with the types of social behavior that this entails, may be characteristic of other types of societies as well (1965, 311, footnote 5).

It is likely, however, that what has been described is particu-

---

[11] For a concise and most informative critical analysis of these phenomena, see Arthur M. Harkins, *Alienation and Related Concepts: Toward a Clarification of Terms,* unpublished M.A. thesis, University of Massachusetts, 1962.

larly endemic to peasants and other people who are characterized by a combination of two crucial factors: on the one hand, a precarious economy, and on the other, recent and radical social change. When these two factors operate together, it is likely that the fundamental conditions of conflict and dissatisfaction inherent in all societies come to full fruition, or at least become more marked in the initial phase of change. It is in this sense that some writers are justified in referring to the current transformations in peasant society as a "Peasant Revolution."

Projected as it is to the city, the peasant community seems now more than ever a worse place to live in, as far as the human cost is concerned. The Industrial Revolution and the Communication Revolution which has followed in its wake have shattered the system of relations and social values of many a peasant community. Citizens of such communities are now bombarded by temptations to abandon their previous mode of life in favor of urban living. Many of the old and simple necessities have now lost their significance; the land, which once may indeed have been revered, has in recent decades increasingly become a place definable in terms of mud, interminable toil, vanishing profit, and above all, social humiliations. In all of these changes, emigration plays a major role.

Even assuming an essentially contented and pacific preexisting system of social relations, with the advent of large-scale emigration the shattering of such a system is inevitable. The reasons are many, but one is paramount: Those who return from the city, "enriched" and transformed, not only deride traditional customs and values but, in putting into circulation the recently acquired capital and values, make havoc in the old economic and social structures.

The citizens of the little peasant community are now projected outward. They cannot wait to reach the new Mecca, the city: a place of wealth, recreation, luxury, and, in appearance at least, of relative rest, justice, and freedom. Many of those who remain in the community feel themselves the victims of a most mortifying weariness of life. Paradoxically enough, what some observers of urban life consider the "ills of the city" have now become for many a peasant the forbidden fruits at their most attractive. Discontent with the traditional way of life is intensified. Like Simmel's "stranger," the peasant is no longer "tied down in his action by habit, piety, and precedent" (Wolff, 1950, 405). In short, today's peasant wants to be a peasant no more. The transition is bound to be fraught with painful stress and discontent. But, as subsequent chapters will show, an amelioration in the economic status quickly yields some very positive counteractive forces.

REFERENCES

Banfield, Edward C. 1958. *The Moral Basis of a Backward Society.* Glencoe, Ill.: The Free Press.

Dahrendorf, Ralf. 1959. *Social Class and Social Conflict in Industrial Society.* Stanford: Stanford University Press.

Foster, George M. 1948. *Empire's Children: The People of Tzintzuntzan.* Mexico: Imprenta Nuevo Mundo.

Foster, George M. 1960–1961. "Interpersonal Relations in Peasant Society," *Human Organization,* 19, Winter.

Foster, George M. 1965. "Peasant Society and the Image of Limited Good," *American Anthropologist,* 67, April.

Hagen, Everett E. 1962. *On the Theory of Social Change.* Homewood, Ill.: The Dorsey Press.

Lewis, Oscar. 1951. *Life in a Mexican Village: Tepoztlán Restudied.* Urbana, Ill.: University of Illinois Press.

Lewis, Oscar. 1959. *Five Families.* New York: Basic Books, Inc.

Lewis, Oscar. 1961. *Children of Sanchez: Autobiography of a Mexican Family.* New York: Random House.

Lipset, Seymour M., and Reinhard Bendix. 1959. *Social Mobility in Industrial Society.* Berkeley: University of California Press.

Lombardi Satriani, Luigi M. 1964. "Far bene è delitto," in *Gazzetta del Sud.* May 26.

Lombardi Satriani, Luigi M. 1965. "Taccuino Calabrese," in *Rassegna Calabrese.* March 31. [English translation mine]

Lombardi Satriani, Raffaele. 1963. "E va fa beni, va!" in *Racconti Popolari Calabresi,* Vol. IV. Cosenza: Editrice "Casa del Libro." [English translation mine]

Lombardi Satriani, Raffaele. 1965. "Il sentimento del destino in una favola calabrese: il calzolaio scalzo," in *Quaderni Calabresi*, Anno II, No. 1, January. Translated into Italian from the Calabrian dialect and analyzed by Luigi M. Lombardi Satriani. [English translation mine]

Lopreato, Joseph. 1961. "Social Stratification and Mobility in a South Italian Town," *American Sociological Review*, 26, August.

Martindale, Don. 1960. *The Nature and Types of Sociological Theory*. Boston: Houghton Mifflin Company.

Pareto, Vilfredo. 1935. *The Mind and Society*. New York: Harcourt, Brace and Company, Inc.

Pitt-Rivers, J. A. 1954. *The People of Sierra*. London: Weidensfeld and Nicolson.

Ratzenhofer, Gustav. 1898. *Die soziologische Erkenntnis*. Leipzig: F. A. Brockhaus.

Ratzenhofer, Gustav. 1907. *Soziologie*. Leipzig: F. A. Brockhaus.

Redfield, Robert. 1930. *Tepoztlán: A Mexican Village*. Chicago: The University of Chicago Press.

Redfield, Robert. 1941. *The Folk Culture of Yucatan*. Chicago: The University of Chicago Press.

Redfield, Robert. 1947. "The Folk Society," *American Journal of Sociology*, LII, January.

Redfield, Robert. 1953. "The Natural History of the Folk Society," *Social Forces*, XXXI, March.

Redfield, Robert. 1960. *The Little Community* and *Peasant Society and Culture*. Chicago: The University of Chicago Press, Phoenix Books.

Reichel-Dolmatoff, Gerardo, and Alicia Reichel-Dolmatoff. 1961. *The People of Aritama: The Cultural Personality of a Colombian Mestizo Village*. Chicago: The University of Chicago Press.

Silone, Ignazio. 1961. *Fontamara*. New York: Dell Publishing Co., Inc.

Small, Albion. 1905. *General Sociology*. Chicago: The University of Chicago Press.

Thomas, William I. 1923. *The Unadjusted Girl*. Boston: Little, Brown.

Tumin, Melvin M. 1952. *Caste in a Peasant Society*. Princeton: Princeton University Press.

Vidich, Arthur J., and Joseph Bensman. 1960. *Small Town in Mass Society*. New York: Anchor Books, Doubleday and Company, Inc.

Weber, Max. 1958. *The Protestant Ethic and the Spirit of Capitalism*, translated by Talcott Parsons. New York: Charles Scribner's Sons.

Wolf, Eric R. 1959. "The Indian in Mexican Society," in Charles Leslie, ed., *The Social Anthropology of Middle America, Alpha Kappa Deltan*, Special Issue, XXX, December.

Wolff, Kurt H., ed. 1950. *The Sociology of Georg Simmel*. Glencoe, Ill.: The Free Press.

Yang, Martin C. 1945. *A Chinese Village, Taitou, Shantung Province*. New York: Columbia University Press.

Part Two

*Social Stratification
and Change in
the Community:
Effects of Emigration*

V THE COMMUNITY SETTING

In preceding chapters, some of the major economic and social characteristics of peasants throughout southern Italy have been described and explained. Beginning with an historical perspective of the subject matter, a picture was constructed wherein the peasants were represented as a group of traditionally impoverished, discontented, and conflict-ridden people. At some points, however, the suggestion was also made that the life conditions of many southern peasants have, in recent times, been undergoing a process of radical transformation. Among the various factors which underlie such a transformation, one appears to be outstanding, namely, the heavy wave of peasant emigration during the present century. This part of the book will pursue the implications of this phenomenon, with attention to a few of its chief effects. To accomplish this task, extensive analysis has been sacrificed in favor of intensive analysis, and attention has been focused on one agricultural community, Franza, to which brief reference has already been made. This chapter describes the community setting.

General Conditions

Politically and territorially, Franza, a farming village, comprises a population of about 2750 and a land possession of roughly 2000 hectares. Of the 2750 Franzini, however, approximately 450 are physically and socially part of a neighboring town, and for this reason are excluded from the present discussion.

The village is situated on the Tyrrhenian side of Calabria, the southernmost region of continental Italy, about midway between Reggio Calabria, looking across the Straits of Messina toward Sicily, and Catanzaro, the seat of the provincial offices. At an average of about 1000 feet above sea level, the village territory spreads out in a series of now steep, now gently sloping hills consisting of approximately the same clays and loams that characterize most of the southern Italian territory.

The exact temperatures of Franza are not known, but they are not unlike those found in Catanzaro, where average temperatures are around 45°F. in the winter, 58° in the spring, 78° in the summer, and 72° in the autumn. Low temperatures occur generally in January and February, when they rarely sink below the freezing level or rise above 55°; high temperatures occur in July and August and on rare occasions reach as high as 100°.

Precipitation is very uneven, the rainy season falling roughly between November and February. In some years, rain is completely lacking between April and September, and sometimes for even longer periods of time. The Italian Central Institute of Statistics reports that in 1961 the total precipitation for the Tyrrhenian side of Calabria was about 23.3 inches (1963, Table 11, 11). This amount was divided approximately as follows: winter, 10.2 inches; spring, 4 inches; summer, 0.8 inches; and autumn, 8.3 inches.

Until a few years ago, Franza was linked to the outside world mostly through a series of farm roads which, when passable, led toward the mountain villages to the east, where local peasants went on the occasion of the annual farm fair, and whence came donkeyloads of lignite for local use. A fairly well-kept though unpaved provincial road led in one direction to the nearby market town of Montelitigio,[1] seat of the court, the secondary schools, and various public and private offices. In the other direction, the road led to another farm village, somewhat larger than Franza, with which meaningful contacts were mediated mostly by the yearly fair and by an occasional marriage.

More recently, while the farm roads have changed little, the provincial road has been paved, thus facilitating access to the market town, where scores of children from Franza go to high school and learn the ways of the city. Their fathers get their papers here and buy their passage for places north or overseas, while their mothers spend some of their newly acquired money on the products and services of the city.

A close look at the village community brings forth the image of a typical southern agricultural town of up to 10,000 population. One- or two-story houses of one to four rooms, built largely of lime and unworked stone, are strung together and clustered along several streets, which lead to the public square. On the square can be found one or two shade trees and a monument in honor of the war dead. Here congregate in idle conversation a group of elders, well off or else too old to work; a group of children at play; students taking time off from their studies; and more recently a group of elderly gentlemen (the *"Americani"*) who, after a number of years in the United States, have returned to their native village to enjoy the fruits of their labor, typically invested in several plots of local land.

To one side of the square stands one of the public fountains installed in the mid-1920's, when water was first piped into the village. Until a few years ago, one could practically isolate the lower strata within the local prestige structure by noting the women and children who came in an interminable procession to draw public water. The act of going to the public fountain indicated that these families were unable to channel water from

---

[1] "Montelitigio" is like "Franza," a pseudonym.

the public main into their houses, and this in turn was a rather clear indication of the low status of these families. To a large extent, this consideration remains valid today, but the situation is undergoing change. As a result of the massive wave of emigration, which began at the end of World War II, many local families who have been recipients of remittances from abroad have recently channeled the public water for their private use. However, as more families have brought the pipeline into their houses and water has been used less sparingly, the supply has become inadequate. For many families the private tap has now assumed the character of a dubious symbol of prestige as they often find it necessary to continue drawing water from the public fountain which, due to the greater pressure, yields a steadier supply. Despite the recent installation, financed by government funds, of a public and allegedly abundant water main, in the continuing absence of a remodeled and enlarged pipe system, for many people, water is now scarcer than ever.

Franza has no railroad facilities, no central school building, and no hospital. A central school was built during the Fascist period, but a combination of poor construction and vandalism quickly reduced it to a useless shambles. Consequently, the community has had to rely on a number of unheated, unequipped, and poorly built private houses as classrooms for the several sections of the five local grades.

A few years ago, under the auspices of the Cassa per il Mezzogiorno, a new school was planned and the construction started. But for various unfathomable reasons, adequate funds were not forthcoming, and the initiated building has been serving since as a public latrine.

With several exceptions, the local teachers are strangers who come to the village in the morning and leave it in the afternoon, after four hours of teaching that usually has little influence on the upbringing and the cultural views of their pupils. Due to the peculiar practice in the state-run school system of assigning teaching positions without regard to physical inconvenience, many teachers consider themselves as being in exile and contribute little to the functions of the school beyond merely "putting in time."

Then, too, the children lack proficiency in the Italian language, and the teachers are only too willing to indulge in the local dialect. Equipment, even such essentials as books, blackboard, and chalk, is lacking. Finally, mention must be made of the poor training of most of the teachers who, in accordance with Italian requirements, are not college-educated, and do not possess much beyond a sprinkling of notions about the arts and sciences. It is a peculiar fact that elementary-school teachers are trained in a type of high school whose graduates are still barred from the Italian university, except for one or two faculties. To make matters worse, many of the teachers came to their positions after a long series of failures in higher-quality high schools.

Like most other southern villages, Franza has a medical doctor assigned to it by the Public Health Commissioner. Much of the time, however, the doctor has had to work and live elsewhere, so that the Franzini could not rely on steady medical care. Fortunately, however, one or two other physicians with part-time private practices are available to those who care to utilize their services. But factional and family hostilities, an excessive and apparently erroneous tendency among the people to distinguish between "good" and "bad" doctors, and economic difficulties do not always make the use of such services possible.

A priest ministers to the spiritual needs of his flock which, given a long-standing tradition and the peculiar demographic make-up of the population, consists largely of old women and young children. His activities are limited to performing the daily mass and vesper services of the main church as well as an occasional baptism, wedding, and funeral. From time to time, he also heads the seasonal religious celebrations of the other three local churches in his charge.

The priest is not a popular or central figure in the village. On the contrary, he is the object of considerable controversy and hostility, and as a partial consequence of this, he usually maintains himself at a distance from most of the local people. He has not, for instance, developed the practice, common to clerics elsewhere, of paying periodical visits to the members of his flock, or to the ill. Indeed, he is rarely present in the village, usually leaving after mass in the morning to return just before the vespers in the evening. When questioned about the priest's unenviable position in the village, many informants explained that it is due to "his excessive financial demands on pious and ignorant old ladies, whose husbands or children slave away abroad," to his being "a playboy in another village," and to his "treachery" manifested in "his readiness to drop a real friend for a false but more convenient one." Although it is not impossible that these accusations are at least in part well founded, it is likely that the priest, rarely a popular figure in any southern Italian village, has provided the people in Franza with a convenient scapegoat. They vent their traditional resentments toward the gentry on him, and use the dissension as an excuse to engage openly in the hostilities and factionalisms latent in the community. The political election, to be discussed in the next chapter, often sets up a similar situation.

The controversy concerning Franza's priest started several years ago when he first came to take charge of his duties under very strained social circumstances. When the previous priest— local-born, held in awe, and widely respected—retired, two factions arose in the village, following roughly a politically derived cleavage which, with some modifications, is still present today. One faction sought to have brought to the village another local-born priest who was serving elsewhere. When all collective requests to the diocese failed, resort was made to threats against the candidate chosen by the bishop. The other faction, perhaps fearing the prestige and power that would accrue to certain families, did all it could to impede the installation of the local-born priest by sending defamatory letters to the bishop and by giving moral support and pledges of concrete aid to the priest whose candidacy finally prevailed. The conflict born of these circumstances was great, and when the day came, the new priest had to be accompanied into the strife-torn village by both the bishop and the police.

Since then he has been unable to reassemble his flock, has supported now one faction, now the other, and has remained a lonely man confronted often by general hostility and gossip. As a result, he is very often absent, thus feeding the suspicions and hostility of his enemies.

The priest, two or three doctors, several schoolteachers, and the postmaster constitute at the present what might be called the local gentry. Their status, however, as can well be imagined, is not secure and well defined. The factionalism expressed through the political activities that began at the end of World War II is one cause of the uncertainty of their status. Another is that Franza is no longer the small community of "simple folk" of a century ago, comprising a group of peasants, artisans, craftsmen-shopkeepers, and menials that dutifully and willingly stood apart from the class of elite. In short, Franza is no longer a "dual-traditional" society (see Hagen, 1962, Chap. 4). The newly emerging elite must cope with the rising of an achievement ideology and a new social resoluteness on the part of the masses. Most of all, it must compete with the local memory of a previous small elite group. This group recently has all but disappeared, but is still remembered by the general population as having built up a large treasure of respect and submission due.

Until the turn of this century, the "simple folk" were almost totally dependent on their gentry for their daily needs—spiritual, cultural, sanitary, educational, and, above all, economic. They did not have the power, and therefore the chance, to question the existing social order and to display whatever independence and individuality they might have secretly coveted. The situation is different today. With one exception, the members of the new gentry are either recently arrived strangers or members of families that are still today part of the common folk. Furthermore, as will be seen in later chapters, the common people have in recent years come to know economic well-being and have acquired, as a result, a self-image which demands mutual respect and egalitarian standards of conduct.

The lower orders of Franza society do not feel that their social structure is not amenable to change. And the fact that at the first sign of economic independence they hastened to question the validity of that social structure, may indicate, contrary to a rather diffuse opinion (Hagen, 1962, 70–71; Pitkin, 1954, 153), that they never did fully accept their inferior status as unalterable.

The careful observer of the southern Italian peasantry can hardly avoid the feeling that "the simple folk" of the past both recognized and learned to live with their lowly status only out of economic necessity. Eventually, through a tortuous evolution of personality formation, they even learned to live in apparent peace with their offended sense of dignity and self-esteem. But latent and seething in their "simple hearts" was always the hope and intention of balancing matters, or altogether overturning them. The recent wave of emigration, of which more will be said later, may be properly viewed as an attempt to achieve economic independence and, through this, to regain their self-respect and possibly to get even with their traditional superiors. It is therefore no surprise that in some cases the social actions of returned emigrants and their families have assumed the character of a veritable revenge.

The 2300 persons of Franza are organized into approximately 700 households averaging a little more than three persons each. The demographic composition of the community is rather unusual due to the recent heavy migration from the village. Whereas in 1947 the typical household consisted of man, wife, and two children, the typical household of today consists of mother and two young children. The father is usually away, working in Piedmont, Switzerland, Australia, or Canada.

Rarely does the household in Franza extend beyond the nucleus of parents and their unmarried children. Nor did the extended family ever exist as a solidary group to any large extent. If the memory of the elders does not betray, their parents and the parents of those before them not infrequently approached old age as lonely individuals in dire want. Thus long before Franza reached a kind of transitional stage between a purely peasant society and an urban-industrial one, the elders did not rule in the way that appears to be the case in many "traditional societies" (Hagen, 1962, 68–69). Nor was their wisdom sought after. Indeed, then as now, the elder was often forsaken, maltreated, and even ridiculed and mortified.[2]

---

[2] Pitkin finds an analogous situation for the present in his study of a Latium community, where elders are pitiful figures to be tolerated at best (1954, 224).

In the old days, the elders must have been considered a drain on a family economy that was too precarious even without their dependence. Today, they are probably worse off than ever—in a social if not in an economic sense. In addition to sometimes being an economic burden, they are almost invariably unable to keep step with the accelerating tempo of cultural change, which they would often hinder. As a result, they are judged stingy, old-fashioned, doting, and stupid. Perhaps as a result of these circumstances, Franzini who reach the age of 65 or 70 are often senile, withdrawn, sullen, and unsociable, particularly in relation to children who compete with them for adult attention and ridicule them for their ancient ways.

The Economy

Until just before the turn of the century, the local economy was simple, largely moneyless and autonomous. Barring the small group of local gentry—consisting usually of the medical doctor, perhaps a pharmacist, the priest, the postmaster—and a dozen shopkeepers and artisans, all were agricultural workers. As tenants, sharecroppers, or farmhands they tilled with the hoe the land of the local gentry or absentee aristocrats. Perhaps a score or two were petty proprietors whose holdings had originated in old leases and in the land reform initiated in 1806.

Their production set the broad contours of the market within which they operated. Working 365 days a year from sunrise to sunset, they managed to produce, in a good year and when in good health, the bare necessities of life beyond that which was due their landlords. Typically, the peasant produced a quantity of corn and sometimes a small amount of wheat with which to make his daily bread and his macaroni; a few sackfuls of beans of various kinds, which in his diet replaced meat, a most rare luxury that could ill be afforded more than once or twice a year; and various kinds of fruits, such as figs, apples, pears, cherries, walnuts, and plums which were consumed in season or, whenever feasible, dried for consumption during the winter months.

In the small garden lot, the more fortunate peasants raised a variety of vegetables: onions, potatoes, squash, tomatoes, and various greens. In the less fortunate cases, the wife and children supplemented the supply with gifts received or earnings in kind, or with the many varieties of wild herbs growing in the fields. To these bare necessities, some of the most fortunate peasants added the cultivation of a small quantity of grapes, which every year yielded a few gallons of precious wine, and a few quintals of olives which were in part pickled for consumption in the winter months and in part pressed to draw the precious oil for cooking. Usually, however, olives and grapes were the exclusive property of landlords.

Sometimes the peasant could also afford a few luxury items. A pig was such an item, which, if sickness and thieves permitted, would ultimately be sold in one of the nearby fairs to yield a little money for medicines and a few items of clothing toward a daughter's dowry. Or perhaps a wife and children would keep half a dozen hens that during the warm months would lay a few eggs to be sold at the market in nearby Montelitigio. Sometimes, eggs might be consumed at home almost as a sacred rite during periods of grave illness. More frequently, however, they were given in homage to the landlord, or offered to the doctor in gratitude for his frequent services.

With the little money she had, the peasant's wife made a variety of small purchases in the local shops: crude salt, matches, a little tobacco that was parceled out to the men of the family and smoked with great frugality, a little quinine against malaria, an occasional liter of wine, salted sardines, on rare occasions a piece of bacon or cheese, and still less frequently a few grams of sugar. To this day, sugar, which is now abundant and much less prohibitive in price, is still used by the people of Franza as a luxury item to be given as a gift to the newly wed, to a pregnant friend or relative, or perhaps to the family of a young man departing or returning from abroad.

Almost everything else that was needed, but not grown on his plot, was bartered for with flour, fruit, beans, and the like. Such needs may have included a pair of shoes made by the local shoemaker, the services of the barber, the patch-up work of the mason, the rare repair of the carpenter, and the grinding of corn at the water mill.

Technology was archaic. The men tilled the land with a heavy, square-bladed hoe. Their women planted grains with a wooden dibble and weeded the field with a hoe similar in shape to that used by their men, but smaller and lighter in weight. The plow, a single-share wooden implement, and perhaps a harrow were very scarce commodities possessed only by a handful of the independent peasants. Such exceptional tools, made possible by economic independence and maintained by the greater work-energy which they themselves generated, were sometimes rented out to the general peasantry to break ground or to transport harvest and seeds. These items were usually owned in combination with a pair of oxen and an accompanying cart. But such technology was scarce and very expensive. More often it happened that those few peasants who were fortunate enough to own a donkey led the poor beast along the muddy or dusty trails with a quintal of cargo on its back each time. More often still, it fell upon the women and the children to haul the burden, bit by bit, along journeys repeated many times over and not infrequently lasting two hours or more.

The corn and wheat were harvested by a hand sickle and threshed by being beaten with wooden tridents and other sticks on the threshing ground. The women then spent days winnowing sievefuls of wheat against an often imaginary wind.

The last major item of farm technology was the olive press. Often operated as a family business, it was powered by a donkey or cow moving around a circle while hitched to a pole that operated a large stone wheel. This wheel, in turn, crushed the olives, squeezing out the golden liquid.

Franza was then a heavily traditional society. The peasants solved the problems of life much as their ancestors had done before them. Life was an arduous affair and offered few comforts beyond those deriving from the inescapable knowledge that it could be worse. If exception be made for an occasional chat with a neighbor or a periodical hour of religious participation, leisure was unknown to all but the very young, the very ill, and the very old. The peasant's almost total dependence and his sense of impotence were translated into the most abject servility toward his superiors and masters. As an elderly Franzino put it recently, "Life then was no joke." The peasant of Franza could therefore be expected to react positively to the transformation that, for various and complex reasons, has taken place during recent decades, and most apparently in very recent years. In fact, his society is now undergoing basic and rapid changes, and he is taking an active and leading part in them.

Franza is still a predominantly agricultural village. At least three-quarters of the adult population is directly engaged in agricultural activities. Furthermore, the essential elements of cultivation and agricultural life have not changed radically. A third of the agricultural population still leads a style of life that is little different from the above description. For this group, leisure is rare, profits scarce, technology traditional, and, as a result, economic insecurity very real. This section of the population, because of one or a combination of factors—ill health, age, abject poverty combined with a total lack of support from friends or relatives, ill fortune, or lack of motivation and enterprise—has not been able to take advantage of the new opportunities, such as the chance to emigrate. Nevertheless, they have not been totally untouched by the events of recent years. Many of them are recipients of small but providential social-security benefits accruing from both local and national sources. Again, owing to the recent massive wave of emigration from the village, land is now plentiful and these peasants no longer need to beg landlords for a tiny plot to be cultivated at all costs and sacrifices, nor for a day's hire in order to bring home the bread and the beans necessary for the minimal needs of their family.

It is possible that this category of peasants represents the class of the rational farmers of tomorrow. With time, it is not unlikely that they will learn to take advantage of the now abundant supply of land, coupled with the great demand for labor, in order to reorganize farming enterprises along more rational lines. That could result in the eventual passage of the property into their own hands. For the present, however, the same factors that have kept them tied to the land have also kept them bound to their traditional existence. They tend to be old or ill; they lack family help, imagination, and enterprise; and above all they lack the know-how and the capital for profitable adventures. Consequently, they continue to live mostly on the profits derived from the pathetically small, though more favorably located, strips of land which they now cultivate under more advantageous contracts than ever before, owing to greater bargaining power as well as to recent interventions by the Italian government. Nevertheless, the larger profits of today are not sufficient to alter substantially their style of life and their relative standing in the community. Their new margin of profit gets lost in the rapidly developing needs that have accompanied the emergence of a money economy, such as the desire for city-made and less durable goods and a greater reliance on pharmaceutical products and on various foodstuffs available only at the city market.

Another third of the agricultural population consists largely of the children and women of recent emigrants who, in the absence of their men, do whatever they can to cultivate as much of their land as possible and raise the basic foodstuffs required by the family. For everything else, they depend on the remittances from the men abroad, and the reserves of the shops in the village or in nearby Montelitigio. For the labor required on the farm, more often than not they must coax members of the first group of agricultural workers, who may welcome the chance to earn a little money, or one of a small group of professionally unemployed farmhands who require a given number of days' work in order to draw unemployment compensation.

A considerable number of the members of the present group have bought all or most of their land (rarely exceeding 20 acres) with proceeds of the work of their emigrant relatives. Many men originally left home with the intention of earning the means to acquire some local land, which they would later cultivate with the help of tenants and farmhands. They well understood that the primary traditional basis of social differentiation in the village has been wealth derived from the land and easily convertible into power and prestige. They, however, failed to foresee the fact that the desire for improvement was general, that the local labor force would soon be depleted, and that, as a consequence, with little or no hired help, their land would lose value. Many today would like to sell their holdings, but can find no buyers. Partly as a result of this situation, they linger on abroad, unable to decide whether to settle there permanently or to return home, hoping all the while to accumulate enough liquid capital to insure in itself a comfortable existence one way or another. In the meantime, the rest of the family marks time at home, the children usually pursuing higher studies in Montelitigio, and the family as a whole enjoying an unusually comfortable mode of life.

The last third of the agricultural population is made up of a number of peasants who have owned all or part of their land for at least several decades. Some of these are representatives of the old migration to the United States who returned permanently to Franza while they were still young enough to work. Others are massari, the elite of the local peasantry, who were the first in the village to come into the possession of a plot of land. This group first owned the technological items and means of transportation mentioned above. The greater comfort, profits, and prestige of these peasants have been such that they have, through the decades, developed an unusually strong sense of attachment to their land. Consequently, their group is proportionately underrepresented in the migratory movement from the village. In a few cases, however, they went abroad, made enough money with which to purchase another relatively good patch of land, and then returned home.

Being a massaro offers considerable economic security, and considerable prestige still attaches to riding an oxcart through the village streets, directing stick in hand, while the bells jingle from the oxen's necks. Today, however, a team of oxen, with cart, is within the means of many, with the result that the category is increasing in number, and at the same time losing in social standing. The phenomenon reflects a movement toward a higher degree of mechanization in agriculture. As an indication of this, a few agricultural innovations that have been introduced in Franza in recent years might be mentioned.

Wheat is no longer threshed by hand, even though it is still so harvested. All take advantage, for a fee payable in kind, of the three threshing machines now in the village. Corn has all but disappeared, being now considered an inappropriate and lowly source of bread, while at the same time it is not yet used as animal feed. Whatever corn is produced, therefore, is sold on the market.

Three or four tractors and other auxiliary implements in the village, although privately owned, are available for hire. Few, however, can take advantage of the implements, in part because of the steepness and irregularity of the terrain, in part because of the expense involved in hiring them, and in part also because of the peasant's old practice of irregularly interspersing his land with fruit trees of various kinds.

The village still has no major industry to speak of. However, four electrically operated olive presses and two flour mills, also electrically operated and rather modern in conception, now make work more convenient and life less burdensome. One of the olive presses is a recent cooperative undertaking organized mostly by a dozen returnees from the old migration to the United States. The cooperative, in addition, owns one of the three threshing machines.

The other three olive presses belong to massaro families, who have owned them for several decades but who have only recently electrified them. One of these families, rich in enterprising and educated children, also owns two of the three threshing machines locally available. Both the olive presses and the threshing machines operate on a seasonal basis, the former lasting from three to five months in good years, and the latter usually from six to eight weeks. Each year, the two types of business employ approximately fifty and fifteen local persons, respectively. On the whole these belong to the lower strata of the agricultural population, for occupational independence is heavily emphasized in Franza.

The two electric flour mills are recent undertakings, replacing the colorful water mills of days gone by. Both mills serve the local people in addition to drawing a considerable part of the business from neighboring towns and villages. One of the mills was installed by an enterprising artisan with a loan from an agency organized by the federal government as part of the southern development program. The other was set up by a small group of particularly intelligent and city-oriented former peasants, one of whom spent a few years as an immigrant in Canada. Each enterprise gives work to half a dozen persons, among them truck drivers, attendants, and "errand boys."

The nonagricultural quarter of the population consists largely of a few professional people, clerks, artisans, shopkeepers, occasional laborers, and increasingly of a number of *operai* (industrial workers), now about eighty in all, who work in the factories of a nearby port city or in the bars, gas stations, and shops of Montelitigio.

The artisans are divided among carpenters and masons, who constitute roughly the elite *maestranza* (stratum of craftsmen), and tailors,[3] shoemakers, and barbers, who represent the less prestigeful of the urban workers. The degree of prestige apparently decreases in direct relation to the amount of bodily contact that the artisan has with his client in the performance of his services. Owing to the recent heavy emigration, there is a considerable amount of money in the community and virtually no competition among the artisans; therefore, it is said that they are doing a thriving business.

The shopkeepers were few till the end of World War II. Since then their number has increased to about a score, although none of them are doing a very profitable business, for their prices are too high, and in any case the clientele prefer to shop in nearby Montelitigio, where a greater variety of items of higher quality can be found. While until recently, the shops carried very few items—mainly dried fish, salt, spaghetti, and a few odds and

---

[3] In addition to these, there are in Franza a considerable number of seamstresses, traditionally the first step among local women who sever direct connection with agricultural activity.

ends—today, partly because of the changing tastes, needs, and economic power of the adult population and partly because of the presence of nearly 100 young students who attend the higher grades in Montelitigio or some university, many "luxury items" are sold, including canned meat and fish, household appliances, and various items of clothing and hardware.

Historical Note

What historical circumstances underlie the transformations just described? About the distant past of the village, nothing is known with certainty. No history is known to have been written of the village, and whatever official records were kept in the past, either by the church or by the town offices, are now lost. About the only available piece of official information concerning Franza goes back to as recent a year as 1805, when, according to Giustiniani, the village was "owned" by the Marchesa della Valle.[4] For a glance into the village's past, we must, therefore, rely either on inferences from the general historical facts of the South in general or, for more recent times, on the memory of local elders.

Doubtless, until the Napoleonic reforms of the first decade of the nineteenth century, the people of Franza were serfs of one feudal lord or another. It is unlikely that prior to this period any independent peasants lived in the village. In fact, despite the various attempts at land reform in the course of the nineteenth century, the Franzini probably were, with few exceptions, virtual serfs well up to the last quarter of that century. However, a few virtually independent peasants were still, at the beginning of 1964, paying a small annual fee known as the *censo* to the church and to at least one absentee baron. This fact would seem to indicate that perhaps as early as 1806 some of the local land was distributed to the people, for it is very likely that the censo

---

[4] Giustiniani also reports here the population of Franza for 1532, when the village was taxed for 10 *fuochi* (fires: hearths, hence families), and for various other years up to 1805, when the population had reached a total of 1450 (1805, Tomo IX, 109).
of 1450 (Giustiniani, 1805, 109).

amounts to an indemnification due the previous owner as a result of the land reform.

In general, whatever little land was distributed during past land reforms was soon lost by the peasants under the pressure of taxation and the unscrupulous stratagems of their spiritual and noble leaders. Thus, the land question in Franza was not substantially altered until overseas migration became the basic driving force behind local affairs. It is possible to estimate, therefore, that just before the end of the nineteenth century, the situation in Franza was approximately as follows.

The greater part of the land was owned by two absentee lords, namely a baron and a count. A considerable portion of it—perhaps as much as 20 percent—was owned by the church and several bourgeois proprietors, the signori who had originated from the first massari as early as the first quarter of the past century: the doctor, the pharmacist, the postmaster, and one or two such others. In addition, a number of fortunate peasants, mostly massari, may have owned as much as 5 percent of the land. The vast majority of the peasants, however, were either tenants or farmhands. In the village, perhaps 5 percent of the total population consisted, in addition to the signori, of artisans, shopkeepers, a few clerks, and a few scavengers.

The people of Franza had then little or no direct contact with the rest of the world. Like most other villages of southern Italy, humbly hidden among the barren mountains, Franza's most important contact with the outside world was provided by its priest and by the handful of signori who went out of the village at one time or another. To be sure, their cultural contact with the peasantry was slight, but their behavior and style of life could be more or less easily observed. Though themselves usually of recent peasant background, their wealth, education, and newly acquired tastes and customs combined to provide for some a strong stimulus for emulation. Moreover, the signori typically behaved in such a way as to deepen the chasm existing between themselves and the rest of the people, for the peasant's existence had until recently been theirs, and now it must be forgotten at all costs. Envy, on the one hand, and well-concealed resentment, on the other, accumulated in the less fortunate. The city, that distant and mysterious world, came to represent the focus of happy change for many. It is quite likely that early in this century these two factors, envy and resentment, combined with economic factors to show the way to the Americas for many hundreds of peasants.

A little contact with the outside world occurred, as has been noted, through the physical mobility of the peasant himself within a small area containing four or five other villages and towns. Here the peasant traveled to buy or sell a donkey, or more frequently a pig. But this type of contact was of little import, for these villages were no less isolated than Franza itself, and in any case the contact was with people of an analogous mode of life and cultural formation. When contact occurred between peasant and urbanite, it was superficial and inconsequential. The peasant was held at a distance.

Just before the turn of the present century, the almost complete isolation of the village broke down. The principal factor involved was a great wave of emigration which reached its peak at the dawn of World War I. Hundreds of local young men traveled in search of work to several countries in North and South America. Those who went to the United States, where economic conditions were better, eventually turned out to be the agents of the most significant form of social change in the history of the village. Some eventually came back to Franza to find wives, then returned abroad to settle permanently and raise American children. Others worked a few years or even a few months and then returned, discouraged, to their home community. While abroad, however, most kept in more or less close contact with their home town—at least for the first few years. Many sent money and new ideas and customs from their place of work. Some who settled abroad are still doing so today. Many who returned to settle in the village bought land and had a relatively comfortable new house built. In a few cases they sent their sons to the higher grades of school and their daughters to learn a trade at the seamstress shop. More important still, in their conception and emulation of a "better life," they became the symbols of a new style of life and the token of a new class. The ranks of the leisurely professionals expanded, and so did those of the less leisurely but still respectable artisans and shopkeepers. The desire to improve one's condition now had a concrete and visible stimulus for the general population. In short, the emigrants ushered in the modern era, the nature of which, as continued by the more recent emigrants, will be the specific focus of the following chapters.

Soon after the peak years of emigration, World War I broke out. The peasants of Franza were recruited en masse to fight a war which they neither liked nor understood. But whether fighting at the front, shoulder to shoulder with other Italians of all kinds, promenading along the luxurious streets of cities, or even living in captivity in prisoners' camps, most of them learned to understand that there was a more comfortable and interesting life away from the little village and from the hoe.

When Fascism later came on the scene, the people of Franza did not understand its political character and purposes. For many peasants, however, Fascism came to represent an instrument of change: a change from an isolated life to the more widely involved type which they had recently come to admire. Public meetings required their participation and demanded their enthusiasm. Radio addresses by high functionaries excited their imagination and encouraged them to feel a part of a much larger and more powerful community. Their children now were compelled to attend school and to wear uniforms which made all alike—at least in appearance. In conveying ideological and bellicose messages, some Fascist slogans glorified the peasant's occupation by the use of agricultural symbols: "It is not the plow which digs the furrow, but it is the blade which defends it [the plow]." Other slogans endeavored to nurse the peasant as a stern but loving mother nurses the awkward but beloved child: "A civilized person neither spits on the ground nor blasphemes." The city people did not take such slogans seriously, but the peasants were probably impressed by them.

Fascism, however, was little more than an incubator. The promises of transformation were many, but the positive actions few. Indeed, Fascism stabilized the conditions of peasant society.

During the Fascist regime, the system of land ownership remained largely intact throughout the South. Various governmental measures were instituted that virtually prohibited migration—both internal and external—exception being made only for the colonists, who were encouraged to go to Africa in order to populate and help develop the new empire. These, however, were to a large extent chosen from the more experienced and rationally trained farmers of central and northern Italy.

It may be said that during the Fascist period, the only factor that sustained the social and economic resolve of the southern Italian peasant was the old migration to the United States. This resolve was sustained more during the prosperous years of the 1920's, when remittances were being transformed into "modern" houses and landed property, and less during the depression years of the 1930's, when many migrants returned home, penniless and demoralized.

World War II again placed hundreds of Franza's young men in contact with distant and strange societies. The vicissitudes of military service and war were painful, but those who went to the city could not but realize that they were a very underprivileged kind of Italian. Not many remained indifferent to this revelation.

But there is more, and it is as ironic as it is incredible. After the privations of peasant life and a difficult war, many found themselves prisoners of an enemy who provided a comfortable existence. Being a prisoner of war was a *pacchia*, some said upon returning—a lazy man's game. As prisoners of war in the United States of America, they were well fed and well dressed. They worked little or not at all, and sometimes they found themselves in the company of civilian friends and relatives, or of young ladies who had come to cheer them up. At the end of the war, they returned home healthy, strong, loaded with sackfuls of valuable personal belongings, and in many cases stirred by the desire to go back as free men. By contrast, many of those who had remained in Italy arrived home after interminable odysseys of fear, hunger, and physical exhaustion. Again, as prisoners of war in Great Britain, the peasants of Franza often found themselves working an easy schedule, occasionally free to frequent public cinemas, and the recipients of a number of calories exceeding by far their past diet as free men.

Upon returning home, immediately following the end of the war, many understood in vivid terms that Italy had lost a disastrous war, and was bearing a pathetic disruption of its social and economic systems. In speaking of this, after more than two decades, many still say that they had to come back home to suffer hunger, cold, and humiliation. As a result, the discontent and motivations of old were reinforced, and when at the end of the war, several countries opened their doors to Italian immigrants, the men of Franza departed like a human flood. Insofar as possible, they preferred to go to English-speaking countries, their first preference being the United States and their second, the country most like it, Canada.[5]

It might be mentioned that the Italian prisoners of war were not the only ones to be favorably impressed by their conquerors. Many civilians reacted in similar fashion. The few English and American soldiers who went through Franza were, on the whole, *brava gente* (nice people). Such was particularly the judgment about the Americans. "They smiled; they joked; they gave a package of cigarettes for a fresh egg; sometimes they gave away canned food, chocolate, and other things; some even spoke Italian." It is the recognition of these circumstances that has recently led an Italian journalist to argue, with understandable exaggeration, that the rural "exodus had entered the blood of peasants at the passage of the armies."[6]

The effects of the old emigration were especially noticeable in Franza during the war years. Indeed, it is not unlikely that the old emigrants were most influential precisely in this period, when, despite severed connections with the migrants abroad, their chil-

---

[5] Indeed, many returnees from Latin America refuse to migrate again unless they can go to one of the English-speaking countries. This is quite at variance with some who hold that "the immigrant naturally has sought his own kind." See, for instance, Kirk and Huyck, 1954, 451.

[6] Ciccone, 1964, 5. Ciccone also argues that the returned emigrants' accounts of life abroad are so positively accepted that the prospective emigrant lies to his wife, relatives, and friends about his alleged sadness in leaving home.

dren, now of age, were seen attending school and developing an urbane demeanor. The families of *"Americani"* had a tremendous impact during the hungry years of World War II when, thanks to their landed property and to the money saved in banks or at the post office, they continued to live a fairly comfortable life while many others were near starvation.

Again, immediately after World War II, money started pouring in from abroad, and with it came also precious goods, such as items of clothing, flour, coffee, sugar, candy, and cigarettes. To be an Americano epitomized well-being and security. Some of the local gentry and petty bourgeoisie did all in their power to captivate the sympathies and good will of the Americani, with the result that their traditional superiority had to undergo an extraordinary exercise in flexibility. The general population saw it and was deeply impressed. As a consequence, the gentry has never since been the same.

What happened then in this connection is analogous to a situation reported by di Lampedusa, who brilliantly captured the flavor of this most interesting phenomenon. Prince Fabrizio and his family were happy to return to Donnafugata after the turmoil of the Garibaldian Revolution and the decline of the Bourbon Dynasty—too happy indeed. After the customary *Te Deum* in the Duomo, the Prince issued dinner invitations to certain members of the local middle class, and then, turning to curious idlers, he added in a moment of enthusiasm: "And after dinner, at nine o'clock, we shall be happy to see all our friends."

For a long time Donnafugata commented on these last words. And the Prince, who had found Donnafugata unchanged, was found very much changed himself, for never before would he have issued so cordial an invitation; and from that moment, invisibly, began the decline of his prestige (di Lampedusa, 1961, 69).

Emigration

As noted, there have been two waves of emigration from Franza. The first began at the turn of the present century and reached its peak around 1913. The other started immediately at the end of World War II and is likely to continue for some time to come. As boys grow into young men, their first thought seems to be to leave the village and join their relatives and friends elsewhere.

Owing to the inadequacy of the village records, it is impossible to determine the exact number of migrants for either period. The best estimate can be obtained for the first period by interviewing old returned emigrants and elders in general. A list carefully compiled in this manner places the total number for the period 1900–1940 at around 1000. Most of these left for the Americas, largely for the United States.

The best estimate for the more recent wave of emigration can be obtained by following, with the help of informed adults, the plan of the village and counting the departures house by house and person by person. This procedure reveals that in the period 1946–1963 approximately 1200 individuals migrated from Franza.

In other ways, a rough estimate can be made of the total number of emigrants in the latter period. For instance, according to local records, at the end of 1945 the resident population of the village was about 2400, while at the end of 1963 it was reported to be 2250. In this same period, births exceeded deaths by a total of 1042. Neglecting the in-migrants, who have been very few, if this figure is added to the difference in population between 1945 and 1963, the total is 1192 departures. Of these, around one-third have migrated to South American countries, usually to Argentina or Venezuela; most in this group have moved away permanently as family units. The rest have gone mostly to Australia, Canada, or to the United States of America; the typical pattern is that of an adult male initially leaving alone, and later calling his family abroad, usually after one or more visits home.

In recent years, as migration overseas has become more restricted, an increasingly larger number of local men have gone to other parts of Italy and Europe. Most of these, however, comprise two major occupational categories: on the one hand, a small group of artisans, craftsmen, and untrained individuals, and, on the other, a group of very poor peasants and farmhands who have not had the economic or moral support to go overseas and have had to seek agricultural work, usually of a seasonal nature, in northern Italy. On the whole, however, the people of Franza look outward. It is their only way of escaping the economic and social difficulties of their peasant society. It is the most effective way so far found to satisfy their basic aspirations.

REFERENCES

Ciccone, Salvatore. 1964. "Una Spinta Motiva Determina l'Esodo Rurale in Capitanata" (Foggia), in *Il Messaggero*, Tuesday, June 9.

Di Lampedusa, Giuseppe. 1961. *The Leopard*. New York: Signet Books. [Original publication 1958]

Giustiniani, Lorenzo. 1805. *Dizionario Geografico-Ragionato del Regno di Napoli*, Tomo IX. Naples.

Hagen, Everett E. 1962. *On the Theory of Social Change*. Homewood, Ill.: The Dorsey Press.

Istituto Centrale di Statistica. 1963. *Annuario Statistico Italiano 1962*. Rome.

Kirk, Dudley, and Earl Huyck. 1954. "Overseas Migration from Europe since World War II," *American Sociological Review*, 19, August.

Pitkin, Donald S. 1954. *Land Tenure and Family Organization in an Italian Village*. Unpublished Ph.D. dissertation, Harvard University.

*VI

THE STRATIFICATION SYSTEM

Now that the community selected for a study of the effects of emigration has been introduced, a major aspect of the social structure of Franza, its stratification system, is to be discussed in this chapter. In subsequent chapters, both structural and normative changes which have occurred within, and about, the stratification system as a result of emigration will be examined.

The Sample

In describing the local stratification system, the unit of analysis is the family conceived of as an interactional entity. Thus, a housewife living in the village, her two unmarried children at home, and her husband and unmarried child in Australia all constitute a single family unit in Franza.

In January, 1959, when the present portion of the research was initiated, 682 families were listed in the official records of Franza. The task was to divide these families according to three degrees of contact with emigrants and take a given number from each category for comparative purposes. The nuclear family, the extended family of close relatives, and the nonkin group provided three declining degrees of contact with emigrants abroad. After a number of exclusions were made, dictated by considerations outlined in Appendix I, a sample was constructed of 120 families, divided into three almost equal groups. Interviews were carried out only with the housewife of each family unit selected.[1] The interested reader is referred to Appendix I for a detailed discussion of the manner in which the sample was drawn.

Stratification Procedures

The fact may be emphasized at this point that, in order to assess the effects of emigration on the community, the derivation of its stratification system is an essential part of the study. The next job, consequently, was to divide the sample into a number of social strata. To accomplish this step, a variation of what is known as the "judges" or "raters" technique was used.[2] For a detailed discussion of this research procedure, the interested reader may turn to Appendix II. The strategy consisted of obtaining from the 120 respondents information on their perception of the number and composition of the social strata as well as on their criteria of classification. This much accomplished, a select number of other individuals in the community—the judges—were relied on to classify in turn the sample families on the basis of the information and the standards these had suggested.

The Social Strata

The distribution by stratum of the 120 families obtained through this procedure is as follows:

---

[1] We might further point out here that with seven exceptions, the migrants claimed by the first group had gone to one of the following countries: Australia, Canada, United States. South American countries were poorly represented because these countries have encouraged the migration of whole family units.

[2] In developing my version of this procedure, the technique developed by Hollingshead was found very useful (1949, Chap. 2).

Stratum	Number	Percentage
I	3	2.5
II	4	3.3
III	25	20.8
IV	40	33.3
V	33	27.5
VI	15	12.5
Total	120	99.9

This distribution varies somewhat from the distribution for the community as a whole. The reason for the discrepancy lies in the fact that the sample is not random. The real percentages for the total population are approximately as follows:

Stratum	Percentage
I	0.5
II	2.0
III	24.0
IV	28.0
V	31.0
VI	14.5
Total	100.0

These figures were derived with the help of two well-informed persons in the community. A description of these strata will occupy our attention in the remainder of this chapter.

STRATUM I

In a few southern villages, one or two families still today can be classified legitimately as members of the old feudal nobility.[3] In other villages, such people are only occasional visitors, and serve merely as reminders of an age now increasingly forgotten. Franza, like many other southern villages, has not had a resident member of the old nobility for a long time. A baron owns a house in the

---

[3] Banfield found one real noble in the village he studied (1958, 70), while in the village studied by Pitkin (1954, 157) there was a prince who was, however, only an occasional visitor.

village, but so far as is known no one now living in Franza has ever seen him. Rather, his *amministratore*, the overseer, comes to the village once or twice a year for brief periods of time for the purpose of collecting the produce due to the baron and shipping it out to the national market.

For a long time, the "aristocracy" of Franza has been represented by a group of four or five families referred to by the local masses as the "signori," "the best," or the *"gente civile"* (the civilized people). However, this group is disappearing from the local scene; indeed, it remains real in the minds of most Franzini only in the historical sense that it is often taken as a reference point against which to appraise, as well as cut down to size, the "excessive pretensions" of the newly rising gentry, that is, the members of Stratum II, who are discussed in the next section.

Only two families belonging to Stratum I are still permanent residents of the village, and the members of one of these are old and have no heirs. The others live away in cities and during some years come to Franza for a brief period during the summer for sentimental reasons, or because this arrangement allows them to look after their property interests. On the whole, the signori are accorded deference by most, especially by the elders, although among the younger people there is a tendency to forget the signori, or deliberately to ignore them.

The members of the present stratum are the descendants of families who as late as the middle of the past century were of massaro status. In speaking of these families, the elders of Franza often state that they remember when Such-and-Such Signore was known as the son or the grandchild of Massaro So-and-So. Their social superiority, in other words, goes back no more than three or four generations at the most. Characteristically, Massaro X, who had managed to retain and perhaps increase the holding he or his father had received during the land reform of the Napoleonic era, was well enough off to send a child or two to the upper grades of school, such as the theological seminary or the university. As a result, the child began his professional career in Franza as a doctor, priest, pharmacist, or perhaps schoolteacher. His male children or other close relatives then followed in his footsteps until recent times. Lately, however, the tendency has been for the new generation to look toward places elsewhere for their professional activities.

Like the upper class elsewhere, the upper stratum of Franza, when its members are in the village, may be portrayed as a group who believe in tradition and in continuity of behavior with the past (Kahl, 1953, 192–193). Wealth, therefore, is not the most important determinant of membership in this stratum. Being a signore is altogether a matter of birth and certain symbols of distinction which are obviously not of current vintage. After family name, education and wealth are next in line as basic attributes of Stratum I, for the signori tend to be well educated and to possess a considerable amount of the local land. However, with the popularization of higher education, recently so common to the children of emigrants, and with the rather general increase of wealth as another consequence of emigration, these two factors are rapidly losing in importance and giving way to lineage as the most important single factor of placement in this stratum.

The signori are distinguished from the rest of the population by a variety of additional cultural symbols that determine a superior social status. Characteristically, their houses are *"palazzi"* (palaces), in reality only masonry structures consisting of two stories and containing eight to ten rooms. Such houses were generally built or remodeled in the second decade of this century, that is, a few years after the terrible earthquake of 1905, which destroyed most local buildings and caused the population to live in government-built shanties. Before the earthquake, the houses of the signori were still "larger and better" than other houses, the local elders remembering them as being of two stories, having iron balconies "with flower pots on them," and "a lot of windows covered with glass," but they were then less imposing, and built largely in cane and lime.

In the course of the past century, Stratum I families accumulated considerable property in dwellings and land, which were rented out to the peasants. As late as 1950, for instance, one such family owned about 150 acres of the local land. More recently, however, coinciding with their gradual disappearance from the local scene, some of their property has been sold, thus contributing in part to the rise of a land-owning "middle class."

The people of Franza agree perfectly about the social position of these families, and members of this stratum in turn do not "err" in classifying themselves. On the whole they perceive a "social chasm" between themselves and the rest of the population, which they tend to see as divided only into a *ceto medio* (middle class) and "common peasants"—whatever their recent success—while a few families at the bottom are singled out as "really poor" or "wretched." [4]

Unlike members of the other strata, among whom interaction is largely unrestricted, Stratum I families rarely interact with members of other strata, and then only on a formal basis for professional or economic reasons. In the past—but to a lesser extent even today for the few who are still in Franza at least occasionally—the signori were largely secluded from the rest of the population. Characteristically, especially the female members of the family withdrew into the private sanctuary of their home, where they were seen only by a handful of local people, such as the servant, one or two especially faithful tenants and part-time servants, and perhaps one or two others of their own social set. [5] The world of the signori was to the general population a mysterious and impenetrable world of silence and dim lights, behind closed shutters and forbidding walls. The signori had little or no interest in local social affairs, [6] and although their prestige was very high and commanded general deference, any power they

---

[4] The relative lack of detail in the gradations made by these people is somewhat discordant with a general finding in the literature that class awareness varies directly with class position. Davis and associates summarize the general finding when they say that the two upper strata make the finest gradations (1941, 72).

[5] An analogous finding is reported by Vidich and Bensman (1960, 294) for a rural New York town, where "the aristocrats withdraw from the affairs of the community and live in a private world made up of their own vanishing set."

[6] One of their number, now deceased, was, however, the local mayor a few decades ago, and he is still remembered as one who did much good in "modernizing" the village.

may have held must be gauged indirectly through the effects of their control over much of the local land.

Since the end of World War II, coinciding with their gradual disappearance from the village, some of the old signori have experienced a greater involvement in the social life of the village. This involvement has been due, in large measure, to the fact that their children have had to attend the higher grades of school in Montelitigio together with the children of the old migrants to the United States. The social contact that this circumstance has entailed has also resulted in two cases of intermarriage with Stratum III, involving children of repatriates from the old migration to the United States. In both cases, a female member of Stratum I has married a male member of Stratum III. In both cases, the wife has a secondary education, while the husband holds a university degree. Both marriages were blessed by the respective families.[7]

It might be said in conclusion of this section of the discussion, that Stratum I [8] is the result of the acquisition of land, during the course of the nineteenth century, by a small number of previously landless but enterprising peasant families. However, time, the social changes—both national and local—of recent decades, and the modern attractions of the urban world have led to the gradual disappearance of these privileged families, and a new upper stratum is now rising.

STRATUM II

This stratum, too, is small, comprising no more than a dozen families. The local people tend to refer to them as "the category of the rich," "the families of so many professional children," and

---

[7] This finding contrasts with what Moss and Cappannari (1962, 287–300) say about a Molisan village, where these authors found that "class endogamy is rigidly fixed in the values of the community."

[8] It may be interesting to suggest here a comparison between the national and the local stratification systems. If we may think of a six-fold system for the whole of Italy, the local members of Stratum I would very likely fall in the national Stratum III, or "the upper-middle class."

"the schoolteachers." With regard to this latter group, it is interesting to note that, though members of the professional group, they are not placed in Stratum I, due mainly to a combination of two factors: (1) they lack a university degree and (2) they lack family lineage. The people of Franza are quick to distinguish the university-educated from those with only a secondary education, though often the latter are honored with academic titles appropriate only to the former, which they obviously appreciate and often demand. Thus, teachers in the elementary grades refer to themselves in all seriousness as professors, and several land surveyors demand to be addressed as engineers. As a result, members of the lower strata often make snide remarks about these *"fastusi"* (inappropriately proud), who would imitate the old signori. All of the professionals, however, receive considerable recognition from the rest of the population because of their higher education and their greater involvement in the institutions of the outside society.

Stratum II would also include any university-educated children of the lower strata who should settle in Franza upon marrying, though, in comparison to the schoolteachers and other nonuniversity-trained professionals, "their superior intelligence and studies" would be more readily honored. Such individuals and their families would eventually be recognized as approximately the equals of the present Stratum I members, possibly after the death of their humble parents and the evidencing of "gentlemanly" and educated manners by their grown children.

A distinguishing characteristic of all members of the stratum is that their present social position has been achieved within the life span of the present family head.[9] By this is meant that they inherited no marked advantages, and their present position is a result of recent mobility from the lower strata. In some cases, the head of the family belongs to the group of nonuniversity-educated persons mentioned above. In several other cases, the

---

[9] This finding is analogous to that reported by Hollingshead for "Elmtown," where about one-half of the families in "Class II" had achieved their position through their own efforts (1949, 90).

head of the family is a returnee from the United States who was particularly successful in having his children educated and who earned, by his greater knowledge of farming techniques and by his particularly pleasant behavior, the respect of the general population. In still other cases, the head of the family is a member of an old massaro family who either never quite reached the economic well-being and professional standing of the old signori or, for some reason, lost it in the course of past decades. In one or two cases, such families had fallen greatly in prestige until, through emigration, they recently reinforced their standing in the community.

The typical family of this stratum is aware of the social distance between itself and those of Stratum I, but it aspires to membership in the upper stratum and identifies with it. Consequently, very active efforts are made to "command the respect" which the upper stratum commands automatically. Stratum II members are not always willing, however, to verbalize this social distance, and in an interview they sometimes explain that Stratum I families "have had their sunset." Stratum I members may have been important at one time, but "they are disappearing from the scene" and no longer perform any useful function today. One member of Stratum II went so far as to say that now they are "like a fungus—parasitic, unnecessary, useless."

Some members of Stratum II view high status in the community in terms of a monopolization of authority and power. The desire to "get there first" and become the exclusive leader is very strong, and as a result the competition is fierce.[10] The struggle for control has a largely economic undercurrent, but it expresses itself in the political arena during the periods of elections for the town offices.

The apparent political stakes consist of the offices of mayor and of the fourteen to sixteen councilmen who make up his administration. All technical positions are state appointed. Strictly

---

[10] This is an interesting parallel to a finding by Hollingshead in "Elmtown" where "the class II man focuses his attention upon the aggressive manipulation of economic and political processes . . ." (1949, 90).

speaking, the mayor does not represent the effective political power of the community, which, on the contrary, is vested in the town's secretary, appointed by the prefect or state representative in charge of the provincial offices in Catanzaro. Indeed, the mayor could technically be dismissed by the prefect under recommendation by the secretary, but this rarely happens in practice.[11] In fact, the mayor has much to say about which public works shall be carried out, what taxes shall be paid by whom, which doctor shall be appointed state health officer, and various other important matters.

Administrative elections occur every four years, during which time there is a constant ferment and realignment among the several factions that want the incumbent mayor out. The faction leaders are in most cases members of Stratum II, and political activity is based on no ideological struggle. With the exception of national elections, when several dozen people vote for the Communist Party or for the Socialists, the people of Franza are Christian Democrats as a matter of course. Although only one faction is the official representative of the national Christian Democratic Party, other factions are just as eager to carry their political banner under some form of religious symbol.

Politics in Franza is a matter of patronage interest: interest in being able to control jobs such as town doctor, cemetery attendant, town guards, and street cleaners; interest in receiving favors or gifts for a vote; interest in not being subjected to "a spiteful enemy." Political realignments and hostilities are, therefore, a never-ending process. In Franza, as in Montegrano according to Banfield (1958, 28), no sooner is one elected mayor than he loses many of his previous followers. The small favors that a mayor can do in a small village are indeed many, but due to the excessive factionalism in the community, a favor to one is almost always a wrong to another. Not infrequently, therefore, the mayor loses even the support of the members of his own administration because he will not or cannot offer them special favors, or will not

---

[11] From time to time, however, one reads of such cases in Italian newspapers. Often they involve defrocked priests and communists.

follow their inclination to take revenge against members of the losing factions.

The conflict reaches a gruesome pitch during the campaigning period. At this time the opposing parties, through their leaders, spare each other no manner of spite and abuse. In the village square they alternate in singing each other's faults and defects—real or imagined. They might begin by reminding each other of their respective origins, passing quickly to accusations of robbery while in office, or of an intention of achieving public office in order to defraud the public. Then, they might discuss the motives behind their marriages to their respectives wives. Imagination runs high: one is accused of marrying for money; another learns that he married a girl, with a huge dowry, who was pregnant by another man. Their education, their professional competence, their manner of speaking Italian, and their intelligence are all viciously ridiculed. When nothing concrete is found to say against the antagonist, innuendoes take over.

During political gatherings, small sections of the population—the faithful clientele of each leader—engage in behavior that substantially adds to the public caricature. While the speaker is busy publicizing the inglorious nature of his opponent, the faithful followers laugh, applaud, and cheer, or they tune up on "Bronx cheers" and shout back courtesies in kind, as the occasion demands.

The bulk of the population listens and laughs, enjoying it all, for this situation created by Stratum II politicians is not only amusing in itself; it also serves the function of undermining the aura of social superiority that they are intent upon building around themselves, encouraging as a consequence the shrinking of social distance between themselves and the masses. Their behavior in the public square dramatically distinguishes these aspirants for general recognition from "the real signori." The latter live in peaceful privacy in the dark of their houses, and no one knows what defects they may have. No one has seen them fight "like street urchins"; indeed, no one has ever heard them even talk in a loud voice. To this extent, they are socially invulnerable. In the age of economic well-being and excessive public noise, social distinction consists more and more of being able to afford silence, and less and less of having money and education. The members of Stratum II in general, and the politically active in particular, are loud; therefore, they are considered vulgar.

Away from the forum, each candidate busies himself in collecting promises of favorable votes. For these, he or his representatives make all manner of promises: a future loan; the redress of an old grievance about the local tax; support in an attempt to obtain a pension or a shopkeeper's license; help in finding a job; and many such others. The poorest are encouraged through small gifts of spaghetti, other foodstuffs, or a small amount of money to vote for a given candidate.

Local politics is a serious business in Franza, and an understanding of it is essential to an understanding of the local situation in general and of the nature of Stratum II in particular. Through the process of politics, a new power structure is seeking to crystallize; the contenders for the upper hand are understandably fighting fiercely. The common men seem to enjoy the fight both for the role it plays in washing publicly the dirty linen of pretentious individuals, and for the chance it affords them to avenge, through the upstarts, their century-old humiliations. Contemporary political conflict in Franza reminds one of a session in group psychotherapy, a sort of group catharsis. Through it is unwound and released the crippling burden of century-old degradations suffered at the hands of the more powerful, as well as the resentments accumulated against friends and relatives alike in the ancient struggle not to be submerged by other contenders for the economic pie.

If conflict is particularly marked in times of political elections, it is because the political arena is a legitimate, public, almost sportsmanlike context within which to give vent to the old pent-up emotions and hatreds. A middle-aged woman put her finger on the truth when, several years ago, she volunteered in a meditative mood that

There has always been animosity in this village, but now—may God have mercy on us!—we are all a handful of Judases. With the excuse of these political elections, we are all pitted brother against brother and sister against sister.

The political competition between members of Stratum II has some positive and concrete consequences for the community as a whole. For instance, in their attempt to outdistance each other in all respects, the leaders of the factions acquire such items from the city as bathtubs, electric heaters, gas stoves, refrigerators, and automobiles. Their behavior then reinforces the city-oriented behavior of the families of successful emigrants and contributes a little to the eventual adoption of these items by the general population. More important still, the mayor has been making special efforts in favor of the community, with the result that he has fully or partially succeeded in introducing much-needed improvements into the village: a more adequate water supply, a new school building still to be completed, repair of the main road, more considerate service to the people at the town hall, a club with a television set for adults and children alike, and a variety of lesser innovations. These successes are partly due to the current activities of the national government, but they also result from the active interest of a mayor who is roused to particularly effective action by the competition for power and popularity.

Because of the local factionalism, disagreement is considerable in the classification of Stratum II families. In fact, the position of these families is, more than for any other stratum, a result of statistical averaging, as in most cases they are classified either in Stratum I or in Stratum III, depending apparently on the good or ill will they evoke in the classifier. This circumstance also attests to the fact that Stratum II families are still mobile and have not yet achieved the coveted position and concomitant prestige of the upper stratum. They, in turn, tend to hold a view of the local prestige structure that is in almost perfect agreement with the system as presented here. Specifically, though sometimes begrudgingly, they recognize the superiority of the old signori, while below themselves, "the professionals," they see the "old *benestanti*" (well-to-do), the "new benestanti," the "common peasants," and "the very poor" or "wretched," in this given order.

Stratum II families have no palazzi, but their houses are well kept and spacious. Furthermore, they have been among the first in the community to acquire the new conveniences from the city, such as bathtubs, electric heaters, gas stoves, refrigerators, television sets, and automobiles. These and a certain tendency to emulate urban styles make their houses the most "modern" in the village. Indeed, like the upper-middle class in the United States described by Kahl, some members of Stratum II, more than others, are "interested in the latest styles for their homes, their clothes, their cars, and their thoughts" (1953, 194). Others, less educated, will have to depend on their children to pursue such interests.

The children are in all cases oriented toward the university, or at least toward a high-school diploma. A professional status is prescribed for them at birth, and in this respect they are completely like the children of the old signori whom eventually they will entirely replace.

The question of intermarriage is difficult to assess for this group. The family heads have in most cases originated in Stratum III or even below. Those who were wed to local women married their peers, with the exception of one who married downward one stratum. Several of them, however, married girls from other villages or towns, and in such cases it is impossible to determine to what extent the marriage was class-endogamous, though it appears that there was in no case much difference one way or another.

The fact that they have tended to marry local girls, or women from nearby communities, suggests a further distinction between the families of this stratum and those above. By and large, they are oriented toward the local culture, bringing to it, of course, a sense of personal superiority and achievement. When they look beyond the local boundaries, they rarely think farther than Montelitigio. Indeed, the members of this stratum manifest a marked attachment to the local community. It would seem that they have deliberately chosen Franza as the social universe within which to pursue their aspirations. It remains to be seen how well and how fast these new local leaders will learn to pursue the collective interests, and help effect the economic and cultural rapprochement that Italians throughout the nation have been hoping and working for.

STRATUM III

The members of this stratum are "those who can afford to live well," "the old Americani," "the massari," "the artisans," "the well-to-do," and "the solid citizens." The basic objective difference between this stratum and the one preceding it lies in the greater education of the family heads of the former, or in some cases their larger property holdings. Many in Stratum III fail, however, to see any difference between themselves and the stratum above and tend to resent the efforts by some members of Stratum II to "take over the village."

Stratum III families constitute a little less than one-fourth of the community. They include most shopkeepers and skilled artisans, most massari, those families of emigrants who own between 16 and 40 acres of land, and several families with one or two children who are university graduates. With the exception of a few massari and artisan families who have held their present position for several generations, most families in this stratum owe their present position to the conversion of the proceeds from emigrant relatives into appropriate social symbols, such as commodious dwellings, landed property, and the education of their children. The Franzino who has only recently achieved a position in this stratum is clearly oriented toward the top stratum, though he recognizes that he has "a long distance to travel." He correctly perceives, however, that a university education will eventually enable his children's children to achieve such a position for themselves.

The families of the old migrants to the United States who returned to settle permanently in Franza were most instrumental in giving rise to what might be called "a middle class." In so doing, they have represented a phenomenon that is generally applicable to much of agricultural southern Italy. In discussing "the social classes since 1900," Guido Vincelli goes even further and argues that the "old class of *Galantuomini*" (signori or gentlemen) was already, at the end of World War I, being replaced by "new elements, fresh with energy from overseas, desirous of improvement and recognition, who constituted then as now the stratum of innovators" (1958, 32–33).

With the money acquired abroad, the returned emigrants bought plots of land from the absentee baron or from the old signori, thus achieving the coveted economic independence. They embellished or constructed anew their old one- or-two-room hovels, and also made it possible for the members of their family to dress and eat better than the average. Their children have often gone to school beyond the five grades locally available and achieved professional status after being educated at the high school or the university. Above all, the economic and moral support which they received in the host society gave them the psychological strength to challenge the traditional order of local social relations. In so undermining the old social system, they have also been aided by their educated children, who accelerate the flow of city ways and tastes into the village.

It is likely that the prestige accruing to the old returnees is due almost exclusively to the economic and educational achievements of their families. As persons, barring a few exceptions, the returnees do not appear to be particularly esteemed. Most of them managed to accumulate a little capital abroad at the cost of terrific personal sacrifices. This circumstance, together with the fact that they had no family with them, made it difficult for them to interact with others and benefit from the urban culture of the host society, which in Franza goes under the name of *civiltà*.

Typically, while abroad they normally worked long hours in construction or other menial jobs. After a long day's work, they went home to a bleak room in an old apartment house or in a cellar, and there cooked their own meal, a plate of spaghetti and a slice of fried meat. When energy and finances permitted, they went to the Italian club, or to the house of a *paesano* (fellow townsman), to play cards for beer, wine, or small amounts of money. On Sunday they went to the bocce grounds and passed the time away bowling and drinking wine or beer.

Their conversation was by necessity limited to problems encountered on the job, to gossip about other paesani in their city or elsewhere, and to the exchange of information about the events in the old village as reported in letters written by relatives, or brought back by those who had returned from visits to their families.

The language spoken was, in general, the dialect of Franza, as they had known it years or decades previously. But this had been modified by other southern dialects spoken by fellow *Americani* and by English words, properly altered to have an Italian sound. Thus "shop" became "scioppa," "store" was rendered into "storu," "job" was changed into "giobba," and so on. These words either had no corresponding terms in the old dialect or related to phenomena which occupied recondite corners of the cultural heritage of the former peasants. What happened to their power of communication was, therefore, simple to understand. They did not learn much English; at the same time they forgot the purity of the old dialect. And of course, while away, they could not partake of the growing "Italianization" of the old dialect which was occurring in their home town under the influence of spreading education and the new media of communication. To top it all, their relative isolation abroad rendered them somewhat asocial, confused, *stupidi* by Franza standards. So, when they returned home, to many they were persons to be pitied at best.

Their manner of dress, too, was striking only by its outdated eccentricity. Many returned home with clothes they had worn for many years or picked up as garbage collectors. While their social isolation militated against any preoccupation with styles, saving was a goal to pursue by all means, while wages were low and the expenses incurred in migrating very high.

Upon returning home, however, they rightly felt that they had personally achieved something important and that, after all, they had "*girato il mondo*" (seen the world). They could scarcely imagine that those who had not emigrated had also "seen the world," many having seen it, irony of ironies, through the very changes that the "*fessi Americani*" (American blockheads) had helped bring about in the old village. The Americani, therefore, felt it their right to demand acceptance as wise and knowledgeable persons, at least by those of their own family and background. Where their cultural and personal makeup was not sufficient to elicit the proper response on the part of others, they became embittered, and either withdrew into solitude or set out to find ways of drawing attention to themselves. Perhaps for this reason, some of them proceeded to tell fantastic stories about America that made them appear altogether ridiculous. They would tell stories of "trains that run in the sky," of swimmers who stay underwater 30 minutes "without breathing," of children who must pay room and board to their parents in order to live with them, and a great variety of other such phantasies—some of them near-truths—that even local "troglodytes" perceived as indications that the emigrants had failed to understand the world they had seen.

All of this must not be construed to mean that the returnees are totally rejected. Very few in Franza fail to credit them with the merit of having done much for their families and, indirectly, for their community as well. Despite the personal peculiarities of returnees, the general tendency is to judge them by the objective criteria of achievement, such as the education of their children and their property holdings. Educated teen-agers, eager to ridicule the past, detract most from them, or from their image of themselves. Educated people in general and the artisans, who react to the Americani as to *parvenus*, also detract. "*Cafoni signorilizzati*" (presumptuous cads), they are called in the village studied by Moss and Cappannari (1962, 295). "Fessi Americani," they are called sometimes in Franza.[12]

The vast majority of the people, however, have no difficulty in classifying the Americani. Asked why they place them in Stratum III, they mention their relative well-being and especially

---

[12] There is a tendency among southern Italian "intellectuals" (of the provincial, narrowly educated type) to judge the United States through the actions of their own returned fellow citizens. In so doing, they commit a most grotesque mistake and at the same time perpetrate a pathetic affront against their own culture, which is the main cause of the excessive marginality of the emigrant: culturally deprived in his own world more than in that of his host.

their success in having their children educated. Indeed, the most important characteristic of this group, as well as most of the stratum directly below it, is that they represent a relatively recent and still current development in Franza (and in much of southern Italy) of a group of landed, though recently landless, peasants who have invested or are investing much of their capital in the education of their children. This means that for some time to come these two strata will be an important source of personnel for the two upper strata.

Next to the families of returned emigrants come the families of the massari, most of whom fall in Stratum III, though a handful belong to Stratum II, and a few others to Stratum IV. The development of a massari group in Franza can be traced to the first decades of the last century. At that time, a small number of peasants who had profited from the distribution of the feudal lands managed to hold onto their shares, and through the years succeeded in rising above the socioeconomic position of the masses. Since the small profits of their labors did not have to be turned over to the landlords, some of them increased their holdings and invested the profits in a team of oxen, an oxcart, and often a wooden plow. By local standards these items constituted precious capital, which in turn required the construction on the land of at least a straw barn to protect the animals from the elements and from thieves. This farmstead type of land settlement now made possible a more effective and profitable cultivation of the land.[13] The massari became an elite group within the peasant estate. Their labor sometimes resulted in sufficient wealth to enable them, as already noted, to send one or more sons to the university or to the theological seminary.

Various other advantages accrued to the massari. Not only were they able to cultivate their land more effectively, owing to

---

[13] Despite the fact that peasants generally live in the village, there have always been two or three occasions each year when many of them sleep in the country. Moreover, a few massari have always resided in the country as a matter of course. Typically, in such cases it is the men and boys in the family who live on the farm, while their women continue to live in the village.

their settlement on it and their more efficient technology; in general, they were also able to work more land than the average peasant. In such cases, they turned for the additional land to the signori and the absentee landowners, who recognized the massari as expert and efficient cultivators, worthy of the best lands. In addition, the massari's sustained presence on their land and the possession of a few animals that this facilitated tended to make them experts on plants, animals, the seasons, and the like. Finally, the massari came to be called upon by the common peasants to break their land with oxen and plow; at harvest time they became the local "truckers." All these factors favored an increase in both the profits and the prestige of the massari, and resulted in considerable consciousness of kind, in self-pride, and in a tendency to resist changes in traditional social relationships.

The massari as a whole are very jealous of their social position. Among the emigrants, they are the least responsible for the introduction of egalitarian norms into the community. As a rule, moreover, they are among the most attached to a farming way of life. In fact, they are overrepresented among those emigrants who returned from abroad to settle permanently in Franza after only a short period away, during which time they made haste to extend their property holdings and to improve their farm technology. Among the old migrants to the United States, for instance, two types of persons lasted only a relatively short time abroad: first, those who could not endure the heavy and sustained work on the railroad or in the ditch, and, second, the massari, for whom the lowly status of laborer in America dramatized their relatively high status in the old community.

Many of the other old emigrants, on the other hand, repatriated when they were already old and could no longer farm. Consequently, those who are still alive live on whatever income they may derive from renting their land out to others, on their savings, and in most cases also on the pension that they receive from the Social Security Administration in the United States. In a few cases this amounts to as much as $200 a month, which by local standards is a large amount of money. Such an income is, in fact, comparable to the average monthly salary of schoolteachers and other nonuniversity-educated professionals.

A number of families in Stratum III are, therefore, very wealthy by local standards, being worth as much as from $10,000 to $20,000. Their wealth is in turn a source of considerable power and prestige, for they are the new landlords; they are the families who can offer or afford "a good marriage"; they can well afford luxuries in food and dress; and above all, they are foremost among the local moneylenders.

The last major category falling in Stratum III consists of artisans and shopkeepers. Not all such people, however, belong to this stratum. In a few cases, present-day shopkeepers, for instance, are recent incumbents of this occupational category, which on the whole appears to have a high rate of turnover. Some "open up shop" as a last resort. They are relatively impoverished villagers who have no trade and cannot, or will not, engage in farming labor. In some instances, the village administration has granted them a license as a form of public charity or as a reward for wounds sustained during the last war. Such businessmen generally sell only very few and cheap items, for their capital is scanty. As a result, their businesses do not survive long, and their prestige is low.

Several other shopkeepers are recently returned emigrants who bring to the occupation whatever prestige they have gained as a result of emigration. Probably, they are marginal to Stratum III, but if they last as shopkeepers, and keep their shops well stocked, they will be permanent members of this stratum within the course of a decade or two. Finally, there are several relatively successful families who come from a long tradition of shopkeepers or belong to families of prestigeful artisans. These represent the core of the shopkeepers' group and are readily accorded membership in Stratum III.

Similarly, not all artisans belong to Stratum III. From the viewpoint of prestige, two types of artisans live in Franza. On the one hand, a few families are descendants of a line of masons, carpenters, and seamstresses. Like the more successful massari, they are the oldest claimants to a position in the present stratum, and they are readily accorded such a position by the rest of the population. On the other hand, there has always been in Franza a group of generally unemployed individuals who sometimes pass themselves off as masons or carpenters and as such find a day's work. They usually belong to poor families, and their general style of life keeps them back in the lower strata. A few other members of poor families have been regularly trained, but, perhaps due to the stiff competition on the part of the traditional artisans, they have been trained as barbers or shoemakers, or sometimes both, because neither of these occupations is lucrative. As a consequence of family origin, continuing poverty, and the personal nature of the service involved, barbers and shoemakers generally belong to Stratum IV at best.

In Franza there is little intermarriage across the three major occupational lines of professionals, craftsmen-shopkeepers, and peasants—whether common or massari. A particularly good dowry or promise of a comfortable future occasionally does attract individuals of both sexes across occupational lines. Seamstresses, in particular, from time to time marry former peasants who have returned, moneyed and elegantly dressed, from abroad. But such cases are not common. If it is rare for an artisan to marry a peasant, it is usual for an artisan member of an artisan family to marry an artisan member of a peasant family. Barring no major discrepancies in family honor or wealth, the determining factor of intermarriage is the occupational similarity of the bride and groom. At this point, the unit of stratification is not the family but the individual, indicating, on the one hand, the major role played by occupation and, on the other, the readiness with which social acceptance is granted to those who are occupationally mobile.

Finally, people in Stratum III, like those in the stratum directly above them, also hold a view of the local prestige structure that is essentially similar to the system of stratification presented in this chapter. At the top of the prestige hierarchy, they place the old signori. Together with the signori, however, they put also "the professionals," by which they mean almost exclusively those with a university degree. In Stratum II they classify schoolteachers and other professionals without a university degree. None of them, however, put in this stratum any of the few particularly successful but nonprofessional massari and emigrant families that some others classify in Stratum II. They "correctly" classify themselves in Stratum III, referring to themselves as "benestanti" (well-to-do), "massari," "artisans," or "shopkeepers." Below themselves, in Stratum IV, they see a group of "new benestanti" or "new Americani." Below these come the "common peasants," or "common people," followed finally by "the wretched" or "the very poor."

STRATUM IV

The members of Strata II and III tend to be detailed in their perception of the local prestige structure. Beginning, however, with Stratum IV, the awareness of social distinctions is less detailed. The three lower strata are represented by 88 families, or 73 percent of the total sample. Of these, only 24, or 27 percent, perceive six strata. The findings, therefore, are in basic agreement with those of other scholars who have discovered greater detail of class awareness in the upper than in the lower strata, although they do not show the linear trend that some scholars have found.

Stratum IV is the newest social stratum in Franza; nevertheless, it is the second most numerous, containing about 28 percent of all local families, compared to 31 percent for the stratum below it. Most of its members would have been classified with the general peasantry until roughly a decade ago. These, however, are the families that have profited most from the economic and social changes of recent years. The bulk of the present stratum, in fact, consists of families of recent emigrants, although a few shopkeepers and a number of artisans, usually without sufficient skill to be considered "first-degree craftsmen" and without certain basic symbols of social importance, are also included in it.

As a result, the most common expressions used to describe Stratum IV are in the nature of the following: "the new Americani," "the new benestanti," "those who have become rich with all these Americas," "those who are almost as important as the old Americani," and "those who are becoming important now." A few Franzini even call them "the richest." And, indeed, not a few of these families do have liquid and property assets that amount to as much as $20,000. Nevertheless, they are still classified in the lower half of the stratification system. It would seem, therefore, that, although wealth is a very important consideration in the village, there as elsewhere, it is expected to go through an aging process before it is allowed to "buy" a position in the higher reaches of the prestige structure. Probably within the next decade or two a large number of these families will have achieved a position in Stratum III or even Stratum II.[14] In part, this upward movement will be achieved through the education of their children.

A large number of children from this stratum are seeking a higher education. They comprise about half of the approximately 100 local youngsters who in 1964 were pursuing studies beyond the five grades of school available locally. A university degree held by a child is almost invariably a sufficient condition for a Stratum III position for the achieving family. The children themselves would, of course, be members of Stratum II, or perhaps Stratum I, if they were to settle in the village.

At the present, the families of Stratum IV make up the largest group of parvenus in Franza. In addition to educating their children, often with a view to sending them on to the university, they have recently built spacious and comfortable new masonry houses. They have also purchased the bulk of the land sold in the past decade, and, finally, they are conspicuously adopting the ways of the city in diet, dress, and general behavior. Their newly acquired status represents one of the deepest breaches in the traditional system of prestige and power relationships that Franza

---

[14] As an indication of this, we may note that in 1964, ten Stratum IV families of emigrants from the 1959 sample were evaluated again by five of the original 20 raters according to the original procedure. While in 1959 only one of the ten had been classified by at least one rater in Stratum III, three of them were so classified in 1964, and none had fallen into a lower position.

has ever experienced. To make matters all the more annoying for some of the "old families," the new style of life of this stratum often takes the form of a "display of arrogance."

The flamboyance of *nouveaux riches* everywhere is notorious. In Franza, the memory of a recently inferior social status seems at times to evoke excessive boldness, ultradefensive types of behavior, and ultraconspicuous displays of wealth in the families of Stratum IV. A critical informant colorfully suggested that the "new Americani sometimes behave like the person who, having acquired a whole new suit for the first time in his life, proceeds to immerse himself in muddy water in order to christen it." The following statement by a member of Stratum IV lends some support to this view:

We were hungry year in and year out. Particularly around April, when the wheat reserve was invariably exhausted, we practically had to go begging and tip our hat to any shark who was willing to pull us through. When we heard a voice from a radio, while walking on the streets, we wondered what kind of devil there was in that box. Now we thank God that we don't have to worry any more, and to tell the truth, we are making up for what we couldn't have then.

This display of wealth, which in the last analysis is an attempt to "live down" previous poverty and humiliation, angers many Franzini, especially the massari (who were rarely in dire economic circumstances and do not now feel the need to "live it down"), as well as previous friends and peers who have been less fortunate.

The parade of wealth and the conspicuous consumption of Stratum IV families is a major cause of social conflict in Franza at the present. Traditional superiors cannot always accept the change in attitude, the lack of deference, and the obvious attempts at equality of persons who, until only a few years ago, were humble and impoverished common tenants or very small proprietors. As a result, they gossip and engage in all manner of spiteful acts. For their own part, the parvenus react to the "envy" of the "fastusi" with various provocative acts that intensify the conflict. For instance, they blast their radio, phonograph, or television set, leaving doors and windows open, so that neighbors and all who pass may see and hear. Or in referring to their eating habits, they may complain that "nowadays there is nothing to eat but meat." "*Allura*," they say of their traditional superiors, "Well, did they expect to be always on top and the only ones with a full stomach? Let them chew up their liver."

The traditional superiors, on their part, look on and often do indeed "chew up" their liver, despite the fact that their social standing, though challenged, remains higher. "*Ah, mannaja li dinari*," they might say. "*Mo si scordaru 'i cipuji!*" ("Damn the money! They have forgotten when they used to feed on plain onions.")

Perhaps the most intensive conflict, however, arises between the people of Stratum IV and those directly below them, that is, their previous equals. Misery likes company. Without such company, the sense of failure and the pain that often accompanies it are greatly intensified. The distress is all the more marked when the successful make great display of their success. The sense of failure is multiplied manyfold, and the only defense against the development of a totally morbid self-image is the denial of the merit of, or at the least an emphasis on the better fortune of, the successful. "*Na vota non avenu cazi 'o culu; mo si ficiaru randi ca fortuna, ma ancora scarpi grossi sugnu.*" ("Once their pants were all patched up; now luck made them big shots, but they are still uncouth peasants.") The new *Americani*, in turn, often react by avoiding any sustained contact with their previous peers, and this, of course, intensifies the animosity.

Stratum IV is the most fluid stratum in the community. This fluidity, combined with the conspicuous consumption of these people, "their arrogance," and the resentment that they provoke, accounts for the relatively marked disagreement among the raters as to the social position of these families. In fact, those who place them in Stratum IV are not much more numerous than those who classify them in Stratum V. For their part, however, many Stratum IV families tend to see but one class of people above themselves. This class image is due to a number of factors: (1) their strong emphasis on money as a criterion of social importance, (2) their perception of marked fluidity in the stratification system, and (3) their positive orientation to the highest social stratum,[15] which they see as being composed of old families and professionals. Evidently, their recent and impressive achievements cause them to disregard entirely the factor of lineage as a possible distinction between old signori and new. To themselves they modestly refer as "neither rich nor poor," "the common people," or more frequently "the good honest and hard-working people." Below them come the "poor peasants," followed, in turn, by the usual "wretched" or "miserable" bottom stratum.

STRATUM V

Stratum V comprises almost one-third of the local families. With few exceptions, they are tenants or petty proprietors owning up to five acres of land. Unlike the members of Stratum IV, who "are getting somewhere," and those in Stratum VI, who are "utterly destitute," the members of Stratum V are thought of, and consider themselves, as just "respectable workers" and "poor but honest people" who "never seem to make enough for the family needs." They take pride in the fact that they are not so badly off as the people in the bottom stratum, and distinguish sharply between themselves and those below them in moral terms, characterizing them as "*poveri disgraziati*" (wretched), "vagabondi," "famished," and in some cases even "half-witted" and "morally loose." [16]

The most important characteristic of Stratum V is that it has traditionally been the main source from which the higher strata have sprung, and is, therefore, the largest and oldest social stratum in Franza—the common peasantry. The fact that this stratum has traditionally been the source of personnel for the higher strata, coupled with the increasing urbanization of Italian society, explains why this stratum has gradually but greatly decreased in

---

[15] My evidence, therefore, lends support to an interesting suggestion made by Merton to the effect that in a system of stratification which is "under wide dispute," the members of a given stratum are likely to manifest "anticipatory socialization" toward members of distant upper strata (Merton, 1957, 266–268).

[16] An analogous tendency is found by Hollingshead (1949, 103).

size. While up to the turn of the century it probably comprised as much as 80 percent of the total population, at present it is only slightly larger than its two major offshoots, Strata III and IV.

Inasmuch as the increase in social opportunities and the proliferation of social strata are to a large extent the result of emigration, it may be seen that one fundamental consequence of emigration has been a systemic or structural change in the local society. In recent decades Franza has experienced not merely a circulation or exchange of personnel across the existing strata, which would in itself denote an essentially static social structure, but a reorganization of the structure through the actual development of additional social strata. Together, the new strata constitute what might be thought of as "the middle class." In matters of social mobility, in other words, emigration has been for Franza—and we might indeed generalize to the agricultural South as a whole—an effective functional alternative to the phenomenon of industrialization experienced elsewhere in more urban societies.

Emigration, however, has not operated alone in determining structural change. The role that the recent changes in the Italian nation as a whole have played in the transformations occurring today in Franza should be mentioned again. Thus, without going into this question in great detail, the cultural impulses that, through the modern media of communication, have been transmitted from urban centers in the years since World War II, the various welfare measures instituted by the Italian state, and the proliferation of industrial jobs all have undoubtedly influenced local social phenomena. Among the various specific influences, three seem to stand out and deserve at least passing attention. In the first place, national conditions have increasingly facilitated the benefits of emigration. For instance, as the occupational opportunities and cultural advantages of the cities have multiplied, local landowners have found it more convenient to settle in the city, thus releasing land for sale to the families of emigrants, and making room for the rise of a new elite from the previously underprivileged strata. Again, the recent democratization of the school system is making it easier for economic gains to be accompanied by social gains.

Second, the efforts of the Italian government in this period since World War II in favor of what T. H. Marshall (1950) has called "citizenship rights" has unquestionably helped lift the economic and social status of the Italian masses throughout the nation. Foremost among the citizenship rights that have benefited the people of Franza are those which involve old-age pensions, unemployment benefits, and public-health insurance. As can well be imagined, such measures have been especially helpful to the most underprivileged and destitute.

Finally, the industrialization of the country has not failed to have some repercussions in Franza. As previously noted, a considerable number of local people are now employed in Montelitigio and in its harbor as factory workers, bartenders, gas-station attendants, and the like. A few others work at the local mills and olive presses. In short, internally and externally, changes have been mutually supportive. Basically while through emigration Franza has experienced the rise of a land-owning middle class yielding forth an intellectual elite, through the industrialization impulses deriving from the city, the community is now experiencing the rise of an industrial middle class.

In view of the fact that the common peasants have constituted the major stream from which social tributaries have formed, Stratum V families have numerous relatives in the higher strata. These kinship ties are important in preventing the members of the present stratum from seeing detailed social distinctions in the prestige structure, although in part this phenomenon is also a reaction to the "parade of wealth" previously noted. Members of Stratum V often stress their kinship to families in the higher strata and claim equality with them. Many feel, moreover, that members of Stratum III, and especially Stratum IV, put on airs that are totally unjustifiable, for "until only yesterday they toiled like dogs with us." Similarly, a few members of this stratum are not willing to admit the "social superiority" of townspeople, the artisans in particular, arguing poetically that *"pancia piena canta e non camicia bianca"* ("a full stomach sings, not a white shirt"). Artisans no longer go hungry, but the argument had some validity until recent times. In the past, the common peasants, though subject to great hardships, could always treat themselves to a potful of wild herbs for the evening meal. A few impoverished townsmen, on the other hand, often had to rely on the good will of peasant neighbors for a handful of beans or a bunch of vegetables.

A considerable number of people in Stratum V have a tendency to divide the local population into the three conventional occupational categories of professionals, artisans, and peasants. In such cases no distinctions are made among those falling in the last category. One of them put it as follows:

Peasants are all the same; we live in dirt, eat dirt, look like dirt, and are treated like dirt. We have mud in our blood. It makes no difference if some give themselves airs; we are all cousins of the donkey, even though some are a little richer than others.

Most, however, perceive a four-fold division, at the top of which are put together "the signori and professionals," followed next by "the rich" or "benestanti." Next comes their own stratum, generally referred to as "most of us common people," while below them are to be found "the wretched," "the beggars," and the like.

A few see only two strata and speak of those above them as "the rich who live in comfort" and of themselves as "the mass of workers." This view may be due to their historical function as caretakers of other people's land and to their awareness of centuries of servility to the landlords. It may represent, in other words, the dichotomous class image that, as Willener notes, is typical of the "inferior" categories of people. Willener found in French Switzerland that while the "superior" categories tended toward a view of multiple and continuous social strata, the lower strata, in turn, tended to respond predominantly in terms of social classes, which is to say that they had a dichotomous and potentially conflict-laden view of the social structure.[17]

The style of life in Stratum V is still one of many hardships. Typically, the peasants work a couple of tracts of land of three or

---

[17] 1957, 206. For some support of this finding, see Bott, 1954, 259–286. For a review of similar findings, see also Dahrendorf, 1959, 280–289.

four acres each, which in some cases are miles from each other and from the village. As a result, as noted, the peasant sometimes puts in two or three hours of walking each day in order to attend to his daily tasks, which engage him from sunrise to sunset. Much time and energy are thus fruitlessly expended. His food supply, which is preponderantly beans, vegetables, and bread, is becoming more nearly adequate. Nevertheless, in some cases it is still a source of insecurity late in the spring, just before the new harvest. His house typically consists of one or two rooms which he sometimes shares with a family of five or more and with a donkey, a goat, or a pig. Poverty and hard work tend to make his health poor. He frequently suffers from rheumatism, hernia, and "liver trouble," which may indicate a variety of ailments of the heart, stomach, and other internal organs.

The precariousness of the economy is reflected in various ways. First of all, the male members of this group, being apparently the least affluent among the peasants, could not initially take advantage of the migration opportunities offered a few years ago by such countries as Canada and Australia. Later, some of them could perhaps have obtained a loan from a relative or friend abroad, or from someone else in the community. But for most it was now too late, for the doors of relatively free immigration were closed. As a result, some went to other parts of Italy and Europe, but most Franzini have no confidence in a place that is "not a real America."

The economic insecurity of people in this stratum is reflected in the fact that their children very rarely go to school beyond the five grades locally available. Many do not even go that long, but the situation in this respect, may soon change. Beginning in the fall of 1963, all Italian children have been required to complete eight years of schooling, or stay in school until 14 years of age. The new policy may eventually draw these youngsters into the expanding educational opportunities. However, in view of the traditional laxity in law enforcement in this respect, and given the scarcity of teachers, classrooms, and equipment, it may be many years before they profit fully from the new law and, through education, compete more effectively for developing opportunities.

Furthermore, children are often needed on the farm, to say nothing of the fact that, even when it is free, school is costly, involving expenses for clothes, books, equipment, and above all, for the city tastes that the children invariably develop. These expenses are especially burdensome when the school to be attended is not in the village, as is the case with the grades beyond the fifth, for which children have to travel daily to nearby Montelitigio.

The chief hope for a more secure and respectable future for the people of Stratum V appears to lie in their possible migration from the village, or at least in the continuing emigration of others. If the latter possibility materializes, they may in a few decades turn to more rational cultivation of larger and more fertile plots of land, a circumstance rendered increasingly possible by the scarcity of manpower in the village. In this, however, the peasant will need the help of his government and the educated classes to teach him new and more efficient ways of farming. However, in view of the fact that agricultural studies are still largely neglected in Italian universities, present hopes for such help seem to be more in the nature of kindly wishes than concrete possibilities.

STRATUM VI

The people classified at the bottom of the stratification system comprise about one-seventh of the population, and are generally thought of as "destitute," "very poor," "half-witted," or "lazy-do-nothings." They, in turn, think of themselves as "poor and unfortunate Christians" and as "honest workers who have been forsaken by God." Like people at the bottom of the prestige structure everywhere, they are a category of laborers, errand boys, and scavengers. They perform seasonal tasks as farmhands (olive pickers, wheat cutters, or the like), or they assist the village masons or run errands for one or the other of the local shopkeepers. A few are totally unemployed and live on public welfare. Their livelihood is, therefore, haphazard. When they work, they are frequently paid in kind rather than in money, and this arrangement keeps them dependent on others for handouts of flour, beans, fruits, and the like. "Bread for today at any cost" seems to be their basic value orientation.

These poor people perform a most important and interesting function, which has been noted elsewhere by students of stratification. In speaking of the category of people whom many of their informants refer to as "the shack people," Vidich and Bensman, for instance, suggest that "their social function . . . for the other classes is to serve as a 'baseline' against which individuals in other groups can make favorable comparisons of themselves" (1960, 71). In Franza, as could be seen clearly in noting the self-evaluation of persons in Stratum V, members of the lowest stratum represent a kind of warning to others, especially those in the stratum immediately above them, that there is still a lower level of existence into which they might slip. To this extent, not only do they serve for others as a reference point for self "conferral of superiority" (Johnson, 1960, 42), but they also provide for those above themselves a terrifying stimulus to work hard and to maintain at least their present position.

A rough indication of the life conditions of Stratum VI is provided by the following statement made recently by a laborer in Franza:

My family has been working on the land ever since the Lord said "plow," but as far as I can remember, and from what I could hear from my parents, never a day has passed in which we did not have to worry about having enough to eat. We have never had a piece of land of our own. Right now it would be easy to rent one, but it does not pay. Look at it this way: as a hired hand, working about 200 days in a year, I can make about L. 400,000 ($640) a year. With a wife and four children this is not enough: if you don't work a piece of land, you have to buy everything, and prices are sky high. But just the same, could I clear that much if I worked any piece of rented land? No, sir—not even half of it.

At least in a few cases, however, this rueful description applies more to the recent past than to the immediate present. The economic conditions of this stratum have improved somewhat in recent years. Some previous laborers are now becoming farm tenants, and as such they are on the way to joining Stratum V, where there is still poverty but somewhat more security. A few of them also combine their meager agricultural earnings with unemployment compensation received by virtue of periodic arrangements of work and of the government's tacit recognition that theirs is underemployment at best. The errand boys and such others also profit from unemployment compensation, and, given the lack of manpower, their services are now more in demand than ever and their remuneration somewhat higher.

What at present best distinguishes this stratum from the one just above it is a combination of erratic employment and the near impossibility of significant personal achievement. This circumstance is, in turn, due to the effective exclusion of Stratum VI members from the regular distribution of the economic pie. If a simile be permitted, members of Stratum VI receive only the crumbs that fall on the floor in the process of division.

Factors other than personal achievement also account for the very low status of the people falling in Stratum VI. For instance, until recent years, a considerable number of Stratum VI families still lived in the *baracche* (one-room wooden frames) built after the 1905 earthquake. Since 1922, many of them have been moved, in three different waves, to *case popolari* (subsidized government apartments). Though basically comfortable and modern in appearance, these, however, are of the lowest possible quality, and not infrequently consist only of one or two rooms plus a brick-furnace kitchen, to be shared by two families, and a toilet without running water. Their residence in these apartments contributes to their low status, for most in Franza consider it "proprio basso" (very lowly) to "live from charity." The additional fact that the roads going by these subsidized apartment buildings have not yet been paved also contributes to the low prestige attaching to this kind of housing.

Perhaps because of their almost absolute dependence on the occasional errand or the *giornata* (day's hire) for their subsistence, the members of this stratum are at once the most resentful and the most deferential in the community. For them there is an extravagant number of *dons, donnas*, and professori in the village. Yet, it is the members of this stratum who, more than others, recognize

two classes alone: "the poor" and "the rich" or "big shots." [18]
They frequently explain that "we are all products of the earth."
When asked what single factor more than any other makes for
"social importance" in the community, their answer almost invariably is "money," or "wealth." When they consider making finer
social divisions, they limit themselves to singling out for distinction a small group among "the rich" whom they call "the real
signori." These, of course, are the old families in Stratum I.
Others below them might be "pretentious" and "stuck up," but
they are still "just rich." In fact, many Stratum VI members are
so resentful of the low status accorded to them that in interviews
they often offer spontaneous complaints by way of engaging in
genealogical reconstructions. Upwardly mobile families of Strata
III and IV are sometimes even singled out as cases of those who
"only yesterday were our dear friends at dinner time, and now
they won't even talk to us."

Conclusions

In concluding this chapter, note that the people of Franza are
quick to recognize social differences, which are most frequently
clustered into six strata. Moreover, there is high agreement among
them as to who belongs where in the stratification system.

Money plays a predominant role in determining the divisions
of the social structure. It is a fundamental basis of social position
because it commands the cultural symbols appropriate to given
positions. Above all, it provides for the acquisition of landed
property, which is still one of the bases of social importance in
the community. The role of money also explains the seeming
paradox inherent in the fact that, although the stratification system is characterized by high fluidity, there is high agreement
among the rating judges in their classification of the sample

---

[18] An analogous finding is made by Archibald (1953, 397) who reports
in her study of shipyard workers that "the shipyard worker's antagonism
to authority increased in direct ratio with his external servility. . . ."

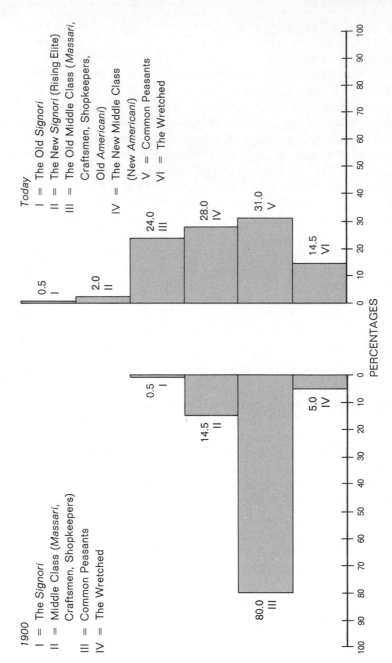

FIGURE 2. The Social Strata of Franza around 1900 and the Present

respondents. The community, in other words, confers ready recognition on those who acquire money and convert it into the appropriate cultural symbols. Money, however, takes time to be effectively converted into these symbols and into the appropriate behaviors that go with it. For this reason, certain families receive more prestige than others even though they may be less rich at a given time. A case in point is represented by the old signori in relation to the new upper stratum. Another is represented by most artisans in relation to members of Stratum IV.

Before closing this chapter, it will now be useful to present diagrammatically the prestige structure that has been described. As a way of emphasizing the changes registered in recent decades by the prestige structure of Franza, in Figure 2 the representation of the structure around 1900, according to a rough calculus projecting present criteria backwards, is in juxtaposition to the structure as it is represented today.

As a glance will show, there has been no change at the very top of the structure. The changes that have occurred in the middle of the structure, however, are dramatic. Whereas in 1900 there were two middle strata, there are now four, demonstrating largely the profound structural effects of emigration. The greatest loss, as previously indicated, has been sustained in the category of common peasants, from which has sprung most of the population that now constitutes the new strata. But it would seem that today there are almost three times as many "wretched" people as there were around 1900. This point is relative. In 1900, most peasants were greatly impoverished, and the wretched were only those few who were totally miserable, such as the scavengers and the beggars. Today, when opportunities for achievement have multiplied, the attribute of "wretched" seems to apply to those who have been absolutely unable to take advantage of these opportunities: they are apparently still a considerable portion of the total population.

A final point is in order. Despite the decision to accept a six-fold division, in Franza as elsewhere, the social-stratification system looks different to the various persons in the community. Before closing the chapter, therefore, it may well be worthwhile

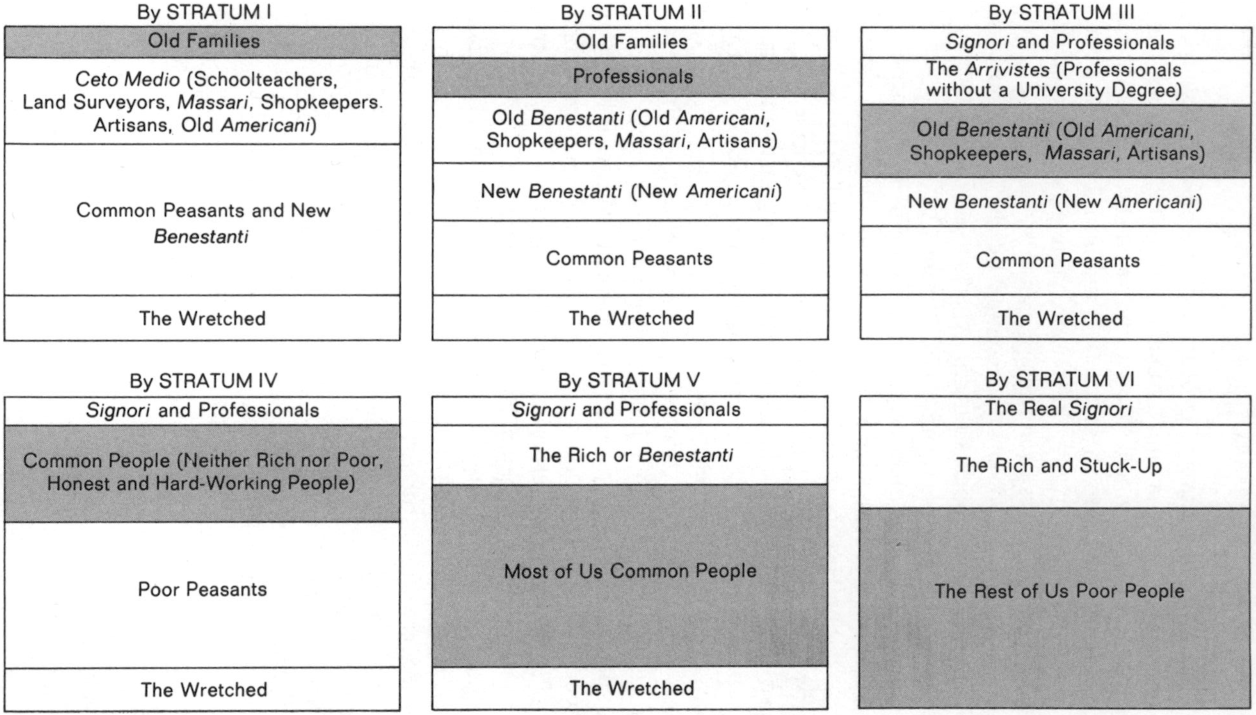

FIGURE 3. The Stratification System as Perceived by the Six Strata. Self-identification is indicated by shading. The six profiles are only roughly indicative of the actual stratum proportions.

to present diagrammatically the prestige structure of Franza as it is variously viewed by the local people.

Figure 3 indicates that, with the obvious exception of Stratum I, all groups recognize at least one stratum above themselves. Similarly, all groups except Stratum VI recognize at least one stratum below themselves. Social perception, however, is most detailed in Strata II and III, wherein the perceived prestige structure corresponds identically to the system as presented in this chapter.

The basis of social distinctions also varies from stratum to stratum, the major difference being between the upper three strata as a group and the lower three, again taken as a group. Thus, while the upper three strata use a variety of criteria, including lineage, occupational activity, and wealth, the lower three tend to emphasize more the single factor of wealth. Stratum IV, however, recognizes to some extent the factor of lineage, and the people in Stratum V especially recognize the moral factor in distinguishing themselves from those in the group below them.

REFERENCES

Archibald, Katherine. 1953. "Status Orientations among Shipyard Workers," in Reinhard Bendix and Seymour M. Lipset, eds., *Class, Status and Power*. Glencoe, Ill.: The Free Press.

Banfield, Edward C. 1958. *The Moral Basis of a Backward Society*. Glencoe, Ill.: The Free Press.

Bott, Elizabeth. 1954. "The Concept of Class as a Reference Group," *Human Relations*, VII, August.

Dahrendorf, Ralf. 1959. *Social Class and Social Conflict in Industrial Society*. Stanford: Stanford University Press.

Davis, Allison, Burleigh B. Gardner, and Mary R. Gardner. 1941. *Deep South: A Social-Anthropological Study of Caste and Class*. Chicago: University of Chicago Press.

Hollingshead, August B. 1949. *Elmtown's Youth*. New York: John Wiley.

Johnson, Harry M. 1960. *Sociology*. New York: Harcourt, Brace and Company.

Kahl, Joseph A. 1953. *The American Class Structure.* New York: Rinehart & Company, Inc.

Marshall, T. H. 1950. *Citizenship and Social Class.* Cambridge: Cambridge University Press.

Merton, Robert K. 1957. *Social Theory and Social Structure.* Glencoe, Ill.: The Free Press.

Moss, Leonard W., and Stephen C. Cappannari. 1962. "Estate and Class in a South Italian Hill Village," *American Anthropologist,* 64, April.

Pitkin, Donald S. 1954. *Land Tenure and Family Organization in an Italian Village.* Unpublished Ph.D. dissertation, Harvard University.

Vidich, Arthur J., and Joseph Bensman. 1960. *Small Town in Mass Society.* New York: Anchor Books, Doubleday and Company, Inc. [Original publication 1958]

Vincelli, Guido. 1958. *Una Comunità Meridionale.* Torino: Casa Editrice Taylor.

Willener, Alfred. 1957. *Images de la société et classes sociales.* Berne.

❋ VII SOCIAL MOBILITY

The outstanding aims of this book are two. The first has been to discuss the economic and social problems of southern Italian peasants as they developed through the centuries and as they linger at the present time. In pursuing this goal, it has been convenient to examine the critical factors underlying the decision of great numbers of people to interrupt the routine of their culture and families and emigrate for permanent or temporary periods of time, an action entailing both clearcut advantages and various types of sacrifices. This task was completed in Part One of the book.

The second aim has been to analyze certain changes in the emigrants' communities of origin which may be looked upon as consequences of emigration. To this task, Part Two of this book is devoted. The social changes of interest are of two types: (1) those that are structural in nature, in the sense that they manifest themselves in the reorganization of the community—these are the specific objects of the present chapter; (2) those that are of a normative character and manifest themselves in a reorientation of behavior among the people in the community—to this aim the bulk of the remaining discussion in this volume shall be devoted.

In Chapter VI, the strata that comprise the social pyramid of Franza, the prototype of communities of origin, were described. The observation was made that the present system of stratification constitutes a major structural alteration of the system as it was in the years prior to the first wave of emigration. Thus, at least two strata now recognizable in the community are largely recent offshoots of the traditional peasantry, having grown out of the two waves of emigration referred to previously. In other words, in that chapter what has happened in recent decades to the stratification system was viewed somewhat in the abstract. In the present chapter, people will be brought more directly into the discussion, and the social movement they have experienced while the stratification system itself was changing will be looked at. This task shall be accomplished by examining the following hypothesis: *Upward social mobility among the community families varies directly with the degree of contact they maintain with emigrants abroad.* It is predicted, in other words, that the greater the degree of association a Franza family has with emigrants abroad, the greater the probability that the family has moved up in the local stratification system during the period since the migrants' departure from the community.

Before proceeding to discuss a test of the above hypothesis, it may be well to remember that the sample under study consists of 120 families, divided into three groups on the basis of degree of contact with emigrants, as follows: Group I comprises 41 families claiming as emigrant the husband or at least one unmarried child. The degree of contact here is high. Group II—medium contact—contains 40 families in which one or both spouses claim as emigrant one or more relatives of the following types: parent, sibling, or married child. Finally, Group III—low contact—consists of 39 families without emigrant relatives or with emigrant relatives of a lesser degree than any of the above.

The Key Status Index: A Measure of Social Mobility

Testing of the hypothesis on social mobility presented a distinctive problem. The hypothesis required classification of the 120 families in the sample at two points in time, namely, both in the "base year" [1] and at the time the study was conducted. Most students of stratification would probably agree that the judges' technique, discussed in detail in Appendix II, is a valid tool with which to describe the stratification system of a little community like Franza *in the present*. Indeed, when focusing on prestige phenomena, as in the present case, such a research tool is particularly useful for small collectivities, where "face-to-face" association makes possible "total-status" evaluation of a person.

Few scholars, however, would be likely to concede that the same technique is also useful for measuring prestige at a point in time past. For such a task, a more objective technique is necessary. Accordingly, a tool had to be found that would be appropriate both for the present and the past, correlate it with the judges' technique, and then, if the result of such a correlation warranted it, use the objective tool alone for both the present and the past. The solution of this problem was an important methodological aspect of this study.

Several objective tools of stratification already in use among American scholars were considered. Among these were Hollingshead's Two-Factor Index of Social Position (1957) and Warner's Index of Status Characteristics (1960, 121–159). The first allows the researcher to classify a group of people by giving each individual a score, or index, according to preestablished procedures and on the basis of objectively derived information concerning

---

[1] The "base year" refers to the year from which mobility is measured. In the case of the first and second groups, the base year is a datum received from the respondents themselves during the interview, and refers to the year of emigration of the first-claimed emigrant. In the case of the third group, where contact with emigrants is either slight or nonexistent, the base year is taken to be 1949, that is, the midpoint between the first and last years of the emigration period considered for purposes of this study.

the individual's *occupation* and *education*. The second, though less rigorous and more intuitive, makes use, in an analogous fashion, of as many as seven such factors, or "characteristics," but normally only the following four: *source of income, house type, occupation,* and *dwelling area*. It soon became apparent, however, that in view of the largely agricultural and relatively homogeneous nature of Franza society, in contrast with the more urban American communities for which these two scales were developed, neither of them would apply to the problem at hand. Consequently, it was decided to let the local people themselves solve the problem.

An account of the simple manner in which the research tool, hereafter referred to as the Key Status Index, was constructed, follows: After each of the 19 local judges [2] had classified the 120 families of the sample in one of the six strata, he was given the following instructions:

Now let us forget for the moment what we have been doing so far and let us do something a little different. Tell me: If I had not given you the things to keep in mind in placing these families in a given class, what kind of family would you have put in Class I, what in Class II, and so on?

None of the judges had any problem in answering this question. In giving examples of families which they would have classified in each stratum, all of them, though some more and others less, provided a number of status characteristics for each of the six strata. Needless to say, some of the information received was superficial, repetitive, or useless. Much of it was very helpful. Moreover, a considerable number of factors were common to most of the judges, indicating that the raters were to a large extent guided by similar cultural criteria in placing families in given strata. Of these common factors, those which were objective or easily objectifiable were chosen for each of the six strata, and the Key Status Index was thus constructed to contain a number of placement criteria for each of the six strata composing

---

[2] This writer excluded.

it. The interested reader will find the Key Status Index in Appendix III.

To determine whether the Index was indeed useful for my purposes, each family in the sample was given a stratum position according to the Index. The set of scores so derived was next compared to the set of scores previously obtained through the use of the judges' technique. The comparison was made on the basis of Kendall rank correlation coefficient (Tau) (Siegel, 1956, 213–223), which is designed to give a measure of association between "two ordered series," such as the two sets of ranked scores dealt with here. The two series are presented in Appendix IV, where it can be observed that, despite a slight tendency for the Index to depress social position, the degree of correlation between the judges' technique and the Index is significantly high. This finding can also be surmised from Table 4 where a more

TABLE 4. Stratum Distribution of Families, According to Judges' Technique and Key Status Index, 1959

Stratum	Judges' Technique		Key Status Index	
	N	%	N	%
I	3	2.5	2	1.7
II	4	3.3	4	3.3
III	25	20.8	24	20.0
IV	40	33.3	36	30.0
V	33	27.5	33	27.5
VI	15	12.5	21	17.5
Total	120	99.9	120	100.0

synoptic distribution of the families by stratum is presented according to both techniques.

With a significant correlation established between the two instruments of stratification, the Key Status Index alone could now be used to stratify the sample both for 1959—the year in which the present part of the study was carried out—and for the base year. The difference between the two scores gives a measure of social mobility from the base year to 1959.

Before discussing social mobility proper, it will be worthwhile to make a few other brief remarks about the nature and use of the Key Status Index. It should be pointed out at the outset that each family in the sample was classified on the basis of one and *only one* placement criterion, namely, *the highest* that could be found for that family on the Index. Thus, for instance, Family X, whose head is a schoolteacher, would normally fall in Stratum II; but if by chance that family should also own 150 acres of land or more, a characteristic of Stratum I, the family would automatically be classified in Stratum I rather than II, regardless of all other considerations.

This point is critical. Students of social stratification have generally assumed that knowledge of certain key statuses and qualities, such as education, wealth, and occupation, is sufficient information for attributing an individual to a given class or stratum position. Indeed, this basic rationale underlies all known objective measures of social position, such as the various indexes of social position and the many occupational scales. So far so good. But this assumption is then grafted onto another and more problematic one, namely, that the criteria of the given scale or index are equally applicable for everyone in the population being classified.

Indeed, reflection on the nature of the judges' technique itself readily reveals that such an assumption is patently false. In using that technique, students of stratification have invariably discovered that in evaluating each other, the people of a certain community often shift criteria as they rate one family and then another. Thus, Family X is classified in Stratum I by Judge Y because of "family name," "traditions," "nobility," and the like. The same judge then classifies Family Z in Stratum II on the basis of wealth, or income. Yet, as has often been noted, "family name" does not always imply wealth, for "impoverished aristocrats" are everywhere as real as their implacable pursuers, the "boorish rich."[3] In evaluating each other, human beings apply

---

[3] For the analytical distinction between "economic power" and "social honor," see Weber in Gerth and Mills, 1958, 180–195.

different standards for different persons. As far as studies of prestige are concerned, this finding obviously indicates that different attributes and qualities are differentially critical for different individuals.

The Index constructed in Franza with the help of the raters is based on this idea—that different qualities are differentially utilized—and constitutes an attempt to formalize it. The Index, however, reduces considerably the complexity of the judges' technique. Whereas in the latter procedure, the raters often take several factors into consideration for an evaluation of their fellow citizens, the Index makes it possible to classify a population by utilizing only one factor for each individual considered. The procedure, therefore, is based on the assumption that there is a "key status" applicable to each individual member of a primary community through which he is best recognized and socially evaluated. That status corresponds to his highest achievement or rank.

The notion is not strange to sociological thinking. As is well known, all normal adults occupy many social positions and play a multitude of roles. Kingsley Davis argues that for the "personal and social efficiency" of each individual, "he must find some coherence in the several positions he fills," and thus "we could expect that in any society certain positions will tend to adhere together in different individuals." To this coherence of positions Davis gives the name of "*station,* meaning by this term a cluster of statuses and offices that tend to be combined in one person as a locus and are publicly recognized as so combined in a great many cases." For Davis, this also defines class (1948, 91–93), and I do not follow him in that extension. I do, however, agree with Davis in his general argument that a person's various positions tend to cohere and thus give that person a generalized or unitary social image and position.

In the last analysis, a person's "station" is a social value conferred by his fellow citizens on the basis of their observation of his social activities. But what are the mental processes through which this value is chosen in the minds of his associates? The various positions occupied by the individual are never fully consistent with one another (Lenski, 1954, 405–413). Conceivably, an individual's associates could derive that value on the basis of a mental calculus that would average the discrepancies. This process of synthesis is one distinct possibility. Another possibility, equally distinct, and probably more realistic, is that a man's associates perceive the generalized value, or station, as being inherent and ready-made in one or another of his various positions.

The evidence from Franza indicates that each individual is characterized by a "synthesizing" or "key" status. In a given community, however, a number of key statuses are possible. These are ranked according to the values prevailing in that community. The people of Franza value most highly landed property and education, and will confer the highest prestige to anyone possessing at least 150 acres of land and a university degree, or both, provided that the holder of such a degree is not engaged in an inappropriately low occupation, such as grammar-school teaching.

However, education—and to a lesser extent property—are not completely "scalable" in Franza because the majority of the people possess very little of either. Variations in education, for instance, are meaningful only at the higher reaches of the hierarchy. Below that, Franzini turn to different criteria of evaluation. Thus, next to having a high education, it is "valuable" to be a shopkeeper or a craftsman, provided that in the latter case, skill be associated with ownership of a house. Following the local hierarchy of values all the way to the bottom, the lowest value is bestowed upon farmhands, uneducated people living in subsidized government housing, and the chronically unemployed poor.

Social Mobility

Let us now proceed to an examination of social mobility among the 120 families comprising the sample. After each of them had been given a stratum position both for 1959 and for the base year, the findings were organized as shown in Table 5. The reader will note that a marked relationship exists between high degree of contact with emigrants and upward social mobility. Fifty-four percent, or a total of 22 families, in Group I have moved from a lower stratum to a higher one since the base year, and one out of 41 families has been downwardly mobile. It is interesting to point out that this case represents the family of an artisan who, after a few years abroad, severed ties with his family, allegedly because they refused to join him. As a result, his wife has had to take on odd jobs as laborer and errand runner. The loss of occupational status combined with the ensuing poverty has moved the family from the Stratum IV position held in the base year to Stratum VI in 1959.

Most of the families in Groups II and III have not been

TABLE 5. Social Mobility of Families from Base Year to 1959, by Degree of Contact with Emigrants

Degree of Contact with Emigrants	Upward		Stable		Downward		Total	
	N	%	N	%	N	%	N	%
I—High	22	53.7	18	43.9	1	2.4	41	100.0
II—Medium	1	2.5	35	87.5	4	10.0	40	100.0
III—Low	2	5.1	36	92.3	1	2.6	39	100.0

socially mobile. Only three of them have achieved higher positions, and five have moved to lower strata. In other words, insofar as movement of families within the stratification system is concerned, it is evident that emigration is the determining factor. Furthermore, in view of the static character of both Groups II and III, it is obvious that emigration is capable of determining a net gain within the stratification system only in the special case of the *nuclear* family claiming one or more of its members abroad. This finding is clarified, as shall be seen later, by the fact that upward social mobility is related to relatively large remittances of money from emigrants. Franza emigrants, as a rule, send only very small gifts of money, and then infrequently, to persons outside of the family nuclei to which they are directly responsible.

Speaking of the sample as a whole, the most noteworthy

finding in Table 5 is that, although in Groups II and III combined there has been slightly more downward than upward mobility since the base year [4] (five families as against three), for the sample as a whole movement has been largely upward. Thus, 25 out of 120 families, or 21 percent of the total, have been upwardly mobile, whereas only six, or 5 percent of the total sample, have been downwardly mobile. This finding is definite evidence that changes in the stratification system of the community have not been merely of the circulatory type. As has been previously

TABLE 6. Stratum Distribution of Families in Base Year and in 1959

| | Number of Families | | | |
| | Base Year | | 1959 | |
Stratum	N	%	N	%
I	2	1.7	2	1.7
II	2	1.7	4	3.3
III	15	12.5	24	20.0
IV	37	30.8	36	30.0
V	45	37.5	33	27.5
VI	19	15.8	21	17.5
Total	120	100.0	120	100.0

pointed out, families in the community have not simply ex-changed social positions with one another; on the contrary, some social strata have increased in numbers while others have sustained a net loss. The point is obviated by a glance at Table 6 which shows a diminution of Stratum V and a remarkable increase in Strata II and III.

The flow of persons from the stratum of the common peasant illustrates in more concrete terms the process underlying the creation of the new strata pointed out in the preceding chapter,

---

[4] For the sake of brevity, hereafter the locution "since the base year" will often be omitted, but understood, in speaking of social mobility of families in this study.

where Strata III and IV were presented as largely recent phenomena coinciding with the two waves of emigration from
Franza. To use Sorokin's colorful terminology, the "profile," or
the number of "stories" in the "social building," has changed since
the turn of the century.[5] The ascending flow is apparently a
continuing one, so that the number of traditional peasants is
diminishing while the middle strata to which they have given rise
continue to grow. Thus, in as short a period as that between the
end of World War II and 1959, Stratum IV replaced Stratum V
as the largest stratum. This in turn is an indication of what again
Sorokin (1959, 136) refers to as the "intensiveness" of social
mobility, namely, the number of strata through which mobile
families have moved. On the whole, within the twelve-year period here in question, mobility has involved one-step movements,
a phenomenon which is in accord with related findings elsewhere.[6] Specifically, with few exceptions, the movement has been
from Stratum V to IV, from IV to III, and in two cases from
Stratum III to the new gentry.

Little or no movement has occurred either into or out of
Strata I or VI. In the former case, while downward mobility is
out of the question, ascension has been lacking due to the brevity
of time under consideration. In the latter case, there have been
two instances of skidding and none of upward mobility. Members
of Stratum I and Stratum VI have not participated in emigration.
By 1959, only one family from the lowest stratum had emigrated
since the end of World War II. This finding is in agreement with
the rather general belief that emigration is "a middle-class phenomenon." Davie, for instance, found that it "is mainly a middle

---

[5] Sorokin, 1959; see especially Chapter IV for an illuminating discussion
of the "fluctuation of the height and the profile of economic stratification."

[6] Thus, Lipset and Bendix (1959, 253) find for the United States that
"the most prevalent form of social mobility in our society involves not
extreme but only moderate improvements in status." Sorokin, too, argues
that "the greater the economic distance to be crossed by an individual the
less is the number of such 'jumpers.'" And again he states that "the majority moves along the vertical line of economic stratification gradually,
without sudden jumps and skipping of the next steps in either direction"
(1959, 472–474).

class that emigrates. The very rich as a rule do not wish to emigrate and the proletariat cannot afford to." [7]

It is a sad fact, nevertheless, that in the interviews it was the members of the lowest stratum who displayed the strongest desire to emigrate. Most manifested a marked desire to "find a way out of here," frequently saying that "the only way you can save yourself is by going to America." When asked why they had not left, they explained that while they had always wanted to go abroad, when emigration first became possible they had neither the means nor the credit to take advantage of the opportunity. By the time they had accumulated the means, through self-deprivation, or had persuaded a friend or relative abroad to lend them the money and file an immigration petition in their favor, it was usually too late. By then, the countries of most frequent destination were imposing heavy restrictions on Italian immigrants. As a particularly perspicacious interviewee from this stratum put it, "For us it is always either too early or too late."

The probability that "the wretched" of Franza will emigrate at any time is very low for another set of reasons. The immigration authorities of foreign governments naturally prefer the better educated and the healthier: in short those who make a favorable impression in an interview. Naturally, the very poor do not fare well in this respect, with the result that the rate of rejection for this stratum is considerably higher than for any other. It is ironic that the very thing these sorry people seek to correct, their excessive poverty, inhibits their chances for improvement. Nothing determines failure more effectively than failure itself. To put it in the language of Weber, their power to dispose of goods or skills for the sake of economic and social betterment is greatly limited by their "class situation" (Weber in Gerth and Mills, 1958, 181).

---

[7] Davie, 1936, 249. MacDonald disagrees on the latter point, arguing that the part played by variations in the ability to pay transportation costs has been exaggerated. However, his findings apply to regional differences rather than to differences within, say, a given community. See MacDonald, 1963, 63.

Factors of Social Mobility

Data have been presented so far to show that a marked difference exists between Group I and the combined Groups II and III in the amount of social mobility experienced. That difference has been attributed to variations between the groups in degree of contact with emigrants, or, more loosely still, to the factor of emigration. To be strict about it, however, neither emigration nor degree of contact with emigrants can in itself be a determinant of social mobility. Something more specific must underlie emigration to account for the incidence of social mobility in the community. What, then, are the specific "causes" of mobility? In seeking an answer to this question, it will be useful to focus on Group I in more detail by comparing the upwardly mobile with the rest of the families in this group on the basis of a number of critical factors of stratification. The first comparison concerns changes since the base year in the amount of landed property owned, as shown in Table 7.

TABLE 7. Amount of Land Owned by Upwardly Mobile and Other Families in Group I at Base Year and in 1959

| Acres Owned | Upwardly Mobile | | | | Others | | | |
| | Base Year | | 1959 | | Base Year | | 1959 | |
	N	%	N	%	N	%	N	%
0	12	54.5	4	18.2	13	68.4	10	52.6
1–10	8	36.4	6	27.3	3	15.8	5	26.3
11–20	1	4.5	8	36.4	2	10.5	1	5.3
21+	1	4.5	4	18.2	1	5.3	3	15.8
Total	22	99.9	22	100.1	19	100.0	19	100.0

This table shows that a majority of the respondents were landless prior to their involvement in emigration. The next major group owned from a minimum of one to a maximum of ten acres, generally averaging about four acres—the most common holding in the community. Among the upwardly mobile families, however, the landless had by 1959 decreased from 12 to 4, the latter being all families of artisans. In all cases of achieving peasant families, therefore, one of the first actions subsequent to emigration was the purchase of a plot of land, thus satisfying their century-long "land hunger."

Table 7 shows that the upwardly mobile families have been far more successful in satisfying that hunger. Whereas the number of landless families in the upwardly mobile group has diminished from more than 54 to only about 18 percent, the majority of families in the other group are still landless. To appreciate better the meaning of this difference, it should be noted that there are no significant differences in occupational composition between the two categories, the majority of the families in both groups belonging to the peasantry. Precise information received during the interviews reveals, moreover, that, whereas the mean holding for the achieving group has increased from 3.4 to 16.6 acres, that of the less successful has risen only from 3.7 to 6.4 acres.

A further comparison between the upwardly mobile and the remaining families of Group I may be made on the basis of changes in the quality of their dwellings. In Franza as elsewhere, the kind of house one lives in is a revealing index of one's style of life and as such is particularly sensitive to changes in prestige. Findings should show, then, that the upwardly mobile families have been more active than other families in improving this very conspicuous symbol of social importance.

The data in Table 8 demonstrate, in fact, that the more socially successful families have had a significantly greater tendency than the less successful to build new houses or to remodel the old, making them larger and more commodious. Thus, 14 out of 22, as compared to 5 out of 19, now have either a new house or one remodeled to include many of the conveniences of modern life as they are understood in the community. As things stand now, these typically include a four-room house, one room of which is generally a kitchen-storage combination containing water tap and sink, and an indoor toilet, in contrast to the old outdoor arrangement. In a few cases, the house includes also a bath, which in Franza is still an item of luxury. In many cases the kitchen contains such items as a refrigerator and a gas stove, which are increasingly considered essential to family comfort and social status. Finally, of rising frequency of appearance are the radio and the television set, which in Franza are foremost among the symbols of *modernità* and social importance.

Thus, concomitant with changes in the social position of families of emigrants there have also been increments in the landed property of those families and improvements in the quality

Table 8. Changes in the Dwelling of Group I Families since Base Year, by Social Mobility

Changes in Dwelling	Upwardly Mobile		Others	
	N	%	N	%
New and better dwelling, or remodeling of the old with added rooms or other items, such as indoor toilet and fountain	14	63.6	5	26.3
Improvements without additions, such as repair of walls, floors, and façade.	5	22.7	6	31.6
No change	3	13.6	8	42.1
Total	22	99.9	19	100.0

of their houses. The assumption has been that these factors play a major role in the mode of life that the people of Franza are building for themselves. The value of these factors lies in the fact that they incorporate in clearly visible fashion highly valued symbols of social status. Of particular importance is landed property, which for the peasant signifies a sharp and final rupture of the old link to a feudal system in which he was a serf totally dependent on others for the sustenance of his family. Similarly, the kind of house in which he lives is a gauge of the degree to which he has broken with the habits and discomforts of the old times, when his family shared a one-room hovel with animals and produce. His house is a sign of the commitment he has made to a civilized and modern way of life.

But how was the acquisition of these highly valued items of

culture possible? An answer to this question may be found by showing one final comparison between the achieving and nonachieving families of Group I, concerning the amount of money received from abroad. Although, as has been noted on several occasions, wealth is not in itself always a determinant of high social status, money is almost always a prerequisite to the acquisition of those cultural symbols and behavior patterns upon which high status is based. In the last analysis, when emigration is spoken

TABLE 9. Average Yearly Amount of Money Received from Emigrants by Group I Families, by Social Mobility

Type of Mobility	Amount						No Information		Total	
	$0–500		$501–1000		$1001 +					
	N	%	N	%	N	%	N	%	N	%
Upwardly mobile	—	—	9	41.0	12	54.5	1	4.5	22 *	100.0
Others	4	21.1	12	63.2	1	5.3	2	10.5	19 **	100.1

* Yearly average per family: $1150.
** Yearly average per family: $675.

of as a determinant of social mobility, what is really meant is the capital that the emigrants earn abroad, which is then converted into the appropriate tokens of social importance in Franza. That the money in itself is *not* a sufficient cause of social mobility is evidenced by the persistent social stability of a few of the cases in the sample. Although allegedly among the richest in money derived from abroad, the recipients have not yet invested it in any of the major ways discussed, preferring instead to "keep it safe" in the bank or in postal bonds. As a result, these families are considered avaricious and backward hicks and their status has not measurably changed in recent years.

Table 9 shows that the upwardly mobile families have received significantly larger remittances than the other families. By their own admission, they have received a yearly average of

$1150 per family, compared to a little more than half this amount for the socially less successful families.

For the peasants of Franza, accustomed for centuries to the most abject and pertinacious poverty, anything above a few hundred dollars is a large amount of money. To be sure, as the standard of living rises, money is needed in ever greater quantities, and an income of $1000 to $2000 is no longer considered a fortune. Nevertheless, some families have received from their relatives abroad amounts sufficient to allow them to break the economic basis of their ancient privations. In so doing, they have also undermined the foundations of their equally ancient humiliations.

So far in examining the phenomenon of social mobility, an objective perspective has been taken: mobility has been studied from the vantage point of the observer. The subjective or psychological dimension of this phenomenon is, in principle, totally independent of the objective experience. A person objectively mobile may perceive himself as having been stationary. As Tumin and Feldman point out, an individual objectively defined as upwardly mobile may perceive himself as downwardly mobile under certain circumstances, when, for example, in his aspirations and self-image he has been surpassed by his effective "others" (1957, 283). This discrepancy naturally would have important behavioral consequences, a fact which provides a major rationale for studies of mobility in the first place.

Let us, therefore, look into this question of perceived social mobility. During the interview, each respondent was asked to state whether she thought her family had moved in the local prestige structure in recent years, and, if so, in what direction. Table 10 again brings together all three groups in the sample, organizing information in such a way as to compare perceived mobility with actual mobility as objectively measured by the Key Status Index. The first thing to note is the rather high degree of agreement between the two measures of mobility, indicating in effect that the people of Franza have realistically absorbed the social changes of their community into their personal experiences. To the extent that these experiences have been satisfactory to the self-concept of at least some of the respondents, the finding would seem to constitute a strong indication that the beneficial effects flowing from emigration have been undermining many of the ancient ills earlier attributed to the traditional peasantry of Franza.

We shall return to this crucial point in more detail. For the moment, it is best to continue the discussion of the findings in Table 10. Two are especially deserving of attention. In the first place, among those who have actually been upwardly mobile, there is a slight tendency to understate the degree of their social

TABLE 10. Perceived Mobility of Sample Families, Compared to Actual Mobility

Actual Mobility	Perceived Mobility									
	Upward		None		Downward		Unknown		Total	
	N	%	N	%	N	%	N	%	N	%
Upward	16	64.0	6	24.0	—	—	3	12.0	25	100.0
None	13	14.6	62	69.7	12	13.5	2	2.2	89	100.0
Downward	—	—	4	66.7	2	33.3	—	—	6	100.0

success. Specifically, about one-third either do not perceive themselves as having been upwardly mobile or cannot pass judgment on this question at all. This tendency may be due to the sort of mechanism suggested earlier: that an absolute gain may not in fact be perceived as such when it is compared to the gain of significant others. In the second place, allowing for the fact that the numbers dealt with are very small, those who are in an objective sense downwardly mobile tend to be a little more buoyant than expected, in the sense that, although none of them claim upward mobility, 4 out of 6 feel they have remained stationary. This finding, in turn, is perhaps to be explained by a natural reluctance to concede "backsliding," which is common to people everywhere, as well as by the possibility that their economic condition has improved even if their relative social status has deteriorated.

In discussing the factors underlying social mobility, three

have been singled out as having been of distinct importance: landed property, quality of residence, and money. In view of the concern with psychological dimensions of social mobility, it might now be worthwhile to inquire whether the respondents perceive the factors of mobility in a manner that is congruous with objective findings. Accordingly, Table 11 compares the

TABLE 11. Factors of Social Importance Perceived, by Degree of Contact with Emigrants

| Factors of Social Importance | Degree of Contact with Emigrants | | | | | |
| | I = High | | II = Medium | | III = Low | |
	N	%	N	%	N	%
Money	13	31.7	10	25.0	24	61.5
Property	14	34.1	13	32.5	7	17.9
Secondary or college education in any member of the family	9	22.0	8	20.0	4	10.3
Family name	4	9.8	4	10.0	2	5.1
Other *	1	2.4	5	12.5	2	5.1
Total	41	100.0	40	100.0	39	99.9

* This category includes a variety of factors, such as "good behavior" and "honesty."

three sample groups in terms of the one factor which more than any other is thought to make a family "socially important" in the community. The criteria suggested by the respondents are referred to as "factors of social importance."

The findings show that while Groups I and II tend to emphasize about equally the two factors of money and property, the tendency in Group III is to stress money almost to the exclusion of all other factors. In fact, while Groups I and II even slightly favor the ownership of property over simple and pure money, Group III leans heavily toward the latter, choosing it almost two-thirds of the time. It is interesting to note, however, that taking the sample as a whole, the emphasis falls clearly on the combination of money-property, comprising about 68 percent of the total. No specific reference to housing is found. Instead, mention is made of "a good education" by nearly 18 percent of the sample, and to family lineage by about 8 percent.

In view of the great emphasis on money, it is now necessary to reiterate that what might be termed an intimate acquaintance with a money economy is a relatively recent phenomenon in Franza. Moreover, it has coincided with what appears to the local population as a massive and rapid change in the status structure of the community. Under the circumstances, the great accent on the social value of money is understandable. The focus on wealth is particularly marked in the answers given to the following question: "What would you say are the reasons why families in Franza have gone from a lower category to a higher one since the end of the last war?" Seventy-six respondents, or 63 percent of the total, mentioned specifically "money from emigrants," while 92, or 77 percent, singled out either "money from emigrants" or money in general.

This heavy stress on money is not inconsistent with an earlier statement that it is not money per se that accounts for social mobility but the cultural characteristics which "money can buy." The respondents' emphasis on money comes in the form of an ellipsis. "He who has not is nobody," is their first thought. Asked about the meaning of this saying, they explain that "money makes the blind sing." Pressed further, they then explain that "with money you can buy the important things of life." Evidence of this kind of thinking can be found in the following statement provided by an unusually articulate and imaginative member of Group III:

Give me money, and I shall be as good as the best. I shall send my son to the University of Rome; I shall eat steak every day, and four other dishes besides; I shall get a servant; I shall buy the whole territory of Franza, and I might even build a castle. Money is all I need!

The relatively greater emphasis of Group III members on money can also be easily appreciated. Lacking property, they begin at the beginning, as it were. The situation is a little different within Groups I and II, where property ownership is less uncommon. A token possession of land on their part leads them to be more explicitly aware of its role in the local prestige system. Hence, a small landowner explained:

If I had about 40 or 50 acres of land I should be a great deal more important, and I could buy a lot of the things the family needs.

In concluding this section, the relationship between emigration and social mobility can be briefly summarized in the following way. When emigrants leave their immediate families, a substantial portion of their earnings abroad is sent back to the home community. The remittances are invested in the local economy in the form of property, a better home, and other symbols of prestige, such as better dress and a higher education for the children. The result is a decided improvement in the style of life of the recipients of capital and, consequently, an improved social position in the local prestige structure. As Bernard Barber has put it, in the long run wealth and social position tend to be congruent with one another, for wealth is a most effective means of commanding the social resources necessary to enter into or learn a social role and thereby achieve its associated class position (Barber, 1957, 374).

Mobility among the Old Americani

Before closing this chapter, one other very interesting question should be looked at briefly. In the preceding pages the concern has been with measuring social mobility in relation to emigration. For convenience sake, however, assessment has been limited to changes in the social structure of Franza since the end of World War II, that is, since the beginning of the most recent wave of emigration. As repeatedly noted, however, Franza has been involved in two major waves of emigration, the first reaching a peak around 1913. Furthermore, it has been suggested that as a result of this earlier emigration, many families formerly belonging to the common peasantry are now classified in Stratum III, and a few have even reached Stratum II. It will be fruitful now to look at the consequences of this earlier emigration somewhat more specifically.

In Franza in 1959, a number of families had male heads who had, at one time or another, spent at least five years in the United States. Thirty-four of these families, randomly selected, were

TABLE 12. Social Position of Families of Old Emigrants prior to Emigration and in 1959

	Past		*Present*	
Stratum	N	%	N	%
I	—	—	—	—
II	—	—	2	5.9
III	6	17.6	21	61.8
IV	7	20.6	9	26.5
V	19	55.9	2	5.9
VI	2	5.9	—	—
Total	34	100.0	34	100.1

listed in alphabetical order. The list was given to six of the oldest of the nineteen local judges, who had spent all their lives in the village. The raters were asked to place these families in the present prestige structure and to indicate in each case how many steps each family had moved up or down since its involvement in the old emigration. An attempt was made to project the present stratification system into the past, and to compare the families of old emigrants to themselves at two different points in time on the basis of the single criterion of "general importance." Specifically, the judges were asked (1) to imagine that prior to the old emigration, the prestige structure of the community was similar to the present one, and (2) to classify the same families at both points in time in terms of general importance.

Table 12 shows that, whereas most families of old emigrants "would have occupied" a Stratum V position prior to emigration, at the present, a majority of them fall into Stratum III. The finding is striking. Emigration, or the more specific factors which flow from it, have moved most of these families from what might be called an "upper lower class" to an "upper middle class." This finding strengthens the argument that emigration has been an effective determinant of upward social mobility and structural reorganization in the community.

In conclusion, among the various consequences of emigration for the people of Franza, one is outstanding: many of the emigrants and their families have realized opportunities in their community that until a few decades ago were almost unthinkable. Such achievements have been of profound significance both for the community as a whole and for the achievers themselves. If, in the first case, the traditional social structure has been broadened to make room for a substantial middle class—outstanding among all features of modern society—social achievement has also signified a more resolute social attitude and a greater sense of security on the part of the achievers. To those new characteristics of the changing peasant, the remainder of this book shall be addressed.

❅

REFERENCES

Barber, Bernard. 1957. *Social Stratification.* New York: Harcourt, Brace and Company, Inc.

Davie, Maurice R. 1936. *World Immigration.* New York: The Macmillan Company.

Davis, Kingsley. 1948. *Human Society.* New York: The Macmillan Company.

Hollingshead, August B. 1957. *Two-Factor Index of Social Position.* Mimeographed (copyright by Hollingshead).

Lenski, Gerhard E. 1954. "Status Crystallization: A Non-Vertical Dimension of Social Status," *American Sociological Review,* 19, August.

Lipset, Seymour, and Reinhard Bendix. 1959. *Social Mobility in Industrial Society.* Berkeley: University of California Press.

MacDonald, John S. 1963. "Agricultural Organization, Migration and Labour Militancy in Rural Italy," *The Economic History Review,* XVI, No. 1.

Siegel, Sidney. 1956. *Nonparametric Statistics for the Behavioral Sciences.* New York: McGraw-Hill Book Co., Inc.

Sorokin, Pitirim A. 1959. *Social and Cultural Mobility.* New York: The Free Press of Glencoe.

Tumin, Melvin M., and Arnold S. Feldman. 1957. "Theory and Measurement of Occupational Mobility," *American Sociological Review,* 22, June.

Warner, Lloyd W., *et al.* 1960. *Social Class in America.* New York: Harper and Brothers Torchbooks.

Weber, Max. 1958. In H. H. Gerth and C. Wright Mills, eds., *From Max Weber: Essays in Sociology.* New York: Oxford University Press, Galaxy Books.

VIII CLASS RELATIONS REDEFINED

So far-reaching and complex are the effects of emigration that, as Robert Foerster once stated, "one must despair of following them into their remoter courses." They visibly touch so many aspects of community life that the insidious danger of ignoring the influence of other and independent forces is ever present. Some changes are the direct or indirect results of the permanent or temporary abstraction or diminution of certain groups of the population, while others proceed more directly from the return of the emigrants or from the remittance of their earnings (Foerster, 1919, 445). Still others result from the emigrants' absorption, while abroad, of ideological elements which, though basically foreign to the reality of their own home culture, are suitable to its inevitable assimilation into the changing culture of the industrializing nation. This latter type of emigration effect will engage our interest in this chapter.

Emigration and Ideology

It has been submitted that the peasant of southern Italy emigrates not merely to seek his fortune but also to escape the afflictions of the social relations characteristic of his society, wherein he holds the lowest status. It should not be surprising, therefore, to find the returned emigrants, or their immediate families in the home community, displaying the attitudes of egalitarianism that they experienced in the host societies, the English-speaking countries in particular.

The cultural conditions that surround an individual while abroad have a pronounced effect upon his innovative potential and upon the potential of the group to which he belongs. That effect is magnified by the "deprivation of essentials," that is, of those things that "a person believes he has the right to expect," which is in itself a powerful incentive to cultural change (Barnett, 1953, 80). Such deprivation keeps the individual in a continuous state of anticipation; innovation naturally flourishes in such an atmosphere. The effect of anticipation on cultural change is, in turn, a function of numbers. The greater the number of people desiring change, the greater the certainty that new ideas will appear (Barnett, 1953, 56). As Sorokin aptly puts it, whether a culture object or value catches on "depends upon the demand" (Sorokin, 1959, 620). Finally, the effectiveness of emigrants as agents of change in their home community can be said to depend, at least in part, upon their own numbers (Barnett, 1953, 302).

Given the large volume of emigrants from Franza, unless personal contacts have been very brief and superficial, foreign experiences may be expected to produce important changes in the tastes, the ideological orientation, and the social attitudes of their families. The changes produce the psychological thrust required to consolidate their materially derived achievements in the prestige structure of their community.

That attitudes acquired by the emigrants abroad actually crop out and introduce new elements into the life of their village groups has been found in various societies (Thomas and Znaniecki, 1927; Kulp, 1925). Writing early in this century, Emily Balch reported that in Croatia she was often asked why it was that returned emigrants refused to take off their hats to, or display deference toward, those who had traditionally been their social superiors. Such behavior, while scandalizing some—the traditional superiors in particular—was admired by many others (Balch, 1910, 61).

The Mediterranean Basin has provided particularly strong evidence of this type of change. Writing about Greek returnees, the historian Saloutos observes:

One important influence was the spirit of progress that animated returning Greek-Americans. It was evidenced by the innovations attempted by the repatriate, the construction of new homes, the purchases of land, and the provisions he made for his family. This spirit was contagious and soon affected . . . even those who had never been to the United States, breeding in them a spirit of discontent (Saloutos, 1956, 123).

In relation to the Italian peninsula itself, Foerster argued early in this century that returned emigrants manifested a certain self-assurance, a challenging disposition, even a sort of vainglory, which contrasted sharply with their former servility. This attitude had, among its many consequences, one of "epochal value," namely, a more resolute attitude toward traditional superiors (Foerster, 1919, 459).

"Why can't the Italians, who practically live with the pope, behave like good Christians, as the Americans do?" an emigrant once complained aboard ship while returning to Canada after a brief visit to his family in the Abruzzi. So powerful an influence does a returnee's identification with his host society have on his own people, that a few years ago the novelist Carlo Levi was led to comment in reference to the people of a rural village in southern Italy:

. . . what never failed to strike me most of all—and by now I had been in almost every house—were the eyes of the two inseparable guardian angels that looked at me from the wall over the bed. On one side was the black, scowling face, with its large, inhuman eyes, of the Madonna of Viggiano; on the other a colored print of the sparkling eyes, behind gleaming glasses, and the hearty grin of President Roosevelt. I never saw other pictures or images than these: not the King nor the Duce, nor even Garibaldi; no famous Italian of any kind, nor any one of the appropriate saints; only Roosevelt and the Madonna of Viggiano never failed to be present. . . . Yes, New York, rather than Rome or Naples, would be the real capital of the peasants of Lucania, if these men without a country could have a capital at all (Levi, 1947, 122–123).

From Montegrano, Banfield reports that, according to the Communist tailor, "When America occupied Italy, she should have stayed. It would have been much better for us" (Banfield, 1958, 23).

In Franza it has often been said that "America should have made another of its states out of Italy. She would have cleaned up the mess here." And echoing almost verbatim a statement made about the people of the United States by de Tocqueville (in Heffner, 1956, 26) over a century and a quarter ago, a Franzino, until yesterday a "humble and ignorant" peasant, said that "nothing struck me more forcibly than the lack of distinctions among the people in Toronto."

The people of Franza are keenly sensitive to social distinctions and to the possibility of lifting their status to a more respectable level. When asked why they emigrate, they readily offer three major reasons: (1) to find bread and work, (2) to be able to buy a plot of land, and (3) to get "to be somebody." As Vincelli notes in his study of a southern Italian community not very unlike Franza, the emigrant has had a goal to reach at all costs, namely, that of improving his social position (Vincelli, 1958, 234).

Are returned emigrants aware of the social changes now occurring in their home town? And are they, further, aware of themselves as the agents of such changes? A positive reply to such questions will strengthen the argument concerning the relationship between emigration and social change.

Between December, 1958, and July, 1964, during which period repeated visits were made to Franza, at least 75 emigrants returned to the community from abroad. Most came to spend

Christmas or Easter with their families, and then returned to their places of work early in the summer. Most of them had been absent from the village from four to seven years; this was their first return home since their initial departure. The vast majority returned from Canada, Australia, or some other English-speaking country. Many of these returnees were interviewed, for a three-fold purpose: (1) to determine their perception of the changes developed in Franza since their departure, (2) to establish their view of the causes of those changes, and (3) to learn whether they specifically perceived themselves as agents of those innovations.

Taking the last of the above three points first, it was found that returnees invariably thought of themselves as the vehicles of social change. The tendency was to consider themselves as bearers of modern culture, showing to their families, relatives, and friends "right ways" of doing things, ranging from "the correct way of playing poker" to the right way of "giving a greeting if one is received."

As to the second question, the returnees were in almost perfect agreement in their claim that emigration was *the only* cause of change in the community. One returnee forcefully stated the matter as follows:

If you put a couple of armed policemen just outside the village to see to it that not a single dollar would come in, within six months the people would start eating each other up, and eventually the population would starve to death. . . . It might even be that out of spite the Italian government would throw us to the lions, for how could we pay taxes without money from America? . . . And it's not just a question of money. The people in this village are dead. They still have ideas from the Dark Ages. The worst ones are all these professori and students. They don't know a blessed thing about the modern world. They are like a dried-up fig tree.

Finally, the repatriates feel that the principal type of change is economic in nature, manifesting itself in a variety of ways, but most dramatically in the people's diet. The people of Franza have an almost obsessive preoccupation with eating, nearly as if they were intent on canceling out with a single meal all the pangs of centuries of hunger. "The biggest and best thing that has happened here," a returnee said accordingly, "is that now we can eat, and be fussy about what we eat."

After the economic changes were mentioned changes in *civiltà*—a wide array of things, including dressing in city clothes, sedate and calm play or conversation, an ability and willingness to consume ready-made goods, an appreciation of the value of higher education as reflected in the sending of children to the higher grades of school, and above all the ability to "feel equal to anyone else and to respect those who respect you." Consequently, next to seeing themselves as a source of capital, the returnees consider themselves propagators of civiltà, at the heart of which lies the value that "everyone is equal."

Attitudes of Egalitarianism

This finding and the various other considerations made so far in this chapter have led to the formulation of the hypothesis that *attitudes of egalitarianism in the sending community vary directly with contact with emigrants.*

The data required for a test of this hypothesis were obtained in the following manner. When the formal interview schedule was still in the exploratory stage, a handful of individuals belonging to the "better families" in Franza were interviewed in order to determine their perception of recent changes in the local status structure, as well as their reactions to those developments. The information received from such persons revealed two basic themes, the nature of which is given by the following two quotations: (1) "Too many people nowadays are presumptuous enough to expect even the doctor to address them formally." (2) "Too many have lost respect for the good families which once gave them bread and work."

These two themes provided the basis for two apposite questions later included in the interview of the 120 respondents. Table 13 shows the distribution of responses to the following question suggested by the first of the above remarks: "Do you think it is right if an important person your age or younger addresses you informally while he expects you to address him formally?" The answers to this question shall be considered as a measure of acceptance of the traditional custom of deference.

The findings show that those who are in closest contact with emigrants are least likely to accept the traditional custom according to which an upper-stratum person, such as a doctor, may address with *tu* (the personal pronoun grammatically appropriate with close relatives of the same age, with friends, and with children and animals) a person in a lower stratum, even though the latter may be 50 years his senior. Only nine out of 41 in Group I

TABLE 13. Acceptance of the Traditional Custom of Deference to Individuals, by Degree of Contact with Emigrants

Degree of Contact with Emigrants	Acceptance							
	Yes		Uncertain		No		Total	
	N	%	N	%	N	%	N	%
I = High	9	22.0	5	12.2	27	65.9	41	100.1
II = Medium	19	47.5	11	27.5	10	25.0	40	100.0
III = Low	22	56.4	6	15.4	11	28.2	39	100.0

manifest a deferential inclination, while 27, or two-thirds of the total, show a definite egalitarian tendency. By contrast, a total of 41 persons, or almost 52 percent of the combined Groups II and III, accept the traditional custom of deference, while only 21, or less than 27 percent, repudiate it.

What is even more interesting is that persons in Group I who repudiate this custom very frequently go on to explain that "In America everyone is a mister, and all give each other the *voi* [you]; only in Italy some people think that Christians [1] are animals." This frequent reference to "America" as a place where

---

[1] Among the people of Franza, the word "Christian" is often used as a synonym for "human being."

"Christians are more humane and just" lends weight to the hypothesized role of emigration in the erosion of the custom in question. In attacking local practices of servility, Franzini draw courage and justification from what they conceive to be "just" practices in "America." A more detailed examination of their answers shows, further, that it is precisely those who object to the custom of deference who are also apt to go further and inveigh against it and the "Italian buffoons." The finding would indicate that it is unlikely that peasants are characterized by an "authoritarian personality," as is sometimes argued, and that as such they feel satisfaction in being dominated by superiors (Hagen, 1962, 71–85). In any case, if that curious interpretation of peasant psychology is correct, the need for submission is quickly lost as a result of contact with an urban culture.

But why are individuals in Groups II and III still highly obsequious? On the basis of the general argument that a new wind of change is sweeping the countryside of southern Italy, the inclination is to expect a lower deferential tendency than here displayed on the part of persons in these two groups. It should be noted, however, that these people remain in many respects dependent upon the services and favors that locally important persons can still provide. Possibly, lacking economic vitality as well as the moral support of the egalitarian "Americans," these individuals continue to find it at least convenient to defer to their traditional superiors. In other words, it is economic autonomy coupled with a greater tendency on the part of "the new Americani" to appraise the local situation through the perspective of "America" that determines the difference between this group and the other two, yielding in it that psychological thrust required to undermine one of the oldest and most deeply entrenched practices of interclass relations in southern Italy.

Nevertheless, the findings do not preclude the possibility that deference to one particular individual is considered proper and just because of reasons not directly related to attitudes of egalitarianism. An especially high intelligence or some particular achievement by an individual, whatever his class position, may be the factor. This type of "respectfulness" might then be more evident in the membership of Groups II and III, due to the possibility that women in Group I, given the eye-opening experiences of having their men abroad, now overreact to any manifestation of deference at home. In the long run, therefore, the interest is in the acceptance or rejection of the custom of deference in relation to groups rather than individuals. This response will give a more direct expression of interclass relations.

Table 14 now shows the distribution of respondents on the

TABLE 14. Acceptance of the Traditional Custom of Deference to Families, by Degree of Contact with Emigrants

Degree of Contact with Emigrants	Acceptance							
	Yes		Uncertain		No		Total	
	N	%	N	%	N	%	N	%
I = High	11	26.8	4	9.8	26	63.4	41	100.0
II = Medium	19	47.5	8	20.0	13	32.5	40	100.0
III = Low	15	38.5	15	38.5	9	23.1	39	100.1

basis of their answers to the following question suggested by the second of the two above remarks obtained from members of "better families": "Some people claim that certain families in Franza are socially superior to others and should, therefore, be treated with deference. Do you agree with this?" Those most closely involved in the phenomenon of emigration continue to differ markedly from the others in their greater tendency to denounce the local practice of deference. Nearly two-thirds express what is considered egalitarianism, while only about 27 percent consider deferential behavior appropriate. By contrast, taking Groups II and III together, only a little more than one-fourth renounce the custom of deference, and more than two-fifths view it as suitable.

It is interesting to note, however, that where the members of Group I by and large express themselves in yes-or-no terms, only one in ten being unable to take a definite stand either way, the number of uncertainties increases greatly as Group III is approached. This finding seems to support an earlier suggestion. Although the attitude of egalitarianism is becoming general throughout the community, it may still be in a stage of vacillation. This is true among those who, due to their lesser contact with urban culture, do not yet possess an adequate reference point on which to rely for support in possible attempts to sever ties with more traditional behavior patterns.

Evidence in support of the hypothesis that attitudes of egalitarianism in the sending community vary directly with contact with emigrants is now quite substantial. Nevertheless, the findings cannot yet be accepted as conclusive. The three groups are not equally distributed in the stratification system. Indeed, as we move from Group I to Group III, the distribution of families tends to concentrate more and more in the lower strata. Are the present valuational differences among the three groups related to present social position? And again, are valuational changes not changes at all, in the sense that differences existing today among the three groups already existed in the base year? In other words, did people in Group I hold more egalitarian attitudes already in the base year? I shall try to answer this latter question first. The problem involved is complex; nevertheless, some insights may be gained by making the following considerations.

Prior to the recent wave of emigration, after World War II, the people of Franza had had three major contacts with the outside world in recent decades, one provided by the first wave of emigration and two others produced by the two World Wars. All such contacts were mediated by the men of the community, for women, who alone are included in the sample, neither went to war, nor migrated, except in rare cases. As a result, it is reasonable to assume that whatever differences in egalitarianism may have existed in the past among the respondents could probably be traced to the male members of their immediate families.

Recall that in drawing the sample, an attempt was made to separate contact provided by the old wave of emigration. At that time, families were excluded from the sample if either or both spouses could claim one or more close relatives (father, mother, spouse, child, sibling) in the old emigration. Hence, influence from the earlier emigration can be omitted from the present consideration. The task remains of taking into account contacts produced by the two World Wars. In this connection, let us assume that differential experiences in war and, more specifically, varying types of contact provided by military service in Italian cities and by internship in prisoners' camps, might indicate significant differences, with respect to the variable now being measured, prior to involvement in emigration.

The participation of Franza males in World War II is especially worthy of consideration. That conflict scattered them far and wide, and some, more than others, came in contact with

TABLE 15. Localities of Service of Respondents' Male Relatives Who Took Part in World War II, by Respondents' Degree of Contact with Emigrants

Degree of Contact with Emigrants	Locale													
	South Italy		North Italy		Italian Empire		Europe, Except England		British Empire		Other Anglo-Saxon Areas		Other		Total	
	N	%	N	%	N	%	N	%	N	%	N	%	N	%	N	%
I = High	4	8.2	7	14.3	11	22.4	9	18.4	13	26.5	3	6.1	2	4.1	49	1.000
II = Medium	5	9.4	6	11.3	16	30.2	7	13.2	17	32.1	—	—	2	3.8	53	100.0
III = Low	8	14.0	9	15.8	9	15.8	13	22.8	11	19.3	2	3.5	5	8.8	57	100.0

values at variance with those existing in the home community and capable of weakening the grip of the latter.

Table 15 shows the localities in which the male relatives of the 120 sample respondents served during the period of World War II. In this table, each respondent is credited with all close relatives (father, son, brother, husband) who were in the military service during that time. If, for instance, a given respondent had a husband, two brothers, and one son serving in the War, she is credited in the table with four relatives. This procedure is followed for each person in each group without any attempt to eliminate duplications, and to each claimed relative is attributed the locality in which he stayed the longest period of time.

The data show that the three groups in the sample do not differ significantly with respect to external contact due to military service. The respondents declared a total of 159 relatives in the military service during World War II. Of these, 120, or three-quarters, spent more of their service out of Italy than in Italy itself, and 46, or 29 percent of the total, had been prisoners of war in the English-speaking world. The numbers, however, are rather evenly distributed among the three groups. It can be concluded, therefore, that if this type of contact brought about any valuational changes, it very probably did not operate differentially on the three groups constituting the sample.

The other question raised above remains, concerning the possibility that differences in obsequiousness among the three groups may be associated with differences in present stratum position. To inquire into this possibility, we must return to the question dealt with in Table 14 and reorganize the responses by holding stratum position constant. When this is done, the differences among the three groups in their acceptance of the traditional custom of deference are markedly reduced. Individuals within each social stratum tend to give similar responses to the question regardless of their degree of contact with emigrants. This finding would force rejection of the hypothesis to the effect that attitudes of egalitarianism in the sending community vary directly with contact with emigrants. Additional data, however, prevent complete rejection of the hypothesis, although they may lead to its modification.

These data concern that special group of peasants known as the massari. These peasants almost invariably accepted the traditional custom of deference both to "important persons" and to "better families," regardless of degree of contact with emigrants. It will be recalled that the massari have occupied a special status within the local peasantry. They have been considered by many, and have thought of themselves, as being a special and "better" group, holding greater prestige than common peasants and per-

haps even greater than the artisans. Not only have they traditionally been a category of relatively well-to-do peasants, but, as has
been pointed out, they also provided the personnel for the local
gentry until the first wave of emigration shifted the control of
education into the hands of the early emigrants. As a result, the
massari still hold a special view of the economic and social
changes now going on in their community.

Those massari who have gone abroad have no doubt reaped
some benefits, but only in an absolute sense. Many common
peasants who only a little more than a decade ago were "nobod-
ies," are now climbing close to them, and a few have even
overtaken them. The thought must occur to the massari that for
other peasants, emigration represents a net gain, for they are now
rising in the local social ladder without the preoccupation of
being overtaken by those who once were their "inferiors." Not so
with the massari. They, too, stand to profit from emigration, but
in a largely economic sense, for their prestige as members of the
peasantry was already high. For them, emigration is both a bless-
ing and a curse. They see themselves rising somewhat above their
old friends and their own close relatives who have not been
involved in emigration, but at the same time, in some cases at least,
they also see themselves overtaken by those to whom, as they like
to put it, they once gave "bread and work."

The experiences abroad of several massari have also been less
favorable than those of most other peasants. As is well known,
southern Italian migrants typically engage in what has been
termed "chain migration." A few pioneers soon make it possible
for their friends and relatives to follow. These, in turn, do likewise, with the result that not infrequently a southern Italian
village gives rise abroad to a kind of replica of itself, where many
of the old traditions and practices are maintained. Naturally, the
people inhabiting these "little Italies" or "little Franzas" frequently work in the same place.

The Australian or Canadian employer knows nothing of the
fine distinctions in social honor drawn in the old country between
the massaro and the common peasant. Or if he does, he probably
could not care less. When the occasion arises for him to single out

from within the work group someone to take on supervisory or mediatory tasks, the employer will be guided by rational considerations. Because the massari are on the whole more tradition-bound and therefore more likely to view their stay abroad as strictly temporary, they also tend to be less acculturated to the host society, particularly in matters that require linguistic proficiency. The employer's choice, therefore, almost invariably excludes the massaro, with the result that the latter is sometimes compelled to work under the direct supervision of one who, only a few years previously, was his tenant or a hired hand on his farm. Naturally, such an arrangement causes distress in the self-image of the massaro, a discomfort that he carries back to the old community or conveys by letter to his family. Little wonder that back in his own milieu, where the massaro still holds a special status, he appears to make a special effort to reestablish the old status equilibrium. In an attempt to safeguard his old superior position, the massaro, therefore, insists on the validity of the traditional practice of superordination-subordination, relating him advantageously to the common peasant. One respondent put the matter bluntly: "Thank God: before my husband went to Australia, we always had enough bread to eat, and a lot of respect. Many others had neither the one nor the other. Now they already think they are like you."

That the massari are basically antiegalitarian can be plainly demonstrated. In fact, when the massari are excluded from the entire sample, the remaining respondents are found to differ significantly, and in the direction originally hypothesized, in their acceptance of the custom of deference. In other words, when the massari are excluded from the analysis, contact with emigrants continues to vary directly with egalitarianism even when stratum position is held constant. It may be concluded tentatively, therefore, that social position is not related to deferential behavior, but such a conclusion requires modification of the original hypothesis to read as follows: The greater the degree of contact with emigrants the lower the probability that an inferior social status in self-comparison with "traditional superiors" will be accepted, *provided*, however, that denial of an inferior social status in relation to traditional superiors does not at the same time erase one's own social superiority in relation to "traditional inferiors." In short, it would seem that people would rather be superior to some and inferior to others than equal to all.

This qualification in the basic hypothesis is based on the behavior of the massari, but the argument should not be construed to suggest that these are the only people in Franza who display a measure of antiegalitarianism. The massari were merely more evident in their display. As a matter of fact, there is reason to believe that, in varying degrees, this same phenomenon is characteristic of all classes of people everywhere. The deepest and undoubtedly the most obvious need of most Franzini is an improvement of both their economic and their social positions. But an urge to improve one's social position, even when accompanied by resentment against social superiors, does not necessarily constitute "egalitarianism," although conceivably it may foster it. On the contrary, it may be that when the desire to improve one's social position is very strong, there is also a strong tendency to desire asymmetry in social relations. Indeed, it is likely that the urge to improve one's social position increases with the commitment to a system of social inequalities. Resentment against the possessors of privilege is not necessarily broadened into resentment against privilege itself. In her study of status orientations among shipyard workers, Archibald found that, much as the worker complained against the surfeit of the rich, so far as the worker "entertained the hope that through a lucky shift in circumstance he too might some day live in the mansions of the mighty and eat his food from the finest Dresden plates, thus far was he discouraged from any consistent or basic criticism of the social hierarchy . . ." (in Bendix and Lipset, 1953, 401).

If the country-club set were abolished, as Kahl puts it, "how could anyone have the fun of maneuvering to get accepted as a member?" (1953, 160). The sentiment that is very inappropriately named *equality*, Pareto argues, sometimes appears to be so fresh and strong precisely because it is not, in fact, a sentiment of equality. It is rather the reflection of the direct interests of individuals who are bent on escaping certain inequalities not in their favor, while setting up new discrepancies which will be to their advantage (1935, Sec. 1227). People everywhere agitate for equality to get equality in general, but then go on to make "countless numbers of distinctions to deny it in the particular. Equality is to belong to all—but it is granted only to the few" (Pareto, 1935, Sec. 1222).

In this chapter, an attempt has been made to determine the extent to which the cultural conditions experienced abroad by migrants from Franza have produced attitudes of egalitarianism among their families in the home community. By and large, to this question an affirmative answer is possible. Egalitarianism, however, must be understood in a special sense, namely, as the desire of the previous inferiors to become the equals of, and where possible, even the superiors of their previous superiors. The people of Franza, like people everywhere, are interested more in equality for themselves, in relation to those who are worthy of emulation, than in equality in general. True equality would amount for many to a reduction of their own social status relative to many others. Most human beings plainly cannot tolerate this type of loss. Nevertheless, a critical link in the ancient chain of powerlessness and almost bovine docility has been broken. The event is of great significance. It promises a future in which domination is lifted from the individual, and human energies are directed to the satisfaction of growing wants rather than to the prevention of encroachments on the most basic needs. Such a future might also be less fraught with social tensions and more conducive to mutual trust and beneficial collaboration.

REFERENCES

Archibald, Katherine. 1953. "Status Orientations among Shipyard Workers," in Reinhard Bendix and Seymour M. Lipset, eds., *Class, Status and Power*. Glencoe, Ill.: The Free Press.

Balch, Emily G. 1910. *Our Slavic Fellow Citizens*. New York: Charities Publication Committee.

Banfield, Edward C. 1958. *The Moral Basis of a Backward Society.* Glencoe, Ill.: The Free Press.

Barnett, H. G. 1953. *Innovation.* New York: McGraw-Hill Book Company.

de Tocqueville, Alexis. 1956. In Richard D. Heffner, ed., *Democracy in America.* New York: Mentor Books.

Foerster, Robert F. 1919. *The Italian Emigration of Our Times.* Cambridge: Harvard University Press.

Hagen, Everett E. 1962. *On the Theory of Social Change.* Homewood, Ill.: The Dorsey Press.

Kahl, Joseph A. 1953. *The American Class Structure.* New York: Rinehart & Company, Inc.

Kulp, Daniel H., II. 1925. *Country Life in South China.* New York: Columbia University Publications, Teachers College.

Levi, Carlo. 1947. *Christ Stopped at Eboli.* New York: Farrar, Straus & Co.

Pareto, Vilfredo. 1935. *The Mind and Society.* New York: Harcourt, Brace and Company, Inc.

Saloutos, Theodore. 1956. *They Remember America.* Berkeley: University of California Press.

Sorokin, Pitirim A. 1959. *Social and Cultural Mobility.* New York: The Free Press of Glencoe.

Thomas, William I., and Florian Znaniecki. 1927. *The Polish Peasant in Europe and America.* New York: Alfred A. Knopf.

Vincelli, Guido. 1958. *Una Comunità Meridionale.* Torino: Casa Editrice Taylor.

✱ IX DISPERAZIONE ON THE WANE

The time has come for pulling ideas together and concluding the argument. Let us first summarize briefly. Chapter I examined briefly, in an historical perspective, some of the major factors that were likely to have produced the conditions of economic poverty, social disorder, and personal despair traditionally observed in southern Italian society in general and among the southern peasantry in particular.

In the next three chapters, those conditions were described in some detail, with particular attention to "the natural poverty" of the region, the lowly social status of the peasant, the conflict-ridden nature of his interpersonal relations, the precariousness of his economy, and his dissatisfaction with his society and his lot—all characteristics, it was suggested, of traditional peasants everywhere. Although those unfortunate conditions have been altered by the far-reaching changes of recent decades, we saw that the past of the region is still deeply impressed upon the life

243

style of the people, with at least part of the peasantry still living very much in that past.

In Part Two, attention was turned to the effects of migration from the South in relation to some of the problems singled out in Part One. To accomplish this task more conveniently, examination was centered on a single southern community, rather than the South as a whole. The community was described in Chapter V, and its stratification system discussed in Chapter VI. In Chapter VII, it was found that the families intimately involved in emigration have recently been far more successful than other families in raising their status within the local prestige structure. Moreover, we saw that the social structure of the turn of the present century has undergone a systemic alteration, the two waves of emigration having resulted in the emergence of at least two new middle strata.

Finally, in Chapter VIII, it was noted that the social mobility of families of emigrants has been accompanied by an extraordinary change in the traditional pattern of interclass relations. Evidence indicated that economic and social meliorations have been reinforced by sentiments and ideologies acquired abroad, giving rise, among those closely related to emigrants, to a firmer attitude toward their traditional social superiors, a condition that was termed "egalitarianism."

To conclude, the changes effected by emigration in another important aspect of the peasant's experience, namely, that pitiable state of mind known as "disperazione" or "miseria," will be discussed. There is, as noted before, evidence to show that this phenomenon, still lingering today, was until very recent times widespread among the southern Italian peasantry.

Disperazione Defined

In general, disperazione or miseria implies a deep sense of poverty and insecurity, coupled with an extreme fear of, and feelings of hopelessness about, the future. A petty landowner puts it as follows:

Life here is a perpetual calvary. There is no hope for most of us; that's why so many are leaving the farm to go to America or to the city; that's the only salvation. Today you think you are going to have at least enough to eat, and all of a sudden something happens. Someone steals your donkey—or God takes him away; a child becomes ill; your wheat doesn't get that last needed drop of rain; a daughter needs a dowry for her marriage. There is always something that keeps you down and in desperate circumstances. Sometimes a poor Christian is afraid even to live.

La miseria is described by Banfield in terms of "chronic melancholy" (Banfield, 1958, 63–67), involving hard physical labor, patched rags, a diet that often consists exclusively of bread, and also "worry." Says Banfield:

Having no savings, he must always dread what is likely to happen. What for others are misfortunes are for him calamities. When their hog strangled on its tether, a laborer and his wife were desolate. The woman tore her hair and beat her head against a wall while the husband sat mute and stricken in a corner. The loss of the hog meant they would have no meat that winter, no grease to spread on bread, nothing to sell for cash to pay taxes, and no possibility of acquiring a pig the next spring. Such blows may fall at any time. Fields may be washed away in a flood. Hail may beat down the wheat. Illness may strike. To be a peasant is to stand helpless before these possibilities (Banfield, 1958, 64).

For Banfield, the state of miseria is not an inevitable by-product of natural poverty. It arises from a combination of social and psychological as well as physiological deprivations. Above all, it is a phenomenon closely linked to the southern Italian's inability to engage in cooperative undertakings outside of his narrow family circle. The peasants of Montegrano are "amoral familists." They lack the ability to engage in collective ventures, and their "ethos" breeds a number of basic misfortunes, such as extreme poverty, public corruption, widespread distrust, and general pessimism.

It is not possible to agree with Banfield's explanation. On the whole, he fails to take into account what has for some time been known as "the southern question." His analysis is essentially ahistorical, which is to say that he is too quick to still his etiology on what are in reality the results or symptoms of a much more complex and deep-rooted set of facts. We can, however, agree essentially with Banfield's mere description of the facts, though only to the extent that it is meant to apply to the most impoverished section of the peasantry rather than to the category as a whole.[1]

A Sense of Economic Security

What effect has emigration had on the traditional disperazione or miseria of those implicated in that phenomenon in Franza? Although the state of miseria is not purely economic, the economic undercurrent is a crucial aspect of the larger syndrome, and we shall find it fruitful to pursue inquiry on an economic level.

THE PRESENT

We have already seen in a previous context that those who have left the village in search of more dynamic markets have earned considerable sums of money, which in turn have greatly improved the style of life of their families in the old community. The emigrants and their families themselves are quite aware of this fact. Thus, to the question, "All things considered, do you feel that you are today economically better off than you were 10 years ago?" the members of Group I respond almost in unison,

---

[1] Although Banfield claims to have interviewed seventy persons, "most of them peasants," nowhere in the book are these seventy persons treated as a sample. The burden of his argument falls on the evidence provided by several individuals from the particularly impoverished class of laborers and farmhands. This serious problem arises because Banfield felt that "It was not practical to employ sophisticated sampling techniques. (To have done so would have left no time for interviewing)" (Banfield, 1958, 10). I find it difficult to appreciate this argument. Personal experience in communities analogous to Montegrano indicates that the application of sampling techniques does not impose an intolerable burden on the research enterprise. On the contrary, it contributes to the efficient use of research time.

and without reservation, that they have experienced significant economic improvement. On the other hand, most members of both Groups II and III state that they have experienced no noteworthy changes, while only a few admit without reservation to an economic amelioration.

These findings are in themselves remarkable. Nevertheless, in terms of interest in the often mentioned phenomenon of miseria, it must be appreciated that to admit that things have been going better is one thing; to have arrived at a feeling of security today is quite another. It is necessary, therefore, to take a further step in the analysis. Table 16 organizes the answers to the following question posed to the 120 Franzini: "If things continue as they are at the present, would you say that you are economically secure?"

TABLE 16. Perceived Economic Security, by Degree of Contact with Emigrants

Degree of Contact with Emigrants	Perceived Security											
	Yes		Yes Qualified		Un- certain		No Quali- fied		No		Total	
	N	%	N	%	N	%	N	%	N	%	N	%
I	28	68.3	6	14.6	2	4.9	2	4.9	3	7.3	41	100.0
II	7	17.5	9	22.5	4	10.0	2	5.0	18	45.0	40	100.0
III	4	10.5	11	28.9	1	2.6	3	7.9	19	50.0	38 *	99.9

* One "no answer" excluded.

The findings in this table clearly show that, while the people represented in Groups II and III are still apt to manifest the penurious feelings and the worry characteristic of a pertinacious miseria, the group of "Americani" are generally freed of such feelings. The economic improvements experienced since their implication in emigration have apparently been translated into a comfortable sense of security. These findings are all the more remarkable if we consider the fact that in many cases the members of Groups I and II are blood relatives who until a few years ago shared a basically identical style of life. The following remark by a particularly reflective and articulate woman provides outstanding evidence of the beneficial effects of emigration:

Let's praise the Lord. Well, what do we lack? We need no longer worry. The only sacrifice is my husband's distance. But, God willing, he will work only a couple of more years, and then he will come home and rest his bones. Years ago, I used to say: "Peppi [Joseph—her husband], how are we going to make something for the child? Time flies and soon she will be of age to marry. If God only guarded our little pig for five or six years!" My heart was always under a stone. Today the girl is married, thanks to America, and even if my husband returned now, we wouldn't have to worry about the future. Sometimes I have such a light heart that I feel like singing. [I interject: "Didn't you ever sing before?"] Well, you should know. In order to sing in this mudhole, you have to be either happy or unbalanced. In the old days I knew very few who were happy in Franza.

A people who sings is a happy people—so at least the fortunate Franzini think. Until recently, however, despite the widespread image of southern Italians, they did not sing. In answering the question, another respondent reminisced as follows:

It's almost like living in a dream; I can't even believe that we are the same people who used to struggle in the mud. The difference between the past and the present is like Hell and Heaven. Blessed be the angels! We now have a nice house; we have a piece of land of our own; and modestly speaking, we also have a little money put away. May God bless Canada!

"The thought of what we had to go through until a few years ago," still another respondent informed, "*m'accuppa 'u cori*" (". . . encases and compresses my heart"). Their hearts are now free. This achievement is of the first magnitude and is one, it should be added, that is not always adequately appreciated by students of the Italian South.

For instance, in discussing the transformation of the agricultural South, even as profound a scholar of that region as Rossi Doria speaks of emigration as a revolution, but a "revolution without fruit." To be sure, he sees some beneficial effects of emigration. For instance, he notes that more land now belongs to the peasants. But the change has not been sufficient, according to him, to substantially alter the fortunes of those who own it, or to quench once and for all their land hunger. Rossi Doria argues that peasants have often sold everything they owned in order to go abroad, where they undergo tremendous sacrifices, without a house or a family, "with hardly anything human" for a number of years, only to return with all their savings and buy a very small plot of land, "thereby enclosing themselves within the small circle of the ancient miseria" (Rossi Doria, 1955, 142–143).

A brilliant and compassionate observer of the Italian South, Rossi Doria is understandably interested in bringing about fundamental transformation in the region. Nevertheless, the note of skepticism in his analysis of the effects of emigration on "the ancient miseria" may be totally unwarranted. To be sure, in Franza, not all returned emigrants or the families of those still abroad have freed themselves of that wretched state of being and mind. But many have done so.

It might be added that in anything other than the most minute and intensive analysis of the effects of emigration, it is quite unlikely that findings would be unearthed that reveal any major changes from the traditional past in the mode of peasant life. After all, the agricultural people of southern Italy still possess, or merely cultivate, tracts of land that by modern standards are pitifully small. They still live in houses that, though sometimes embellished by urban middle-class appliances, remain more like caves with at best a hint of a "civilized" future that is too slow coming. And—to touch on one more aspect—they still manifest what must appear, to anyone completely caught up in the stream of urban-industrial civilization, as a mentality that is basically "feudal," confined, and "retrograde." In short, they are still peasants, recognizable kin and descendants of the troglodytes and serfs of scarcely 100 years ago.

Appearances from a distant perspective are misleading, however. The fact remains that there are more landowners today as a result of emigration. And, however tiny his holding may be, to the peasant himself it is much worse to be both totally impoverished and completely dependent on the wealth of others for his livelihood than to be poor but his own master. The peasants are acutely sensitive on this point and to differences in their midst in the quality of dwellings, diet, over-all style of life, and general mentality. In short, a close scrutiny of their life situation from within reveals that there are "kings in their midst." Things are changing in locally very significant ways, and emigration has a major responsibility for these changes.

The current transformation, of course, runs the risk of being seriously hindered, if not arrested, unless national and regional conditions complement and enhance the newly emerging economic and psychological vigor. There is every indication, however, that those conditions are slowly but surely being built into the affairs of southern Italian society. To this extent, the endogenously induced changes and those exogenously derived effectively complement one another, and emigration may thus be viewed as a powerful instrument of the envisioned process of economic and cultural rapprochement between the poor, isolated peasant community and the national society. This latent function of emigration serves well a basic aim of present-day Italian society.

The importance of emigration extends beyond the beneficial effects accruing to those directly affected by it. Those in Groups II and III who also claimed a greater sense of economic security today most frequently referred to indirect consequences of emigration, such as the fact that as a result of numerous departures, work has now become both plentiful and more lucrative. A contented respondent from Group III, who preferred to give a general and objective, rather than personal, account of the situation, explained as follows:

Now that so many people have gone to all these Americas, there is plenty of land to work almost for the asking. As for the artisans, they are so few nowadays that you must beg them even to make a coffin when you need it.

It may be seen, therefore, that emigration has not merely helped those who are directly implicated in it; by taking a large number of persons away from the community, it has also resulted in a redistribution of the locally existing resources by which those remaining in the village have increased the size of their previous shares.

THE FUTURE

The beneficial effects of emigration are all the more remarkable when it is seen that they instill in the people, especially those

TABLE 17. Respondents' Confidence That They "Will Be Better Off 5 or 10 Years Hence," by Degree of Contact with Emigrants

| Degree of Contact with Emigrants | Confidence in the Future | | | | | | | | | | |
| | Yes | | Yes Qualified | | Uncertain | | No Qualified | | No | | Total | |
	N	%	N	%	N	%	N	%	N	%	N	%
I	13	31.7	8	19.5	9	22.0	5	12.2	6	14.6	41	100.0
II	3	7.5	6	15.0	12	30.0	9	22.5	10	25.0	40	100.0
III	3	7.9	5	13.2	10	26.3	6	15.8	14	36.8	38 *	100.0

* One "no answer" excluded.

most directly affected, not only a sense of security with respect to the present situation, but a faith in times to come as well. Thus, Table 17 reveals that more than half of those in Group I are confident that they "will be better off five or ten years hence." The following answer to the question, offered by a member of this group, accurately summarizes the comments made by those who are optimistic about the future:

Yes, God willing. By then we hope to have another piece of land and to have the children either settled or well on their way to a fine profession. The best thing about America is that we poor tamarri [earthworms] get to eat more, have more, and the children don't have to struggle in the mud. Do you see all these *Americani* of the past [reference to families of returnees from the previous emigration]? Their children are teachers, doctors, lawyers. They and also their parents now have much respect. I remember some of these families when they were nobody. Even *pani 'ndianu* [corn bread] was a luxury. Today they lack nothing, and they are among the best families in the village. If it were not for America! Italy can't do anything for us. She is too poor, and besides, there are too many *mangiuni* [grafters]. Who would have money in the bank or the Post Office if it were not for America?

The Need for Achievement and Achievement Motivation

The evidence shows that among the peasants of southern Italy, the hopelessness, disperazione, and miseria that have often been observed as outstanding characteristics in the psychology of the people are now on the wane. Their gradual disappearance is due to the influx of substantial sums of money, deriving from local emigrants abroad, which is invested at home to buy cultural symbols of affluence and influence, such as property and education. This and the other beneficial effects of emigration already discussed constitute an achievement of great proportions. Simultaneously, they provide distinct evidence of a strong motivation to achieve, while the ensuing style of life also provides the basis and the inducement for the sustained endeavors that are required for the continued success of the individual as well as for the social and economic development that the larger society is engaged in bringing about.

Without getting involved in a complex theoretical issue, a pervasive tendency to measure the "need for achievement" [2] in terms of hypothetical risk-taking among school children in highly industrial societies may now be pointed out. As a result, it is no

---

[2] McClelland defines this phenomenon as "a desire to do well, not so much for the sake of social recognition or prestige, but to attain an inner feeling of personal accomplishment." See McClelland, 1963.

surprise that, by almost general agreement, this "motivational structure" is weak in peasants and in underdeveloped peoples generally. This weakness is particularly apparent given the fundamental assumption—sometimes explicitly stated but more often only implicitly held—that a real need for achievement is manifested only when individuals engage in cooperative enterprises. Banfield unwittingly echoes this assumption when he argues that the miseria in Montegrano is in large measure a result of the lack of "a spirit of cooperativeness and initiative." By implication at least, peasants have no one to blame but themselves for their poverty and miseries.

In general, it could be argued that people will expend effort and energy in the pursuit of a given goal when there is at least some expectation of success. Given a long history of unrewarded efforts as well as a continued lack of the means for success, a people is likely to practice a pure and simple "bread-for-today-at-all-costs" policy. Once the conditions for achievement and success have been provided, the previously "inert" may then be expected to develop their motivation and multiply further the conditions for success. Put otherwise, after social changes have once been introduced, and the previously deprived have begun to share the opportunities of their society, attempts to partake of those opportunities can be expected to grow in vigor, and the hope of still greater future prospects will become a more general characteristic. In another part of the national survey mentioned earlier, it was found that not only were the upwardly mobile in Italy more satisfied than those who had inherited their present position from their fathers, but satisfaction and hope of future improvement also varied directly with the intensity of upward mobility. In general, the greater the intergenerational jump, the greater the present satisfaction and faith in the future.

Analogously, Tumin and Feldman argue, on the basis of their findings in Puerto Rico, that

Depending on their past experiences and future prospects, men will hold different views of their lives and their society. Those who see an unbroken line of improvement for themselves, from past times through a projected future date, are likely to have high hopes for the future . . . (Tumin with Feldman, 1961, 202).

In this same connection, Parsons and Weber show that economic advancement is associated with optimism and belief in the possibility of progress (Parsons, 1951, 1958; Weber, 1958).

In short, the chances for success and the motivation to pursue strategies that normally lead to success are not distributed equally in society. To the extent that this is true, it is likely that the lower the chances—real or imagined—of success, the lower the achievement motivation *with respect to the internal conditions of a given stratification system.* This says nothing, however, with respect to the *need for achievement,* which may comprise a constant rather than a variable aspect of human personality. Motivation, moreover, may still remain high in relation to some external system.

We have seen with what readiness the peasants of southern Italy leave their home community for places many thousands of miles away. Some of them depart with their entire families, never to return to the old society. For these, despite the deplorable conditions they leave behind, and despite the hopes and dreams that they nourish for the future, emigration must constitute a risk of the greatest magnitude. Leaving behind familiar surroundings, friends, relatives, and the habits of a lifetime, and converting into a little cash all their meager possessions in the face of a multitude of uncertainties, the emigrants undertake a grave risk. The society of destination will require new language skills, new eating habits, new work skills, and an entirely new outlook: in short, the act of emigrating entails a new process of socialization which must loom as a painful experience to even the most hopeful and optimistic. On top of this, the venture begins for many, who have never before even seen the ocean, with sea voyages that frequently involve an entire month of the most atrocious discomfort and seasickness.

Many of the emigrants leave as individuals, and for these, there is the further knowledge that they must suffer an existence of many years abroad without family, and without any of those simple but essential comforts that only family living—however destitute—makes possible.

Is this not evidence of a high motivation and a high need for achievement? These risks and sacrifices are at least as impressive as any of those hypothetical risks that students of human motivation and achievement contrive and measure within populations of school children.

The question now remains: Why do the peasants of southern Italy not address their motivation or—to put it otherwise—expend more energy in their own society in attempting to fulfill their need for achievement?

Banfield is on indefensible grounds when he argues that the people of Montegrano lack a spirit of initiative, though he is essentially correct in stating that they lack a spirit of cooperativeness and do not organize to pursue their goals at home. But why should they organize and cooperate when it appears to them that there is nothing worth cooperating about as long as they remain at home? As we have noted, their region, a country of peasants, is really not suited to agriculture. The most diligent work all too often comes to naught and does nothing to dispel the secular miseria. Moreover, in those few instances in which cooperative enterprises are undertaken, the peasants are quickly and almost invariably swindled without justice or retribution.[3] We could further remind ourselves of the particular nature of their system of inequalities, but so much will suffice.

Southern Italian peasants do not address their motivations and their initiatives more forcefully to local conditions because local conditions are correctly perceived as forbidding. In any

---

[3] A case in point is reported by an Italian sociologist, familiar with the South, in the process of discussing Banfield's book. It seems that some years ago in one of the villages mentioned by Banfield, a group of peasants were tempted to sell their horses and donkeys in order to purchase together a truck and thus facilitate the marketing of their produce. In this enterprise, they were represented by a business-minded accountant from the North. One fine day, however, the accountant went to the city and did not return. And with him disappeared the truck and the peasants' life savings. "Can we," the writer concludes, "really blame those poor peasants if the 'cooperation' argument is now taboo . . . ?" See Marselli, 1962, 125.

case, the risk involved in leaving the system, entirely, by emigrating, appears less than that involved in local enterprise, and success more probable in the former than in the latter. Perhaps this flight—temporary or permanent—is the most effective mechanism of achievement for peasants everywhere and underprivileged people in general. By going out of the system for a period of time, classes of individuals who have been trapped in the vicious cycle of self-perpetuating poverty and miseria, manage to break that cycle. They do so not only because of the economic thrust received from without, but also, and especially, because of the new outlook and self-image they gain abroad. Their absence from the old inferno affords them the opportunity to create, and eventually to project, a new self-image.

The general argument may be summarized by suggesting the over-all process by which the need for achievement among southern Italian peasants has been expressed and has become increasingly compelling during the course of this century. Traditionally, southern Italian peasants were faced with a common set of personal problems arising from the severity of the physical, economic, and social environment. The very severity of this environment, however, prevented individuals from coming together and *collectively* seeking melioration of their problems. The first serious attempts to solve them were, therefore, individual, as represented by the first wave of emigration.

The early emigration, coupled with the development of new channels of communication and the two World Wars, has served to make the problems clearer; but the individualistic tradition has been strengthened by the already obvious example of an individually effective solution by emigration. The structural characteristics of social disorganization, therefore, remain, as is evidenced by the continuing social tension and conflict.

However, as it became evident to the people that their problems were in fact soluble, individual motivations were increasingly aroused, and they, in turn, reinforced the immediate, tangible pressures for solutions. Put otherwise, the motivation was aroused in many by the initial perception that change in one's status was possible by engaging in actions that bypassed the local system. In turn, change functioned to sustain and increase efforts toward fulfilling that possibility.

In conclusion, emigration is recognized by southern Italian peasants as the most rational, perhaps the only feasible, way in which they can guide their destiny. It is the major avenue through which they strive and achieve. Through it, many have achieved in their home society a degree of economic well-being and independence unimaginable until a few decades ago. By emigrating, they have rapidly gained a degree of social recognition that until recent times seemed to be the monopoly of the signorial class. Through it, they have achieved the social and psychological vitality with which to challenge the old social order and to demand the recognition that their achievements deserve. Finally, and more important still, the southern Italian peasant has won a sense of security in relation to the present and the future as well. In short, through emigration, the peasant has broken the formidable bonds of his secular miseria and disperazione.

REFERENCES

Banfield, Edward C. 1958. *The Moral Basis of a Backward Society*. Glencoe, Ill.: The Free Press.

McClelland, David C. 1963. "The Achievement Motive in Economic Growth," in Bert F. Hoselitz and Wilbert E. Moore, eds., *Industrialization and Society*. New York: UNESCO-MOUTON.

Marselli, Gilberto A. 1962. "Sociologi nordoamericani e società contadina italiana: a proposito del libro di Banfield," in Società Italiana di Sociologia Rurale, *Archivio*. Milan: Feltrinelli Editore.

Parsons, Talcott. 1951. *The Social System*. Glencoe, Ill.: The Free Press.

Parsons, Talcott. 1958. "Some Principal Characteristics of Industrial Societies," in *The Challenge of Development*. Jerusalem: Hebrew University.

Rossi Doria, Manlio. 1955. "Cos'è il Mezzogiorno Agrario," in Bruno Caizzi, ed., *Antologia della Questione Meridionale*. Milan: Edizioni di Comunità.

Tumin, Melvin M., with Arnold S. Feldman. 1961. *Social Class and Social Change in Puerto Rico*. Princeton: Princeton University Press.

Weber, Max. 1958. *The Protestant Ethic and the Spirit of Capitalism*. New York: Charles Scribner's Sons. [Original publication 1904–1905]

Appendices

Appendices

Appendix I

The Sample

The first task was to make a list of the 682 families registered in 1959 in the town records. Next, needed information was gathered that the official records did not provide about the 682 families. The local postman was turned to for help, which he gave most competently and generously.

In a small rural community such as Franza, the postman is a particularly good source of information. The discharge of his duties requires personal and often intimate contact with the local people. For instance, when the villagers go to a bank in Montelitigio to cash a check, he often acts as a witness, for since he gets the mail for Franza in Montelitigio, he is known there. Again, in order to deliver the mail to the right persons he must frequently know not only the names of the local people but also their outside contacts, for not infrequently an incoming letter bears only the name of the village and the first and last names of the receiver. Certain surnames are very common, and as a result, the postman must make his delivery more on the basis of what he knows about the sender than of what he knows about the receiver. In short, the postman, who has been at his job for many years, is known locally as "one who knows how many hairs each one of us has." In fact, it later became evident that this colorful hyperbole was surprisingly accurate. The errors of information that the postman made were few and inconsequential.

Specifically, he provided the following types of information for each of the 682 families on the list: age of man and wife; number of relatives who had migrated since the end of World War II; degree of kinship of these to man or wife; marital status of emigrants; year of initial emigration for each emigrant and number of home visits; place of immigration for each migrant; degree of kinship of man and wife to relatives who had emigrated before World War II; and several other necessary details.

The next task was to divide the 682 families into groups according to "degree of contact" with emigrants. Accordingly, the nuclear family, the extended family of close relatives, and the nonkin group were chosen, in this order, as providing three declining degrees of contact with emigrants abroad. Hence, the 682 families were divided into three groups as follows: in the first group were put the 157 families which could claim as emigrant the husband or one or more unmarried children or both; in the second were placed the 311 families in which either or both spouses could claim as an emigrant one or more relatives of the following types: father, mother, brother, sister, or married child. The remaining 214 families fell into the third group.

For various reasons which will become clear as we go along, in proceeding to draw the sample, it was next necessary to make the following four exclusions:

1. All those families were excluded in which either spouse had one or more members of his family of procreation or of orientation directly involved in the old emigration. The restriction facilitated measurement by limiting the cases to a fairly recent and brief period; the findings would thus assume greater validity as well.

2. In view of the interest in measuring the consequences of

emigration after World War II, there was further concern about the possibility that in many cases whatever changes had been initiated by emigration had not had enough time to become sufficiently visible. Consequently, in choosing family units for our first group above, only those families were included which had been involved in the emigration before 1952. In this way, a maximum span was left of twelve years (1947–1959), and a minimum of eight (1951–1959).

3. Families in which the prospective interviewees were over 70 years of age were also excluded in order to avoid problems of communication. Old age in Franza is often characterized by near-blindness, deafness, and, as already noted, senility.

4. Finally, families of migrants to other parts of Italy were excluded. Justification for this decision is that, in 1959, only about a score of local people were in other parts of the country. Of these, eight or nine had little or no contact with persons residing in Franza. Several others were policemen (*carabinieri*) stationed in other southern Italian locations not sufficiently unlike Franza to warrant their inclusion in the present study. Only a handful of local persons were working in central or northern Italy and were keeping in close contact with their old community.

When all the above corrections were made, the first category of contact with emigrants was reduced to a total of 40 families. With these accepted as the first segment of the sample, an equal number of families were drawn from each of the other two contact categories by using the following procedure: the families in both groups were listed alphabetically and enumerated. Then the total of each group was divided by 40, and each quotient was used for its respective group as the interval between any two consecutive numbers to be drawn. In this way, an additional 80 families were drawn, for a total sample of 120. An error of classification was made on one family, and the sample of 120 families was divided into three groups of 41, 40, and 39, respectively.

With one exception (an unmarried male) belonging to the second group, all sample subjects were female and married or, in a few cases, widowed. Control by sex was necessary in view of the fact that most families falling in the first group were implicated in the phenomenon of emigration through the male family head. Therefore, with the single exception mentioned above, women only were interviewed.

Appendix II

Stratification Procedures

The following are the basic steps involved in the raters' technique. One of the questions in the interview schedule required each of the 120 sample respondents to tell how many "social classes" she saw in the community. In addition, she was directed to give examples of local families belonging to each of the classes mentioned as well as to explain the reasons for so classifying such families. At first, the results were discouraging, as the interviewees did not seem to completely understand the question. Despite the fact that interviews were carried out in the local dialect, the respondents were ill at ease and uncommunicative. After considerable hesitation, the tendency was either to name the three occupational estates of "professionals, artisans, and peasants," or to dismiss the question with a "don't know," typically qualified by an "*abbastanza*" (a sufficient number).

The subjects' apparent lack of class awareness was attributed to a variety of factors: (1) their unfamiliarity with the Italian term "*classe*"; (2) their lack of familiarity with a highly structured interview situation in which they were forced to "think out from scratch" a complex phenomenon like the stratification system; and (3) the possibly unsettled nature of the stratification system itself, only recently emerged from a feudal-estate orientation. Fortunately, the 37th interviewee, a remarkably sociological, though illiterate, person came to the rescue with the following information:

Well, I think that if you want to be meticulous about the matter, you will find as many classes here as there are families. However, if you want *categorie* of families, instead of individual families, I think it might help to think of the saying that "*paro para piglia*" [equal marries equal]. In this way, I think you could organize the whole community into five or six *categorie*. By the way, I was saying to my sister just the other day that because of all these Americans, very many families have recently improved a great deal in respect and importance. There are families today with which I would gladly contract marriage ties but which were nobody at all ten years ago.

This statement was a welcome stroke of luck. Many social scientists have pointed out this very factor of intermarriage as a fundamental criterion for class differentiation. Joseph Schumpeter, for instance, relied upon the concept of intermarriage for the very definition of class. For this scholar, the most important symptom of class differences was the ease or difficulty with which members of different classes contract legally and socially recognized marriages. Hence he found "a suitable definition of the class—one that makes it outwardly recognizable and involves no class theory—in the fact that intermarriage prevails among its members, socially rather than legally" (Schumpeter, in Bendix and Lipset, 1953, 77). Again, Hollingshead, investigating the question of "who marries whom," finds strong support for the theory of homogamy and for "the proposition that one's subculture, and one's race, age, and class position in the society effectively determine the kind of person one will marry," although not the exact individual (Hollingshead, 1950, 619–627).

In view of all this, beginning with the 38th interview, the term *classe* in the basic question was replaced with "*classe o categoria d'importanza*" (class or category of importance). Moreover, in their attempt to stratify the community, the respondents were encouraged to think of the saying that *paro para piglia*, and as a result, they became at once considerably more articulate than the previous interviewees had been.[1]

When all 120 interview schedules had been completed, they were analyzed with a view to singling out the following three types of information: (1) number of strata given by each interviewee; (2) examples of families provided for each given stratum; and (3) criteria of placement or classification used. With regard to the first point, 9 respondents denied the existence of social strata, and 14 others had no view at all. Of the remaining 97 informants, 9 saw two strata, 18 saw three, 12 perceived four, 11 gave five, and 41 saw six strata, while 3 perceived seven and 3 others saw eight strata.

Which breakdown should be accepted? On theoretical grounds alone, given this wide array of differences, no particular reason leads to acceptance of any one view instead of the others. For convenience sake, however, the modal response was accepted, and the six-fold stratification system was adopted. The 41 families giving this particular breakdown shall be referred to as the "nucleus." A more detailed analysis of those schedules which presented a breakdown by one, by two, or by three strata revealed that most of these schedules had been completed prior to introducing the factor of intermarriage as a criterion of differentiation. There is no exact way of telling how many of these cases would have fallen in the nucleus of 41 cases, had they also been asked the revised question and invited to consider the saying of *paro para piglia* since there was no reinterviewing. It may be

---

[1] In this kind of procedure there is, no doubt, some "result-guiding." The problem here would involve us in a long-standing controversy in sociology concerning the question of whether "social classes" are *real* or not. Without becoming embroiled in the arguments concerning this problem, it might be pointed out that the question is at best irrelevant. This is not a study of classes in the proper sense of the word, but one of social prestige. Moreover, in this study a system of social stratification is considered a heuristic device, a fact finder, a "scientific construct" to be used for the investigator's purposes.

helpful to point out, however, that out of 83 schedules completed subsequent to the introduction of the criterion of intermarriage, 39, or 46 percent, divided the social structure into six strata. Of the 36 schedules done prior to that point, only two had given a six-fold breakdown.

With regard to the question of the families used as examples of given strata, given the decision to adopt the six-fold break-down, only the 41 schedules of the nucleus were examined. Here it was found that 23 particular families in the community had been consistently placed in the stratification system by all who used them as examples of strata. By this is meant that when these 23 families, hereafter referred to as "the reference group," were used as examples of strata, there was perfect agreement among those who suggested them as to where they belonged. Specifically, 3 out of 23 had been regularly placed in Stratum I, 2 in Stratum II, 5 each in Strata III, IV, and V, and 3 more in Stratum VI.

Finally came the analysis of the placement criteria indicated by the respondents in the nucleus. After looking again at these 41 schedules, it was discovered that, although the number of differently worded and accentuated criteria exceeded 200, at close scrutiny certain major sets of characteristics appeared with regularity. Consequently, the multiplicity of placement criteria were grouped under five general headings as follows: (1) wealth and possessions; (2) family name; (3) achievement of family head or of children in a given occupation; (4) general behavior of the family; and (5) general importance of the family.

To recapitulate briefly, of the 120 persons interviewed, 41, "the nucleus," saw the local prestige structure as being divided into six strata. This response was the most common among the interviewees, and it was decided arbitrarily to accept it as the most "correct" view of the local stratification system. Furthermore, 23 families in the community at large, "the reference group," were uniformly cited by the 41 individuals in the nucleus as representatives of the six social strata. Finally, in making their classifications, those 41 persons had in mind a variety of attributes, or placement criteria, which could be grouped under five general headings.

The next step was now to type on cards the full names (and where possible the nicknames) of the man and wife of each of the 23 families in the reference group. Then, these cards, alphabetically arranged, along with a sheet listing the five major headings of placement criteria, were presented to 10 local persons who were considered to be well informed, who had not been previously interviewed, and who appeared to be widely scattered through the six social strata agreed upon as characterizing the community. These ten "judges," or "raters," were asked to study the family list along with the placement criteria and then to state: (1) whether the families on the list represented "a number of different social classes or *categorie*," and (2) whether the families "exhausted all classes present in the community." The ten raters did not disagree on these two points. Consequently, the procedure was continued and the ten raters were asked to look at the list of placement criteria once more and on the basis of these to arrange the reference group so as to put "equals with equals."

Eight of the 10 judges divided the 23 families into six strata, one into five, and one into three. Agreement among the judges was, therefore, very high, and could be explained, in part, by the fact that the judges were a select group of well-informed persons. In part, however, the high agreement was also due to the fact that the raters were confronted both with a select group of families to be classified and with a specific number of cultural characteristics to guide them in their classification. These facts may also explain the very high concurrence between the eight raters and the 41 respondents in the nucleus who had originally classified the reference group. In fact, three of the eight judges disagreed with the original classification on only one of the 23 families; two disagreed on two families; two others disagreed in three cases; and an eighth rater disagreed on four families. One further point of interest is that in no case did any of the eight judges disagree with the original classification by more than one stratum.

The high agreement between this group of raters and the 41 members of the nucleus as to the number of strata in the community strengthened the conviction that the breakdown agreed upon was both convenient and at least partially valid. A final group of 22 judges was then selected who had not been pre-viously interviewed. Again, they were chosen with a view to possibly including a fair representation of the community on the basis of social position, age, sex, length of time in the community, and degree of contact with emigrants. These persons were given the final task of classifying the 120 families in the sample.

The 22 judges were shown: (1) a sheet listing the five major headings of placement criteria; (2) a sheet containing the refer-ence group distributed by stratum; and (3) a set of 120 cards, one each for the 120 families in the sample. They were asked to: (1) study the breakdown of the reference group, (2) study the placement criteria, (3) state whether they agreed with the break-down of the reference group, and, if yes, (4) find for each of the 120 families in the sample "the best possible equal" from the 23 families in the reference group. Nineteen accepted the distribu-tion of the 23 families as given; three disagreed. Of these, one found only five strata; a second saw three; and the last one made no subdivisions, explaining that in Franza "we are all equal." To facilitate later computations, these three judges were discounted, so that a total of 19 were left. However, the writer himself acted as a rater, bringing the total of final judges to twenty.[2]

When all 120 families in the sample had been classified by the 20 raters, each family was given a mean score, and this was taken as representing that family's social stratum. If a given family, for instance, was placed in Stratum IV by nine judges, in Stratum III by eight judges, and in Stratum V by three, that family received the following value: $[(4 \times 9) + (3 \times 8) + (5 \times 3)] \div 20 = 3.75$. This value puts such a family in Stratum IV. It should be pointed out, however, that the above example is not typical of the amount of agreement found among the 20 judges in classifying the sample

---

[2] In order to avoid being influenced by the other judges, I was the first to rate the 120 families. Later, when my ratings and the ratings of the other 19 judges, properly averaged off, were compared, it was found that the two sets of ratings differed on only 16 of the 120 families, and then in only one case by more than one stratum position. Worth mentioning also is the fact that all 20 judges classified all of the 120 families, a fact which for our purposes at least makes the use of the judges' technique all the more appropriate and useful.

families. The raters were, in fact, in remarkable concurrence among themselves, to the extent that they disagreed by more than one stratum interval on only 26 out of the total 120 families.[3]

REFERENCES

Hollingshead, August B. 1950. "Cultural Factors in the Selection of Marriage Mates," *American Sociological Review*, 15, October.

Schumpeter, Joseph. 1953. In Reinhard Bendix and Seymour M. Lipset, eds., *Class, Status and Power*. Glencoe, Ill.: The Free Press.

Siegel, Sidney. 1956. *Nonparametric Statistics for the Behavioral Sciences*. New York: McGraw-Hill Book Co., Inc.

---

[3] As a test of agreement among the 20 judges, Kendall coefficient of concordance (W), with corrections for tied observations, was computed. This statistical tool is particularly useful in studies of interjudge or intertest reliability. The resulting value of W was .854, and X^2 was computed as a test of significance, obtaining a value of 2,032.52, which is highly significant. See Siegel, 1956, 229–239.

Appendix III

The Key Status Index

Stratum I
1. Families whose heads are university graduates but are not engaged in grammar-school teaching
2. Families owning at least 150 acres of land

Stratum II
1. Families whose heads are grammar-school teachers or other professionals without a university degree
2. Families owning 41 to 149 acres of land provided that they have (had) children in school beyond the grammar grades

Stratum III
1. Massaro families owning 11 to 40 acres of land
2. Families of first-degree craftsmen, provided that they own at least a four-room house
3. Families of shopkeepers or other major retailers of business
4. Nonmassaro families owning 16 to 40 acres of land
5. Families of clerks
6. Families with at least one child who is a university graduate

Stratum IV

1. Families of second-degree craftsmen, with or without a house of their own
2. Nonmassaro families owning 6 to 15 acres of land
3. Massaro families owning less than 11 acres of land
4. Families of policemen or guards (country or town, public or private)
5. Families of millers
6. Families of minor shopkeepers (few items sold)
7. Families of first-degree craftsmen without a house of their own

Stratum V

1. Families whose heads are either third-degree craftsmen or have ever worked as laborers while holding craftsman status
2. All remaining farm families: tenants and small nonmassaro landowners (owning 1 to 5 acres)

Stratum VI

1. Families of laborers: farmhands, olive pickers, construction workers, garbage collectors, "errand boys," and the like
2. All uneducated families living in new *case popolari* (subsidized government housing)
3. Families of the regularly unemployed (but not disabled), though there is poverty in the family

Note:

1. A family is classified according to the highest characteristic applicable to that family.
2. There are three degrees of skill among craftsmen. The rating judges for the total sample also rated sample craftsmen on degree of skill. Mean rating was used to establish degree of skill for each craftsman family.
3. "Bad reputation" in a family or in either parent's family of orientation lowers that family by one stratum. The sample families were rated on this point by six judges.

Appendix IV

Stratum Positions of Sample Families

Stratum Position of Sample Families (in code number), According to Judges' Technique (JT) and Key Status Index (KSI), 1959 *

Family No.	Stratum Position		Family No.	Stratum Position		Family No.	Stratum Position	
	JT	KSI		JT	KSI		JT	KSI
1	V	V	12	V	V	23	III	IV
2	VI	VI	13	V	V	24	III	III
3	II	III	14	V	V	25	II	II
4	II	III	15	IV	IV	26	IV	III
5	IV	IV	16	IV	IV	27	V	V
6	VI	VI	17	IV	IV	28	V	V
7	IV	IV	18	III	III	29	V	V
8	VI	VI	19	V	V	30	VI	VI
9	V	V	20	V	VI	31	V	V
10	III	III	21	III	IV	32	IV	IV
11	V	V	22	III	III	33	IV	IV

Stratum Position of Sample Families (in code number), According to Judges'
Technique (JT) and Key Status Index (KSI), 1959 * (*Continued*)

Family No.	Stratum Position		Family No.	Stratum Position		Family No.	Stratum Position	
	JT	KSI		JT	KSI		JT	KSI
34	IV	III	63	III	III	92	V	V
35	III	III	64	IV	IV	93	IV	V
36	V	VI	65	III	III	94	V	VI
37	V	V	66	IV	IV	95	V	V
38	VI	VI	67	III	III	96	III	III
39	IV	IV	68	VI	VI	97	I	I
40	IV	IV	69	III	III	98	III	III
41	V	VI	70	VI	VI	99	IV	IV
42	IV	IV	71	III	III	100	IV	IV
43	IV	IV	72	III	III	101	II	II
44	V	V	73	V	V	102	IV	IV
45	IV	IV	74	V	V	103	IV	IV
46	III	III	75	III	III	104	VI	VI
47	V	V	76	VI	VI	105	VI	VI
48	III	IV	77	IV	IV	106	IV	IV
49	VI	VI	78	IV	IV	107	IV	IV
50	IV	IV	79	IV	IV	108	V	VI
51	IV	V	80	V	IV	109	III	III
52	V	V	81	IV	V	110	VI	V
53	III	III	82	IV	IV	111	IV	IV
54	IV	III	83	V	V	112	IV	IV
55	IV	IV	84	VI	VI	113	I	I
56	V	VI	85	I	II	114	V	V
57	IV	V	86	V	V	115	IV	IV
58	IV	V	87	IV	V	116	VI	V
59	III	IV	88	IV	V	117	III	III
60	III	III	89	III	III	118	VI	VI
61	III	IV	90	V	V	119	V	VI
62	V	VI	91	IV	IV	120	V	V

* τ (tau) = .76; z = 3.4; p < .0003.

Index

FALVEY MEMORIAL LIBRARY

VILLANOVA UNIVERSITY